Pricing the European Environment

Edited by Ståle Navrud

To my daughter Marte
and all children inheriting the earth

Pricing the European Environment
Edited by Ståle Navrud

Scandinavian
University Press

Scandinavian University Press (Universitetsforlaget AS), 0608 Oslo
Distributed world-wide excluding Norway by
Oxford University Press, Walton Street, Oxford OX2 6DP

Oxford New York Toronto
Delhi Bombay Calcutta Madras Karachi
Kuala Lumpur Singapore Hong Kong Tokyo
Nairobi Dar es Salaam Cape Town
Melbourne Auckland Madrid
and associated companies in Berlin Ibadan

Oxford is a trade mark of Oxford University Press

Published in the United States
by Oxford University Press Inc., New York

© Universitetsforlaget 1992

Cover design by Ellen Larsen

Published with a grant from the Norwegian Research Council for Science and the
Humanities

British Library Cataloguing in Publication Data
Navrud, Ståle
Pricing the European Environment
I. Title
333.7

ISBN 82-00-21505-9

Library of Congress Cataloguing in Publication Data
Data available

Typeset by typer & tall as, Oslo
Printed in Norway by Tangen Grafiske Senter AS, Drammen 1992

Acknowledgements

The idea of this book emerged after experiencing the broad spectrum of European environmental valuation studies presented at the first and second annual conferences of the European Association of Environmental and Resource Economists (EAERE) in Venice (1990) and Stockholm (1991). It struck me that very little of this work was known internationally, as opposed to the large U.S. literature in this field. Although the bulk of methodological development and empirical applications has taken place in the U.S., the activity is increasing in Europe. Also, Australia, Asia, Latin America and Africa have started pricing their environments.

I would like to extend my sincere thanks to my European, Australian and Israeli colleagues for their keen interest and enthusiasm in contributing to this book. Also, I would also like to thank our American colleague, Professor W. Michael Hanemann at the University of California, Berkely for setting the scene, by providing the history and state of the art of environmental pricing in the U.S.A.

I am indebted to NORAGRIC (Norwegian centre for sustainable agriculture and development) and the Agricultural University of Norway for allowing me to spend time on this book project, and to the Norwegian Research Council for Science and the Humanities for their financial support.

Last, but not least, Anne Turner and Ruth Ensby at the Scandinavian University Press have done a great job in easing the burden on the editor. Their colleague, Thor Audun Gulbrandsen, also deserves thanks for encouraging the editor to start the project.

I hope this book will contribute to a greater awareness and appreciation of the value of our environment, and, thus, an economical, ecological and social sustainable development.

Drøbak, July 10 1992

Ståle Navrud

Contents

Preface

W. MICHAEL HANEMANN, DEPARTMENT OF AGRICULTURAL &
RESOURCE ECONOMICS UNIVERSITY OF CALIFORNIA, BERKELEY

Until recently, it could have been said with some accuracy, if no little chauvinism, that placing an economic value on the natural environment was the pastime of a few rich countries – especially the United States. Like some other topics in microeconomics, the economics of environmental valuation might have been seen as exemplifying a typically American tendency to quantify that which is best left unquantified. Among many American economists, environmental valuation was perceived as something of primarily methodological interest – it was an extension of existing benefit-cost techniques to value a rather novel public good, namely, the natural environment. For their part, environmental policy makers generally had relatively little interest in economics: they felt that they could function perfectly well without the benefit of advice from economists.

Within less than a decade, all of this has begun to change. The protection of the environment has moved to the forefront of the political scene in America, Europe, and many other parts of the world. Within the European Community, for example, there has recently been a wave of environmental policymaking as part of the effort to harmonize domestic policies by 1992. In Eastern Europe, since the fall of communism in 1989 it has been recognized that massive degradation of the environment may be one of its most enduring legacies. Longstanding concerns about the harmful environmental side-effects of economic growth are finally receiving attention from international development agencies. The Earth Summit in Rio is, indeed, a testament to the global nature of the concern to protect the environment.

However, a corollary to this heightened sense of concern is that the economic aspects of environmental protection will become correspondingly more important: pollution control is not necessarily cheap, and the resources devoted to it must be allocated wisely. In the US, for example, the Environmental Protection Agency has recently estimated that, by the end of this decade, almost 3 % of the

GNP will be spent on pollution control, either by the private sector or by the federal and state governments. With expenditures on that scale, it will be hard to avoid economic questions such as whether the benefits in particular cases are sufficient to justify the cost.

Hence, this volume dealing with the economic valuation of the natural environment is most timely. Its focus on Europe is particularly useful because of the rapid pace of change there. Moreover, it provides an important corrective to the existing published literature, which mostly deals with the US.

For European readers, however, it may be helpful to give a brief description of how environmental valuation evolved in the US, and to comment on some of the lessons to be learned from this experience. The first point to be made is that environmental valuation grew out of cost-benefit analysis, which itself first emerged as a practical tool of government decisionmaking in the US in the early part of this century. The history since then can be divided roughly into four phases. The first phase lasts through World War II; the second phase is the early post-war era through about 1964; the third phase is from 1965 to about 1980, and the fourth phase is from then to the present.

In the first phase, cost-benefit analysis emerged, in Hammond's [1960] words, as "an administrative device owing nothing to economic theory." It was conceived as a tool for managing the activities of the U.S. Army Corps Engineers. The 1902 River andd Harbor Act created a Board of Engineers to review navigation projects and required the Board, in conducting its review, to consider the commercial benefits from such projects in relation to their costs. The River and Harbor Act of 1920 further required the separate reporting of special, or local, benefits as opposed to general, or national, benefits, for the purposes of ensuring appropriate local cost-sharing. During the New Deal, there was a call to broaden project evaluation in order to recognize larger social concerns, especially unemployment, In 1934, the National Resources Board appointed a Water Resources Committee to consider "the development of an equitable system of distributing the cost of water resource projects, which should include not only private but social accounting." Its report spoke of the need to study "the part played by intangible factors" in assessing the equities, benefits and costs of public-works programs. Some of the Committee's recommendations were embodied in the Flood Control Act of 1936, which added flood control – previously seen as a responsibility of state and local government – to the Corps' mandate and permitted it to participate in such projects "if the benefits to whomsoever they may accrue are in excess of the estimated costs, and if the lives and social security of people are otherwise adversely affected." Hammond comments that, given the political and economic climate of 1936, these words were an open invitation to discover new types of benefits that might justify public works projects.

Over the next decade, other federal agencies rose to this challenge adopting, as they did so, the practice of benefit-cost analysis, and expanding its scope in two ways. First, agencies sought to identify intangible factors that could be counted among the project benefits, such as national defense, saving human lives, or aesthetic or recreational impacts. Second, some agencies – notably the Bureau of Reclamation – attempted, in Hammond's words, "to travel down the chain of economic causation and evoke *secondary* or *indirect* benefits and costs: not content with crediting the dam with the value of the wheat grown on the land it was going to irrigate, they would add the net value of the bread that might be baked from the wheat." Moreover, each agency developed its own approach. There were no attempts at standardization until the late 1940's, which marks the second phase in the history of benefit-cost analysis – a period of consolidation, systematization and, for the first time, academic engagement.

In 1946, the Fedral Inter-Agency River Basin Committee appointed a Subcommittee on Benefits and Costs to investigate the practices of the various federal agencies that engaged in the evaluation of water resources projects and to formulate some "mutually acceptable principles and procedures" which could serve as a common approach. The Subcommittee's review of current practices was presented in interim reports issued in 1947, 1948 and 1949. Then, it turned to the task of developing "a systematic, consistent, and theoretically sound framework for the economic analysis of river basin projects." The resulting report, published in May 1950 and known as the "Green Book", received widespread attention. As Hammond says, for the first time in an official publication it applied the language of conventional welfare economics to the analysis of federal policy. It covered most aspects of project evaluation, including measurement of benefits and costs, correct definition of secondary impacts forecasting future price levels, choice of a discount rate, period of analysis, allowances for risk, treatment of taxes, and cost-allocation for multipurpose projects. With regard to the benefit measurement, it characterized the issue thus: "The ultimate aim of river basin development, in common with all productive activity, is to satisfy human needs and desires. The problem of evaluating, from a public viewpoint, the extent to which a project accomplishes this aim presents a major difficulty ... because there are no common terms in which all effects of a project are normally expressed. All objects and activities which have the power of satisfying human wants ... are referred to ... as "goods and services." The values placed on goods and services through the exchange process afford one means of measuring the degree of want-satisfying power attached to those goods and services by those who participate in the exchange. Most of the effects of projects involve goods and services which are readily evaluated in terms of market prices. Some effects of a project, however, such as improvement of health and enjoyment of recreation, have not been customarily evaluated in the monetary terms used in the market system."

For valuing project effects, the Green Book recommended a tripartite solution. First, use market prices wherever possible. Failing this, use values "derived or estimated indirectly from prices established in the market for similar or analogous [outputs] or ... derived from the most economical cost of producing similar effects by an alternate means." Second, "projects effects which are ordinarily evaluated incompletely or not at all in actual exchange processes should be given, insofar as possible, an adjusted or estimated market value in monetary terms." For example, "for the purpose of establishing a greater comparability among the benefit-cost analyses of the various agencies, a human life might be given, as a minimum, the same economic value as would be payable for a life lost during project construction under compensation arrangements which are normally included in estimates of project costs." Alternatively, "on a broader basis the value might approximate the average ... amount paid for accidental loss of life in court awards." With regard to recreational impacts, "since market prices are not available to express the value of this increase in monetary terms, an estimated or derived value comparable to market value may be used for this purpose. Under one procedure ... the value of recreational benefit to an individual is assumed to be equal to the sum of expenditures by the recreationist for such items as gasoline, food, lodging, and sporting equipment ... This method, however, provides a measure of gross rather than net values and from the project standpoint does not measure benefits creditable to the project." As an alternative, the Green Book suggested measuring recreational benefits on the basis of "informed estimates of the average value of these recreational facilities to prospective users. In estimating or deriving these tangible values, consideration should be given to all pertinent factors, including the charges which the recreationalists who may be expected to use the facilities would be willing to pay and to any actual charges being paid by users for comparble facilities in other areas." The third type of effects was intangibles, i.e, "effects which it is considered impossible or undersirable to express in monetary terms." Examples include "the loss of a scenic or historic site" or "the strengthening of national security and the national economy." The Green Book held that these effects "need to be described with care and should not be overlooked or minimized merely because they do not yield to dollar evaluation." Rather, they should be "considered and described in such a way that their importance and influence on project formulation and selection can be clearly indicated."

Although the Green Book was recognized as a landmark in the application of microeceonomics to policy analysis, its impact was muted in two ways. First, its recommendations were advisory not mandatory: the participating agencies were still free to continue with their existing practices, and some did. Hence, fierce battles continued to be waged during the 1950's – both among rival federal agencies and between the agencies and their outside, especially academic, critics – regarding issues such as the Bureau of Reclamation's treatment of secondary impacts or its choice of a discount rate. Second, while some parts of its economic analysis were of enduring value, other parts were quickly overtaken by contemporaneous developments in welfare economics. The "new welfare economics" created in the late 1930's and 1940's by Bergson, Hicks, Hotelling, Kaldor and Lerner was consolidated and synthesized in such works as Little (1950), Baumol (1952) and Graff (1957) which employed a more technically advanced mode of analysis than that found in the Green Book. Perhaps because of this – and perhaps because of interest aroused by controversies over water projects – benefit-cost analysis quickly became an attractive area for academic research on applied welfare economics, generating an extensive literature in the 1950's and early 1960's, including six major books in as many years, four coming out of Harvard University's Water Program – Eckstein (1958), Krutilla and Eckstein (1958), Maass et al. (1962), and Marglin (1963) – and two from the Rand Corporation – McKean (1958) and Hirshleifer et al. (1960).

Much of the conceptual framework for valuing project outputs came ultimately from Hotelling (1938), who had rediscovered for the Anglo-Saxon world Dupuit's (1844) classic analysis of marginal cost pricing and had reformulated it in modern, welfare-theoretic terms. An important implication was that, while market prices can safely be used to value marginal changes in the supply of market commodities, for non-marginal changes one needs to measure the impact in terms of the change in producer's plus consumer's surplus and this, in turn, requires knowledge not of market prices but of the underlying demand and supply curves. The detailed application of these principles to specific water project outputs, such as irrigation supply, hydropower generation, navigation and flood control, was elucidated in the works of Eckstein and the others. In this respect, to be sure, their analysis represented a significant advance over that presented in the Green Book, with its simplistic emphasis on market prices.

But not in other respects. For, whereas the Green Book emphasized all three kinds of project output – marketed commodities, those non-marketed commodities which still could be given an estimated monetary value, and intangibles – the newer treatments, especially those emanating from Harvard, were far more disposed to write off the latter two categories, preferring to concentrate on a more rigorous analysis of the former. For example, Eckstein's core analysis of recreation reads, in its entirety, as follows: "There have been many attempts to measure the benefits of recreation. Since people actually hire the use of recreational facilities one might expect that one could find prices that would measure willingness to pay. When a dam creates a lake, agencies look to the total expenditures which people make on swimming and fishing. but these expenditures are for travel, equipment, lodging, and so forth, and are not expenditures for the lake. A proper measure of benefit would be to indicate how much managers of the lake could collect in the form of user charges; since there are no charges for use of reservoirs or comparable bodies of water elsewhere, appropriate prices cannot be found. Such purposes as recreation must therefore be judged on other criteria, for the use of benefit-cost analysis for them not only is invalid, but casts general doubt and suspicion on procedures which can effectively serve a high purpose where they are appropriate. ... To assure proper consideration of such immeasurable outputs, an analysis of intangibles should be part of every project report. Verbal discussion of the intangible benefits and costs will communicatae the facts to Congress more clearly than invalid benefit estimates. Relevant figures may be submitted without forcing them into the benefit-cost framework; for example, recreation benefits of a project can be described in terms of expected use."

Eckstein's attitude towards the valuation of recreation in monetary terms might be characterized as: "it can't be done, and you shouldn't try." By contrast, the Green Book had at least said "try." Moreover, there was some reason to believe that it *could* be done. The source was no less than Hotelling. This came about in the following manner. In June 1947, the directorate of the National Park Service

(NPS) was casting about for some way to place an economic value on the services provided by national parks in order to justify the federal government's expenditures on them. Their problem was compounded by the fact that, at that time, there were no entrance fees for visiting the national parks. Hence, the parks generated no revenues: they were a pure drain on the federal budget. The project was assigned to an economist in the Planning Division, Roy Prewitt, and he conceived the idea of sending a letter to 10 distinguished experts soliciting their advice. Almost all of them responded negatively – they counselled that it would be impossible to measure recreational values in monetary terms. The chief exception was Harold Hotelling, then a professor of mathematical statistics at the University of North Carolina. He saw that, from a conceptual standpoint, the question was identical to that considered by Dupuit. Dupuit had sought a criterion for determining the value of social overhead capital such as a road or a bridge and had pointed out that the total value was *more* than the aggregate revenues collected, since many people would be willing, if necessary, to pay more than they actually did for the use of the bridge – an extreme case would be where the bridge was free, but people valued it at some positive amount. Dupuit, and Hotelling following him, argued that the social value of the bridge was measured by the area under people's demand curve for its use. The practical problem was to measure this demand curve. It certainly existed – with a high toll, there would be a low demand to use the bridge while, with a low toll, the demand would undoubtedly be higher – but it was latent: only a single point on the curve was observed, corresponding to the particular price being charged (perhaps zero), and from this nothing could be inferred about the position of the *rest* of the curve. For that, there would have to be some variation in price. Hotelling saw that valuing a national park or a lake was conceptually the same as valuing Dupuit's bridge. But, there was one possible difference which worked in the park's favor, namely that there were other inputs associated with the use of the park, such as travel, equipment or lodging, which could provide the necessary price variation. Eckstein had dismissed these items as "not expenditures for the lake" but they *were* – the costs of travelling to the lake or the park were as much a part of the cost of enjoying its recreational services as an entrance fee: they were not captured by the NPS, but they set a price on visiting the site. Moreover, this price would vary among potential visitors residing at different distances. If this price could be measured, one could construct a demand function for visits to the recreation site, from which its value could be determined.

Prewitt went along with the majority opinion of the other consultants and concluded that "recreational values cannot be measured in dollar terms." The consultants responses and this analysis were published in an NPS report in 1949. Hotelling's response was included in the report but received no attention. It remained buried in obscurity for almost a decade, while the NPS turned to other methods of assigning "judgment values" to outdoor recreation. In 1950, the NPS adopted a policy of assuming, for planning purposes, that primary recreation benefits were approximately equal in value to the costs of providing and maintaining recreation sites, and that secondary recreation benefits were approximately equal to primary benefits; "thus, benefits are always twice as great as costs in NPS calculations." This practice was not without its critics – including Eckstein – and it was abandoned in 1957. In that year Senator Robert Kerr held hearings before his subcommittee on Public Works regarding the evaluation of recreation benefits from reservoirs. Testimony was presented that "failure properly to estimate recreational potentials of reservoir projects had led to dangerous overcrowding with, in many cases, actual recreational use in the first year far exceeding facilities provided." Remedial action was recommended. As a result, both the Corps of Engineers and the NPS decided to adopt a dollar value – initially, $1.60 per visitor day – for the purpose of valuing recreation benefits. This figure was based on a previous study of entrance charges and other costs at several hundred private recreation areas; it was intended as judgment estimate of the consumer's surplus for at typical visitor at a national park – i.e. of the amount that a discriminating monopolist could capture through entrance fees. As the earlier quote indicates, Eckstein did not think much of this method either.

It was just at this time, however, that Hotelling's idea finally resurfaced – ironically, almost simultaneously with the publication of Eckstein's book. In 1956 the State of California was planning the Feather River Project and it retained an economic consulting company to quantify the recreational benefits associated with the project's reservoirs. This company became aware of Hotelling's idea through Harold Ellis, a professor of economics at the University of California, Berkely and fellow consultant to the NPS in 1947, and decided to try it out. Accordingly, a survey of visitors was conducted at several sites in the Sierras during 1956 to obtain information about where they had come from and how much they had spent. On the basis of these data, a rough demand curve was traced out and an approximate estimate of consumer's surplus was constructed. This analysis appeared in Trice and Wood (1958), which is the first published application of what subsequently became known as the "travel-cost" method of estimating the economic value of recreation. The second appeared only a few months later. In 1957, Marion Clawson had initiated a research project at Resources for the Future to collect data on visitation at Yosemite and other major national parks for the purpose of applying the Hotelling method. His preliminary estimates of consumer's surplus based on these data were published in Clawson (1959), which stated as its premise "that it is both theoretically possible and practically manageable to put monetary value on outdoor recreation. The conceptual and theoretical problems, while somewhat novel, are not insurmountable nor perhaps unusually difficult; the problem of getting accurate and dependable data is serious but still manageable." Putting the travel coost method on the map was Clawson's goal, and with this in mind he was soon joined at RFF by Jack Knetsch; their joint work was first circulated in draft form in 1961, and subsequently published as a book, Clawson and Knetsch (1966). Meanwhile, other papers applying the travel cost method were published by Lerner (1962), Ullman and Volk (1962), Knetsch (1963), Brown et al. (1964) and Wennergren (1964).

Two related developments should be mentioned. In 1958, the U.S. Outdoor Recreation Review Commission was appointed to examine the future needs for outdoor recreation resources. As one of several studies, it sponsored a national household survey on outdoor recreation participation in 1960–61. The Commission's report was published in 1962, and it led to the creation of a Bureau of Outdoor Recreation within the Department of Interior for the purpose of planning and coordinating the development of outdoor recreation facilities at the national level. The Bureau sponsored a second national survey of outdoor recreation in 1965; an analysis of the data from the two surveys was subsequently published in Cicchetti, Seneca and Davidson (1969). Secondly, in 1962 recreation was given official status as a primary purpose of federal water projects, alongside navigation, flood control, hydropower, and irrigation, U.S. Senate (1962). The procedures for valuing recreation benefits were promulgated in U.S. Senate (1964); they were based on an updated and expanded version of the 1957 unit-day values.

By this time, it was apparent that benefit-cost analysis had become established as both a legitimate branch of welfare economics and a standard tool for the analysis of government expenditures. In 1960, it had been introduced by Robert McNamara to the Department of Defense in the form of Program Planning and Budgeting (PPB) and, in 1965, President Johnson directed all federal agencies to start using PPB. The range of applications covered in the literature had by now widened from water resource projects to other facets of government activity such as road and rail transportation, [Mohring (1961), Mohring and Harwitz (1962), Foster and Beesley (1963), and Winch (1963], health care [Weisbrod (1960), Mushkin (1962), Klarman (1965)], education and job training [Bowman (1962), Hansen (1963), Becker (1964) and Blaug (1965)], and urban renewal [Rothenberg (1965)]. The first major academic assessments of this new vintage were publishehd in Dorfman (1965) and Prest and Turvey (1965). Like the contemporaneous work on recreation, it valued non-marginal impacts in terms of changes in consumer's plus producer's surplus derived from underlying demand and supply functions and, in order to deal with the demand for an intangible such as health, it found a surrogate in the observed demand correlated marketed commodities such as expenditures on averting or preventative behavior.

With regard to water resources project evaluation, developments since 1965 can be subdivided into two periods: from 1965 to about 1980, and from then to the present. During the first of these periods, much academic attention was focused on refining the travel-cost approach to valuing recreation. In terms of both statistical methodology and consistency with the economic theory of futility-maximizing choice. As a crude index of the growth of this research, while about 5 papers on travel cost were published between 1960 and 1964, about 15 were published between 1965 and 1969 and about 35 between 1970 and 1976. Furthermore, the publication in 1974 of Karl-Goran Maler's treatise on environmental economics represented a landmark in showing how changes in the quality of market goods, and quasi-market goods such as recreation, could be treated rigorously within the framework of utility theory. In reflection of its maturation, when the federal governement's principles and standards for evaluating water projects were revised in 1973 they now listed the travel-cost method as an approved procedure, although they still permitted the use of unit-day values as an interim measure.

The major innovation during this period concerned the valuation of what the Green Book had called intangibles, although these would now be defined as items for which there was no direct market demand function nor could one be inferred, as in the travel-cost method, from the demand for surrogate market commodities. For those items a different approach was required: one would have to interview people and ask them directly for their monetary evaluation. In fact, this approach, known as contingent valuation (CV), had first been suggested in 1947, the same year that Hotelling proposed the travel cost method. It was suggested by S. V. Ciriacy-Wantrup (1947), a professor in the Department of Agricultural Economics at the University of California, Berkeley, in the context of a discussion of measuring the benefits from soil conservation practices, some of which were collective, extra-market goods – his phrase – such as reduced siltation of reservoirs or reduced impairment of scenic resources. He characterized the essential problem as being how to obtain a demand schedule for such goods, and suggested the following solution: "Individuals of a sample or of a social group as a whole may be asked how much money they are willing to pay for successive additional quantities of a collective extra-market good. The choices offered relate to quantities consumed by all members of a social group. If the group interrogated is only a sample ... the modal schedule of the sample is obtained, and each point on this schedule is then multiplied by the number of individuals in the whole social group being investigated." What was thus obtained could be taken as the analog of a market demand schedule for the collective good. Ciriacy-Wantrup went on to consider some possible objections to this evaluation procedure, including the objection that "expectations of the incidence of costs in the form of taxes will bias the responses to interrogation." However, he was confident that "through proper education and proper design of questionnaires or interviews it would seem possible to keep this potential bias small." The same suggestion was repeated in Ciriacy-Wantrup's 1952 book on resource economics. Both times, however, it fell on deaf ears.

Nevertheless, there was considerable intutitive appeal to this notion of surveying people and asking them directly what they would be willing to pay. Thus, when the first applications of CV occurred, the authors conceived the idea independently and were unaware that it had been suggested earlier by Ciriacy-Wantrup. The first such application appears to have been in 1958 at the bequest of none other than the NPS. The circumstances are described by Mack and Myers (1965): "In a survey of the outdoor recreational activities and preferences of persons living in the Delaware River Basin area, respondents were qestioned about their willingness to pap entrance fees. They expressed a general willingness to pay entrance fees for 'satisfactory publicly owned outdoor recreational areas' for day trips. ... The median average amount they said they would consider a reasonable fee was 50 cents per person." To this, Mack and Myers added the followingg qualification: "The interviewers noted, however, that this finding must be interpreted with some caution because people often express a willingness to pay before the fact, but are much less willing when the time comes. But those respondents who are puffing up their status by indicating a willingness to pay a fee are undoubtedly balanced by others who hesitate to admit such willing-nesss lest officials might be moved to institute or raise fees. Such con-flicting biases fatally weaken interpretations that might be drawn from the data. But this does not necessarily signify that the approach itself is barren; rather, it may argue for a more searching methodo-logy ... [One] technique entails the selection of three or four similar large sample groups who would be told that a proposed service or facility would cost a different price long an ascending scale. For example, one group might be told the admission charge was 50 cents, the next group that it was 75 cents, and so on. Each would be asked to indicate on a "reaction scale" the statement that best reflects their own attitude towards this price. The resulting data could indicate when a sizable "resistance point" is reached. "This actually fore-shadows a later development in contingent valuation. Mack and Myers conclude with the assessment that "the approach is worth exploring more fully."

The second application of CV occurred in 1961 when Robert K. Davis (1963) interviewed a sample of hunters and other visitors to the Maine woods for his Harvard Ph. D. dissertation on the benefits of outdoor recreation, and asked them how much they would have been willing to pay (WTP) to engage in these activities. Four years elapsed before the next application. In 1965, influenced by Davis, Ridker (1967) included some WTP question in two surveys that he conduct-ed on attitudes to air pollution in Philadelphia and Syracuse. In 1969, Hammack and Brown (1974) surveyed duck hunters in several western states to elicit both their maximum WTP for the right to hunt waterfowl and their minimum willingness to accept to surrender this right. In 1970, Cicchetti and Smith (1973) surveyed hikers in wilder-ness areas for their WTP to reduce crowding in these areas, and Acton (1973) conducted a CB survey to value health programs which reduced the risk of dying from heart attacks. In 1972, Darling (1973) conducted a CV study on the valuation of amenities at urban parks in California, Alan Randall and colleagues initiated a series of CV studies to value visibility in the Four Corners Area [Randall, Ives and Eastman (1974)]. Indeed, when Hanemann (1978) was conduct-ing a survey of Boston area households in 1974 to collect data for a travel cost model of beach recreation, CV seemed sufficiently well established and a sufficiently obvious thing to do that he included a CV component in his questionnaire. More than a dozen other CV studies were conducted in the US during the next few years. By the end of the decade, this number was growing exponentially. In 1979, official recognition was given to CV when the Water Resources Coun-cil revised the Principles and Standards for water project evaluation:

the new edition included travel cost, CV, and unit day values as the three recommended methods of valuation.

The other important innovations during the period 1965–1980 concerned the conceptual foundations of non-market valuation and grew out of two seminar papers by Burton Weisbrod (1964) and John Krutilla (1967). Both papers started from the premise that the natural environment is not a conventional type of economic commodity, and that some of people's motives for valuing it may differ from those for valuing private market goods. In particular, people may value the natural environment – at least in part – out of considerations unrelated to their own immediate and direct use of it. Weisbrod focused on uncertainty and what became known as "option value": some people who do not now visit a national park, say, may still be wiling to pay money to protect it from destruction or irreversible damage because they want to preserve their option of visiting it in the future. Krutilla focused on what became known as "bequest value" and "existence" or "non-use" value. Some people would be willing to pay because they want to preserve the park for future generations. And, others would be willing to pay even if they knew that neither they nor their children would ever visit it because, as Krutilla put it, they "obtain satisfaction from mere knowledge that part of the wilderness in North America remains, even though they would be appalled by the prospect of being exposed to it." All of these are legitimate sources of value, Krutilla and Weisbrod felt, but they would not be captured by conventional demand analysis, nor would they be respected by private managers of the resource. These arguments have become widely accepted. However, because both authors employed a largely non-mathematical mode of exposition, there was some ambiguity as to the precise definition of the concepts that they were describing. A substantial literature was generated before those issues were largely resolved during the 1980's. A key implication of the consensus definition which has emerged is that non-use value can *only* be measured by the CV method: it cannot be measured through the travel cost or similar methods that rely on the demand for surrogate market goods because it reflects a value placed on the natural environment from quite separate motives.

The other distinctive characteristic of this period was the relatively limited interaction between federal agencies and the academic research community. During the 1950's many of the leading researchers had worked quite closely with the agencies and were personally interested in improving project evaluation practices. The new generation of researchers who became active in the late 1960's and the 1970's were, on the whole, more concerned with benefit-cost analysis as an academic field and had little interest in – perhaps, even some disdain for – what the governement agencies did.

This began to change in the late 1970's. The period since about 1980 has been marked by a heightened level of interaction between the academic community and government agencies, and a renewed interest on the part of the agencies in employing more up-to-date and sophisticated measurement techniques for public decisionmaking. During this period, environmental valuation came of age. As it did so, it has emerged from the academy into the rough and tumble of the outside world.

One of the important influences in this regard was the 1979 Revision of the Principles & Guidelines, but there are many others. For example, in preparation for the 1980 Resource Planning Assessment (RPA), the Forest Service launched a large-scale effort to collect data on the economic values associated with recreational uses of forest lands, in order to balance these against timber production and other uses. This research effort was expanded for the 1985 and 1990 RPAs. Another example is what has become known in the electric utility industry as environmental costing. At the federal level, the Electric Consumers Protection Act of 1986 required the Federal Electric Utility Commission to take account of environmental impacts when issuing licenses for new hydro facilities or relicensing existing ones. At about the same time, some state Public Utility Commissions (PUCs), which regulate the pricing and investment behavior of investor-owned utilities, started becoming interested in the same concept. One of the pioneers was the New York State Energy Research & Development Authority which in 1988, inspired by Hohmeyer's (1988) study of externality costs in Germany, commissioned the first major US study of the environmental costs of electricity generation [Pace (1991)]. Since then, 29 PUCs have required, or are now considering, the incorporation of environmental externality costs in electricity supply planning and resource selection procedures.

However, the greatest impetus to the diffusion of environmental valuation in the US over the past decade has come from Executive Order (EO) 12291 and from CERCLA. EO 12291 was issued by President Reagan a few weeks after he took office in 1981 with the aim of controlling what he regarded as excessive government regulation. In pursuit of this goal, he required all federal agencies to prepare a Regulatory Impact Analysis (RIA) before undertaking any major regulatory action, including both the promulgation of new regulations and the review or revision of existing ones. The RIAs had to be submitted to the Office of Management and Budget (OMB) for review and approval. OMB was given the power both to define what constituted a major regulatory action (and to waive the requirement of a regulatory review, if it so chose) and to specify the procedures to be followed in conducting a RIA. Grubb et al. (1984) reviewed the accomplishments of EO 12291 after two years and found them to be modest. The RIAs that had been conducted were highly variable in quality. For the most part, they were based on off-the-shelf information and very few resources were devoted to their preparation. At worst, they were uninformative and misleading. Moreover, there were obvious signs of bias in their coverage: OMB tended to require a RIA for actions involving more regulation but to waive the RIA for actions involving deregulation or the granting of exemptions from regulation. Besides issuing a vacuous, five-page leaflet, OMB had done nothing to promote consistency in the RIAs or improve their quality. Nevertheless, Grubb et al. concluded, "more important than the absolute number of high-quality analyses under EO 12291 – which is small by any standard – is the fact that benefit-cost analysis seems to be taking its place in the routine procedures associated with the regulatory process. The consciousness that costs and benefits need to be analyzed rather than assumed, that alternatives need to be considered, that information is uncertain and may require sensitivity analyses, that the claims of external interest groups need to be independently checked – all these views are implicit in EO 12291 and are present in the best RIAs that have been performed so far." Almost a decade later, the same conclusion still holds.

While EO 12291 applied to tall federal regulations, its impact fell somewhat disproportionately on environmental regulations. This is partly because of the bias noted above, but also because the EPA responded to it more openly than some of the other agencies. As Andrews (1984) noted, during most of the 1970's the EPA's economic analysis had focused largely on the costs of pollution control as "a flank-protection strategy against potential business attacks;" it did relatively less on the benefits side until the late 1970's, when the growing pressure from the regulatory reform movement forced it to pay more sustained attention to the balancing of benefits against costs. Thus, after the apperance of EO 12291, EPA was one of only two agencies to prepare its own manual on benefit-cost analysis (the other was the Department of Transportation). Moreover, it adopted a strategy of funding basic and applied research on various aspects of benefits analysis. Among the work funded in this way was the research by Smith and Desvousges (1986) on applying the travel cost and CV methods to measure the use and non-use benefits associated with improving water in the Monogahela River, the work by Bockstael, McConnell and Strand (1988) on applying the travel cost and hedonic methods to value improved water quality in Chesapeake Bay, and the 1984 Palo Alto conference assessing the state-of-the-art of the CV method.

A feature of that assessment was the involvement of a review panel of eminent economists and psychologists, including Nobel laureate Kenneth Arrow. At the conference, many leading researchers offered their views about CV's potential as a means of valuing environmental goods [the proceedings were subsequently published in Cummings et al. (1986)]. The lead authors' conclusion was that, while the method showed promise, some real challenges remained. In particular, more focused research was needed on the methodological foundations of CV, including the theory of individual behavior in contingent market settings, the question of incentive compatibility, and the specification of "reference operating conditions" for the accuracy of CV measures. Around the time of the conference there was a quantum leap of interest in CV, and some of the new work addressed in various ways the issues raised at the conference. For example, researchers began to move away from the open-ended questioning that had been the hallmark of the early CV studies to closed-ended questions in which respondents were offered a single dollar amount of payment, to which they could respond "yes" or "no." This format had been mentioned by Mack and Myers (1965) and had first been implemented by Bishop and Heberlein (1979). It was found to be more incentive compatible and, since it could be cast in the form of a referendum, it tended to make the WTP question more realistic for respondents. The new research was also marked by a greater attention to the utility-theoretic interpretation of CV responses and, in many cases for the first time, a heightened sensitivity to the survey research aspects of the CV method. The new point of view was fully reflected in Robert Mitchell and Richard Carson's treatise on CV, published in 1989. This work sought to place CV in a broader context as a technique of social science research, involving elements of economics, sociology, psychology and survey research, and having strong links to public opinion polling and market research. It drew on the literature from all of these fields in order to define what it would take to obtain reliable and valid CV measures. Through its scope it set a new standard for the field.

Compared to EO 12291, CERCLA's impact on environmental valutaion was slower to develop, but ultimately far more dramatic. The term is an acronym for the Comprehensive Environmental Response, Compensation and Liability Act, passed by Congress in December 1980 primarily in response to the notorious case of dioxin contamination at Love Canal, NY that had come to light in 1978.

CERCLA contained two main sets of provisions. By far the better known – at least until recently – were those providing for the creation of Superfund to finance the remedial clean-up of existing hazardous waste sites. The other provisions established a liability on the potentially responsible parties (PRPs) to pay damages for the injuries to natural resources resulting from the spill or release of hazardous substances, in addition to the costs of clean-up, removal, remediation, and any other necessary response costs including the costs of the damage assessment. In order to exercise these liabilities and recover these damages, CERCLA created the legal concept of a resource trustee. The federal and state governments would be the trustees for the natural resources owned or controlled by the federal, state or local governments; in this capacity, they would conduct an assessment of the natural resource damages and then take appropriate steps to recover the damages from the PRPs. How were these damages to be assessed? CERCLA required that, within two years, the President promulgate regulations which would identify the "best available procedures" for determining natural resource damages. Congress almost certainly was thinking of something analogous to the Principle & Guidelines for water projects. It stipulated that the regulations would specify both "(A) standard procedures for simplified assessments requiring minimal field observation, including establishing measures of damage based on units of discharge or release or units of affected area, and (B) alternative protocols for conducting assessments in individual cases to determine the type and extent ... of loss." The Type A assessment, as it became known, would be like using off-the-shelf unit day values, whereas the Type B assessment would be a investigatiion tailored to the specifics to the particular incident: the trustees would decide which type to perform. Finally, CERCLA stipulated that the President review the regulations every two years and revise them as appropriate.

The new Reagan administration was less than enthusiastic about the damage liability provisions of CERCLA and did not hurry to implement them, beyond designating the Department of the Interior (DOI) as the agency responsible for promulgating the regulations. In 1984 several states sued DOI for its failure to issue regulations and obtained a court order compelling action. Drafts of the regulations were published in 1985, and the final regulations were issued in August 1986 (Type B) and March 1987 (Type A). The final Type B regulations contained at least two distinctive features. The first was the "lesser-of" rule: the DOI regulations made the measure of damages either replacement/restoration costs or lost use value, *whichever was the lesser.* The second was the "hierarchy of assessment methods." The regulations specified that the diminution in market price should be used to estimate the damages if there existed a reasonably competitive market for the injured resource. Alternatively, if market prices were not appropriate, the damage estimate should be based on the loss in appraised value using commercial appraisal techniques. Only if the trustee had determined that neither the market price nor the appraisal methodologies were appropriate could non-market valuation methods be used, including travel cost, hedonic pricing, unit day values, and CV. Here, too, there was a hierarchy: the use of CV to measure existence or option value was permitted only if no use values could be ascertained. Thus, both CV and non-use values were firmly relegated to an inferior status. While the lesser-of rule was a standard application of economic principles, the hierarchy of methods was nothing short of bizarre within this context of assessing the public (as opposed to private) losses from injuries to natural resources. As permitted by Congress, appeals were filed against these and other aspects of the regulations with the District of Columbia Circuit of the US Court of Appeals: some state governments and environmental groups attacked the rules for being too narrow, while some industrial groups representing potential PRPs attacked them for being too broad – in particular for being too liberal in permitting the use of CV. The DC Court of Appeals issued its *ruling on* what became known as the case of *Ohio v. US Department of the Interior* on Bastille Day in 1989. On the main issues concering environmental valuation it sided firmly with the states. It threw out the lesser-of rule and held that the Congressional intent was to make restoration costs the proper measure of damages, unless they were "grossly disproportionate" to the lost use values. Moreover, it held that Congress had intended lost use values to *include* non-use values: "option and existence values may represent 'passive use,'" the Court wrote, "but they nonetheless reflect utility derived by humans from a resource, and thus prima facie ought to be included in a damage assessment." In the same vein, the Court struck down the hierarchy of assessment methods as "not a reasonable interpretation of the statute." It directed DOI to permit trustees to derive values for natural resource damages "by summing up all reliably caluculated use values, however measured, so long as the trustee does not double count." Lastly, it dealt with the industry petitioners' objections to the use of CV. They had argued that CV could not possible qualify as a "best available procedure" because of the unreliability of CV responses. The court examined this argument at some length and rejected it in no uncertain terms. For example, in response to the argument that "respondents do not actually pay money, and likely will overstate their willingness to pay" the Court replied that "the simple and obvious safeguard against overstatement … is more sophisticated questioning." It found that CV was a best available procedure and it sustained DOI in its conclusion that CV could be utilized as a "valid, proven technique … when properly structured and professionally applied." DOI was directed to revise its regulations in line with all these findings.

By the time of the *Ohio* ruling these issues were of more than academic interest: after a slow start caused by the novelty of the concept as well as by DOI's delays in issuing the regulations, litigation over natural resource damages had by now become a reality. The first suits for natural resource damages were brought by the state of Colorado in connection with the pollution of groundwater and surface water by mining operations at the Eagle Mine near Gilman and the Idarado Mine near Telluride. During 1985 and 1986 the state conducted something like Type B assessments (this was before the DOI regulations had been issued) that included estimates of lost recreation based on unit-day values and estimates of both use and non-use values based on a CV study. In each case, the defendants countered by presenting estimates of lost use value derived from a travel cost analysis intended to account for the presence of substitute sites [a penetrating analysis of the economic tactics in these cases is provided by Kopp and Smith (1989)]. Although these cases involved the first court test of the CV method, the outcome was inconclusive – the Eagle Mine case was settled without a court decision, and the Idarado case is still in process. In 1983, the fedral government brought its first natural resources damage action in connection with PCB contamination of New Bedford Harbor in Massachusetts. The government's damage assessment was conducted in 1986 and involved travel cost analysis and hedonic property value analysis, but not CV; the defendant conducted similar analyses in 1987. These were not tested in open court, however, and the case was settled in 1990–91. The pace of events quickened in 1988. In April, there was a spill at the Shell Oil refinery near San Francisco and the state of California initiated a natural resources damage action; a CV study was contemplated, but this was not followed up and the damages were estimated on the basis of off-the-shelf information (the case was settled the next year – details on this and other cases are provided in Ward and Duffield (1992). In June, Resources for the Future held a conference on natural resource damage assessment which brought the subject to the attention of many environmental economists for the first time [the proceedings are being published in Kopp and Smith (forthcoming)]. In the fall, the state of Montana announced its intention to initiate a natural resources damage action in connection with mining pollution of the Clark Fork Basin. At the end of December, the barge *Nestucca* ruptured off the coast of state of Washington, and oil killed birds and soiled beaches in Washington and British Columbia. The state of Washington and the Canadian government subsequently brought suit and conducted a CV study at the end of 1990 to measure the damages [Rowe, Shaw and Schulze (1992)].

Then, on March 24, 1989, the tanker *Exxon Valdez* ran aground and spilled 11 million gallons of crude oil into the waters of Prince William Sound, a remote and pristine part of Alaska. This was the largest oil spill in U.S. history: it caused substantial environmental damage and attracted worldwide attention. Within a short period of time the state and federal governments, on the one hand, and Exxon, on the other, retained many prominent environmental economists with a view to the natural resource damages litigation that was likely to follow. This was clearly going to involve natural resource damages that were an order of magnitude larger than in any previous case, and non-use values were likely to play a major role. The *Ohio* ruling, coming a few months later, could not have been more timely!

While the *Exxon Valdez* dominated the scene, it was not the only natural resource damage case under way. In addition to those already mentioned, there were several more oil spills on the East Coast later in 1989 and one on the West Coast in 1990 which genereated actions for natural resource damages . In addition, in March 1990 the federal government announced its intention to bring several suits for PCB or DDT contamination of harbors in California and Washington. All of these cases involved some degree of non-use values and some possibility of CV. Moreover, there was action in Congress: in response to the *Exxon Valdez,* an Oil Pollution Act was passed in August 1990 which superseded CERCLA with respect to oil spills (but not other hazardous releases); this act kept many of the elements off CERCLA, including the notion of the federal and state governments as trustees for injured natural resources, but it substantially extended the scope of recoverable damages and it strongly reaffirmed the elements of the *Ohio* ruling dealing with the lesser-of rule and non-use values. As a sign of Congressional dissatisfaction with DOI, the responsibility for promulgating the regulations for the assessment of natural resource damages under the new act was handed to the Department of Commerce's National Oceanic & Atmospheric Administration (NOAA).

During 1989 and 1990, the state and federal governments worked on separate natural resource damage assessments for the *Exxon Valdez*. Appraently, both included some work on CV. Then, in mid-

March 1991, it was announced that the state and federal governments were ready to settle with Exxon on payment of $ 100 million in criminal fines and $ 900 million in natural resource damages, the latter to be paid over 11 years without interest. According to some newspaper accounts, the notion of a $ 1 billion settlement had originated with Governor-elect Hickel of Alaska in December 1990, a month before he took office. However it was conceived, it bore no known relationship to the findings of the natural resource damage assessments; several newspaper accounts suggested that they put the damages at several billions of dollars. At the request of the Hickel administration, the economic components of both the federal and state damage assessments were not publicly released. At the end of April the settlement was rejected by a federal judge in Alaska as financially inadequate relative to the magnitude of the damages. However, the judge apparently had a change of heart, for he accepted a virtually identical settlement at a hearing on October 8, 1991.

While there are still some private lawsuits by Alaskan recreationists claiming lost consumer's surplus, the settlement ended the bulk of the natural resource damage litigation. But, at least for some of the economists on both sides, the argument continued in other forums. The first grew out of DOI's revision of its regulations, as mandated by the *Ohio* ruling. In September 1989, DOI solicited comments from the public on some aspects of the revisions. The majority of comments came from economists associated with potential industrial PRPs. Most of them argued that CV was unreliable and that the estimation of non-use values should be restricted to a limited class of cases – long-lasting or irreversible damage to unique, well-known resources. In both respects, their position was effectively that the *Ohio* ruling had been wrong. Eighteen months later, in April 1991, DOI issued its new version of the regulations for public comment. These followed the *Ohio* ruling faithfully with respect to the lesser-of rule, but somewhat reluctantly with respect to the hierarchy of methods, CV, and non-use values. The preamble – but not the main text of the regulations – suggested that non-use values be limited along the lines proposed by the PRPs. With regard to the choice of methodologies, DOI remarked that «generally the use value-marketed valuation methodologies are more reliable than the use value-nonmarketed valuation methodologies, which in turn are more reliable than the non-use value-contingent valuation methodology." Moreover, while in the preamble DOI agreed that CV was the *only* method for assessing non-use values, in the main text it opined that, when used to determine non-use values, CV was the least reliable method. To the untrained eye, these statements might seem inconsistent and at variance with the *Ohio* ruling. However, as before, the majority of the public comments came from the PRP side and either supported the regulatins or urged a more restrictive position with regard to to CV and non-use values.

DOI was supposed to have issued its final regulations this spring – but that was overtaken by other events. Starting in April 1991, at the time the settlement was first proposed, Exxon's economic consultants conducted a series of theoretical and empirical studies on CV for public release. That came a year later, on April 2–3 1992, when Exxon held what it described as a seminar in Washington, DC, to which it invited several hundred attorneys and governement officials, along with economists who had been involved on both sides of the *Exxon Valdez* case. This was more of a public relations exercise than a conventional seminar: the only speakers were Exxon's consultants, their oral presentations were polished but light on the details, the written papers were more detailed but were not to be distributed until after the seminar was over, and questions from the floor were tightly controlled. The thrust of all the papers, which are to be published in Hausman (forthcoming), was that CV does not measure an economic value that conforms with the economic theory of preferences, that CV is biased and does not provide reliable estimates for non-use values, and that, because of the impossibility of measuring them accurately, non-use values should be omitted from natural resource damages. This seemed strongly reminiscent of Eckstein's attitude towards the travel cost method 35 years earlier: it can't be done, and you shouldn't even try. Since Exxon has not yet released the data used in the empirical studies, there has been no independent verification of whether they show what the authors claim; some questions to this effect have been raised by Carson and Hanemann (1992) based on inconsistencies in the published papers. The surveys used in these studies seem to have been conducted in a hurried manner and contain obvious potential for error. Moreover, there appear to be some problems with the theoritical analysis of non-use value. Clearly, these are matters which will be debated for a long time to come.

At the same time that Exxon was preparing for this conference, it was also vigorously lobbying the Bush administration to intervene both in DOI's damage regulations and in the regulations that NOAA would start to develop in 1992 for oil spills. The pressure on NOAA grew particularly intense. In response, the week after the Exxon seminar. NOAA's General Counsel announced that he was convening a blue-ribbon panel to advise him on the use of CV in natural resource damage assessments for oil spills. The panel is headed by two Nobel laureats – Kenneth Arrow, who had been retained by Exxon but was not on the program at the April seminar, and Robert Solow, who had been retained by the state of Alaska. The other members are the economists Edward Leamer, Paul Portney and Roy Radner, and the sociologist and survey research expert Howard Schuman. The panel has identified three questions for consideration: "(1) Can constructed market methodologies, including CV, be implemented reliably ... to calculate non-use values for natural resources? If so, under what circumstances and under what guidance? (2) If constructed market methodologies cannot be implemented to reliably calculate non-use values, what additional work or studies should be conducted to refine constructed market methodologies so they can reliably determine non-use values of natural resources? (3) What are the alternatives, if any, to the use of constructed market methodologies to reliably calculate non-use values?" The panel is receiving written testimony on these issues through October 1, 1992, It is expected to deliver its report some time in the fall. Pending its report, both NOAA and DOI have put their rule writing process on hold.

In the U.S., then, this is a somewhat exciting time for those engaged in environmental valuation. CV, in particular, faces a crucial challenge, from which it surely will emerge as a stronger tool. A recent bibliography by Carson et al. (1992) lists almost one thousand CV studies throughout the world. Much as some might wish this, it seems unlikely to vanish overnight. The concern that due weight be given to what were once known as intangibles and are now called non-use values goes back to the very beginnings of benefit-cost analysis in the US in the 1930's. This is no less valid today. It was recognized in the 1960's that benefit-cost analysis may always attract some controversy because of the crucial importance of distributional considerations. Of course, this also applies to the benefit-cost analysis of environmental projects. But, there is a sense in which non-use value plays the same role within environmental valuation that income distribution has played within conventional benefit-cost analysis: it is an indicator of the maturity of the discipline, in that the ability of economics to render an adequate accounting of it becomes the hallmark for judging its success as a social science.

References

Jan P. Acton, *Evaluating Public Programs to Save Lives: The Case of Heart Attacks* Research Report R-73-02, Rand Corporation, Santa Monica, CA, 1973.

Richard N. L. Andrews, "Economics and Environmental Decisions, Past and Present," in V. Kerry Smith (ed.) *Environmental Policy Under Reagan's Executive Order: The Role of Benefit-Cost Analysis* Chapel Hill: University of North Carolina Press. 1984.

K. J. Arrow, *social Choice and Individual Values* New York: John Wiley, 1951.

F. M. Bator, "The Simple Analytics of Welfare Maximization," *American Economic Review* 1957.

W. J. Baumol, *Welfare Economics and the Theory of the State* London: Longmans, 1952.

G. S. Becker, *Human Capital* New York: Columbia University Press, 1964.

Richard C. Bishop and Thomas A. Heberlein, "Measuring Values of Extra-Market Goods: Are Indirect Measures Biased?" *American Journal of Agricultural Economics* 61 (1979) pp. 926–30.

M. Blaug, "The Rate of Return on Investment in Education in Great Britain," *The Manchester School,* Vol. XXXIII, 3, September 1965.

Nancy E. Bockstael, Kenneth E. McConnell, and Ivar E. Strand, *Benefits from Improvements in Chesapeake Bay Water Quality* Report for USEPA Cooperative Agreement CR-811043-01-0, Washington, D. C.: US Environmental Protection Agency, 1988.

Mary J. Bowman, "Social Returns to Education," *International Social Science Journal,* Vol. XIV, No. 4, 1962.

W. G. Brown, E. N. Castle and A. Singh, *An Economic Evaluation of the Oregon Salmon and Steelhead Sport Fishery* Oregon Agricultural Experiment Station Technical Bulletin No. 78, Corvallis, 1964.

R. T. Carson, N. C. Conaway, A. Albelrini, N. Flores, K. Riggs, J. Vencil and J. Winsen, *A Bibliography of Contingent Valuation Studies and Papers* NRDA Inc, La Jolla, CA June, 1992.

Richard T. Carson and W. Michael Hanemann, "A Critique of the Exxon Papers on CV," Working paper, UC Berkeley Department of Agricultural & Resource Economics, presented at the AAEA Annual Meetings, Baltimore MD, August 10, 1992.

C. J. Cicchetti, J. Seneca, and P. Davidson, *The Demand and Supply of Outdoor Recreation.* Washington: D.C.: U.S. Bureau of Outdoor Recreation, June 1969.

Charles J. Cicchetti and V. Kerry Smith, "Congestion, Quality Deterioration, and Optimal Use: Wilderness Recreation in the Spanish Peaks Primitive Area," *Social Science Research* Vol. 2 (1973), pp. 15–30.

S. V. Ciriacy-Wantrup, "Capital Returns from Soil-Conservation Practices," *Journal of Farm Economics* 29 (1947) pp. 1181–1196.

S. V. Ciriacy-Wantrup, *Resource Conservation: Economics and Policies.* Berkeley: University of California Press, 1952.

Marion Clawson, *Methods of Measuring the Demand for and Value of Outdoor Recreation.* Reprint No. 10, Resources for the Future, Inc., Washington, 1959.

Marion Clawson and J. L. Knetsch, *Economics of Outdoor Recreation* Baltimore: Johns Hopkins Press, 1966.

R. G. Cummings, D. S. Brookshire and W. D. Schulze, *Valuing Environmental Goods: An Assessment of the Contingent Valuation Method.* New Jersey: Rowman & Allanheld, 1986.

Arthur H. Darling, "Measuring Benefits Generated by Urban Water Parks," *Land Economics* Vol. 49, No. 1 (1973) pp. 22–34.

Robert K. Davis, *The Value of Outdoor Recreation: An Economic Study of the Maine Woods* Ph.D. Dissertation, Harvard University Department of Economics, 1963.

Robert Dorfman (ed.) *Measuring Benefits of Government Investments* Washington, D. C.: The Brookings Institution, 1965.

Jules Dupuit, "De la Mesure de l'Utilite des Travaux Publics." *Annales des Ponts et Chaussees,* 2nd series, 8 (1944). Reprinted in translation as "On the Measurement of the Utility of Public Works" in *International Economic Papers,* 2 (1952) pp. 83–110.

Otto Eckstein, *Water-Resource Development: The Economics of Project Evaluation* Cambridge: Harvard University Press, 1958.

C. D. Foster and M. E. Beesley, "Estimating the Social Benefit of Constructing an Underground Railway in London," *Journal of the Royal Statistical Society,* Vol. 126, Part 1, 1963.

J. de V. Graff, *Theoretical Welfare Economics* Cambridge: Cambridge University Press, 1957.

W, Norton Grubb, Dale Whittington, and Michael Humphries, "The Ambiguities of Benefit-Cost Analysis: An Evaluation of Regulatory Impact Analyses under Executive Order 12291," in V. Kerry Smith (ed.) *Environmental Policy Under Reagan's Executive Order: The Role of Benefit-Cost Analysis* Chapel Hill: University of North Carolina Press, 1984.

Judd Hammack and Gardner Mallard Brown Jr., *Waterfowl and Wetlands: Toward Bioeconomic Analysis* Baltimore: The Johns Hopkins University Press for Resources for the Future, 1974.

R. J. Hammond, *Benefit-Cost Analysis and Water-Pollution Control* Food Research Institute, Standford University Press, 1960.

W. Michael Hanemann, *A Methodological and Empirical Study of the Recreation Benefits from Water Quality Improvement* Ph. D. Dissertation, Harvard University Department of Economics, 1978.

W. L. Hansen, "Total and Private Returns to Investment in Schooling," *Journal of Political Economy* Vol. LXXI, April 1963.

Jerry A. Hausman (ed) *Contingent Valuation: A Critical Assessment* New York: North-Holland, forthcoming.

Jack Hirshleifer, James C. de Haven, Jerome W. Milliman, *Water Supply: Economics, Technology and Policy* Chicago: University of Chicago Press, 1960.

Olav Hohmeyer, *Social Costs of Energy Consumption: External Effects of Electricity Generation in the Federal Republic of Germany* Berlin: Springer-Verlag, 1988.

Harold Hotelling, "The General Welfare in Relation to Problems of Taxation and of Railway and Utility Rates." *Econometrica* 6 (1938) pp. 242–69.

Inter-Agency River Basin Committee (Sub-Committee on Costs and Budgets), *Proposed Practices for Economic Analysis of River Basin Projects."* Washington, D. C., May 1950.

Herbert E. Klarman, "Syphilis Control Programs," in Robert Dorfman (ed.) *Measuring Benefits of Government Investments* Washington, D. C.: The Brookings Institution, 1965.

Jack L. Knetsch, "Outdoor Recreation Demands and Benefits." *Land Economics* 39 (November 1963)

Raymond J. Kopp and V. Kerry Smith, "Benefit Estimation Goes to Court: The Case of Natural Resource Damage Assessments," *Journal of Policy Analysis and Management* 8 (1989) pp. 593–612.

R. J. Kopp and V. K. Smith (eds.) *Valuing Natural Assets: The Economics of Natural Resource Damage Assessment* Washington, DC: Resources for the Future, forthcoming.

John V. Krutilla, "Conservation Reconsidered," *American Economic Review* Vol. 57, No. 4, September 1967, pp. 777–786.

John V. Krutilla and Otto Eckstein, *Multiple Purpose River Development: Studies in Applied Economics* Baltimore: Johns Hopkins Press, 1958.

Lionel J. Lerner, *Quantitative Indices of Recreational Values,* University of Nevada, Conference Proceedings of the Committee on the Economics of Water Resource Development, Report No. 11, Reno, 1962.

I. M. D. Little, *A Critique of Welfare Economics* Oxford: Oxford University Press, 1950.

Ruth P. Mack and Sumner Myers, "Outdoor Recreation," in Robert Dorfman (ed.) *Measuring Benefits of Government Investments* Washington, D. C.: The Brookings Institution, 1965.

Arthur Maass et al,, *Design of Water-Resource Systems* Cambridge, MA: Harvard University Press, 1962.

Karl-Goran Maler, *Environmental Economics: A Theoretical Inquiry* Baltimore: The Johns Hopkins University Press for Resources for the Future, 1974

Stepen A. Marglin, *Approaches to Dynamic Investment Planning* Amsterdam: North Holland, 1963.

Roland N. McKean, *Efficiency in Government Through Systems Analysis* New York: John Wiley & Sons, 1958.

Robert Cameron Mitchell and Richard T. Carson, *Using Surveys to Value Public Goods: The Contingent Valuation Method* Washington, D. C.: Resources for the Future, 1989.

H. Mohring, "Land Values and the Measurement of Highway Benefits," *Journal of Political Economy,* Vol. LXIX (June, 1961).

H. Mohring and N. Harwitz, *Highway Benefits: An Analytical Framework* North-Western University Press, 1962.

Selma J. Mushkin, "Health as an Investment," *Journal of Political Economy,* Vol. LXX (Supplement), October 1962.

Outdoor Recreation Resources Commission, *Outdoor Recreation for America: A Report to the President and the Congress.* Washington: U. S. Government Printing Office, 1962

Pace University Center for Environmental Legal Studies, *Environmental Costs of Electricty* New York: Oceana Publications, 1991.

A. R. Prest and R. Turvey, "Cost-Benefit Analysis: A Survey. *Economic Journal* December 1965.

Robert D. Rowe, W. Douglas Shaw, and William Schulze, "Nestucca Oil Spill" in Kevin M. Ward and John W. Duffield, *Natural Resource Damages: Law and Economics* New York: John Wiley, 1992.

V. Kerry Smith and William H. Desvousges, *Measuring Water Quality Benefits* Boston: Kluwer Nijhoff, 1986.

A. H. Trice and S. E. Wood, "Measurement of Recreation Benefits," *Land Economics* XXXIV (August, 1958).

Edward L. Ullman & Donald J. Volk, "An Operational Model for Predicting Reservoir Attendance and Benefits: Implications of a Location Approach to Water Recreation," *Papers of the Michigan Academy of Arts and Letters,* Vol. XLVII, 1962, pp. 473–484.

U. S. National Park Service, *The Economics of Public Recreation: An Economic Study of the Monetary Evaluation of Recreation in the National Parks.* Washington DC, 1949.

U. S. Congress, Senate. *Policies, Standards and Procedures in the Formulation, Evaluation, and Review of Plans for Use and Development of Water and Related Land Resources.* Senate Document No. 97, 87th Cong., 2d sess., 1962.

U. S. Congress, Senate. *Evaluating Standard for Primary Outdoor Recreation Benefits* Supplement No. 1, June, 1964.

Kevin M. Ward and John W. Duffield, *Natural Resource Damages: Law and Economics* New York: John Wiley, 1992.

Burton A. Weisbrod, *Economics of Public Health: Measuring the Economic Impact of Diseases* Philadelphia: University of Pennsylvania Press, 1960.

Burton A. Weisbrod, "Collective Consumption Services of Individual-Consumption Goods," *Quarterly Journal of Economics* Vol. 78, No. 3, 1964, pp. 471-7.

E. B. Wennergren, "Valuing Non-Market Priced Recreational Resources," *Land Economics,* Vol. XL, NO. 3 August, 1964.

D. M. Winch, *The Economics of Highway Planning* Toronto: University of Toronto Press, 1963.

Chapter 1
Introduction

STÅLE NAVRUD

1.1 Why value the environment?

There are two main arguments for putting a price on environmental goods such as water and air quality, biodiversity and natural environments. First, we need to know the marginal value of environmental goods to find the socially "right" (optimal) quantity/quality of different environmental goods. Second, if environmental goods are not valued explicitly, they will still be valued implicitly through policy decisions. Since the decisionmakers are often not aware of that they make these valuations, this procedure produces an arbitrary and inconsistent set of prices.

The first argument stems from the increasing awareness among policy makers that the trade-off between environmental quality and economic development can be viewed in economic terms as costs and benefits. According to economic theory, there exists some socially optimal quantity/quality of an environmental good where the marginal cost of supplying the goods is equal to its marginal benefit, expressed as the public's demand for the good. While the costs of supplying environmental quality, i.e. environmental protection costs, can be calculated in a relatively straight forward way, the demand for environmental quality, i.e. environmental protection benefits, are more difficult to value.

Environmental goods have significant "collective good" characteristics since individuals generally cannot be excluded from enjoying environmental improvements nor can they avoid environmental degradation. Thus, these goods are generally not bought and sold in markets, and have no market prices, or have market prices that do not reflect the full, marginal social costs of providing them. However, we need to know the marginal values or prices of environmental goods to be able to compare costs and benefits, and set the socially "right" environmental policy goals. Environmental prices are also needed in cost-benefit analyses to decide upon which regulations and projects are socially most desirable. Thus, these prices are needed at the policy, regulatory and project level.

To illustrate the second argument, let us look at an imaginary, but realistic, project of hydropower development in a Norwegian river. Potential environmental damages of a dam and other installations necessary to produce electricity are carefully mapped. The negative, mostly irreversible, effects on recreational and commercial fisheries, hunting, other outdoor recreational activities, agriculture, forestry, reindeer husbandry, water quality and supply, cultural and historical objects, landscape aesthetics, and the ecosystem in general, are quantified in physical terms or described verbally. However, no attempt is made to value these environmental damages. A cost-benefit analysis, taking into account all social benefits and costs except the environmental costs, shows a net present value of the project of 7 million ECU (European Currency Units). If we assume that the dam and the other installations last for 50 years, and use a 7 % p.a. discount rate, the annual net benefits are about 500,000 ECU.

If the policy makers decide to build the dam, they have implicitly valued the environmental damage as being less than 500,000 ECU per annum. If the construction of the dam has consequences only for a local community of 10.000 households, this means that the policy makers implicitly say that each household is willing to pay less than 50 ECU a year to avoid these environmental damages. If the affected river is of national interest, it means that each of the 1.77 million households in Norway is assumed, on average, to value its average welfare loss due to the environmental damages of the dam at less than 0.28 ECU per annum. However, people have not been asked about their values, and they might be willing to pay more than these amounts to avoid the negative environmental effects. Previous valuation studies in Norway indicate that people are willing to pay larger amounts than those mentioned above to preserve rivers from hydropower development (see chapter 6.2.5). If these estimates can be transferred to our imaginary case (something we know very little about, and which has become a new, important research area) the total social costs will most likely exceed the benefits. From an economic point of view the dam should, then, not be constructed.

In a situation where implicit valuation leads to arbitrary prices on environmental goods, it must be better to use existing methods for explicit valuation to construct a consistent set of appoximate prices of environmental goods.

The marginal environmental costs of producing energy from hydropower could be added as an environmental tax to the current market price of energy. If we assume that the current energy price is corrected for all other market imperfections and exclusive of any environmental cost, the new market price will reflect the full, marginal social costs of producing energy from this source. However, the environmental costs of energy consumption should also be added as a tax. Then, the external costs of the complete fuel cycle for hydropower will be internalized. The external costs of energy from other sources, e.g. coal, oil, natural gas, uranium and renewables like solar and biomass, could be internalized in the same way. The energy market would then give correct signals about the social optimal use of different energy sources, and indirectly also about the optimal level of provision of environmental goods affected by the production and consumption of energy.

Returning to the environmental effects from hydropower development, some of the effects can be valued using dose-response relationships (damage functions) and market prices. These include effects on commercial fisheries, forestry, agriculture, water supply and reindeer farming. Due to the lack of market prices, valuation of effects on recreational activities, cultural and historical objects, landscape aesthetics, water quality and the ecosystem in general requires other valuation techniques. According to applied welfare economics, the marginal value of environmental goods can be measured as affected individuals' aggregate willingness-to-pay (WTP) for marginal changes in quality or quantity of the goods. Over the last 40 years, methods to elicit people's WTP have been developed, and especially in the last two decades much effort has been put into refining them.

1.2 Overview of environmental valuation techniques

Two main approaches to elicit people's WTP for environmental goods have been developed: direct and indirect approaches.

In the direct approach pepole are asked directly about their WTP, while the indirect approach derives the WTP for environmental goods by observing people's behaviour in markets for related private goods. Individuals' WTP to get an improvement, or to avoid a decrement, in environmental quality, can be motivated by both use and non-use values. By use value we mean the money value people place on being able to physically use the resource, e.g. the recreational value of fishing or boating. However, in addition to such consumptive uses, the use value also captures non-consumptive use such as wildlife watching and photography. Non-use values are mainly motivated by the wish to preserve the existence of environmental goods i.e. existence value) and to be able to deliver this existence to future generations (i.e. bequest value). While the direct approaches have the potential of estimating both use and non-use values, the indirect approaches capture mostly use values.

The most popular of the direct approaches is the CVM. Contingent valuation involves asking individuals in surveys (or experimental settings) to reveal their personal evaluation of a hypothetical environmental change. In the survey, the good or amenity is described, and both the current level of provision and the proposed increment or decrement therein. The respondents are also informed about the institutional structure under which the good is to be provided, the method of payment, and (implicitly or explicitly) the decision rule which determines whether to implement the offered program or not. One of the main challenges here is to convey to respondents what a policy maker wants them to take into account in a way that is both theoretically and technically correct, and at the same time understandable and plausible. The respondents are then asked to carefully consider his/her maximum willingness-to-pay (WTP) to get the increment or avoid the decrement in quantity/quality of the commodity in question. Different elicitation procedures are used. The WTP question can be asked through a bidding game procedure, open-ended formats with or without a payment card, or the currently most popular single- and double-bound discrete choice formats. An alternative measure to WTP, although not recommended for most public goods (Mitchell & Carson 1989; 37-38), is to ask about minimum willingness-to-accept (WTA) compensation for not getting an increment or getting a decrement in the level of provision of the good.

In CV surveys, individuals are asked neither about their opinions nor their attitudes, which may be poor predictors of actual behaviour. Rather they are asked about their contingent valuation (i.e. if "this" happens, what would you be willing to pay ?). While questions posed in CV surveys are (arguably) not attitudinal, the "market", the commodity or the payment as they appear in the surveys, are hypothetical. Due to this hypothetical nature, several biases may occur. Mitchell and Carson (1989) give a thorough description of the CVM and its potential biases.

One of the most important biases is "amenity misspecification". This is also related to the concepts "mental account bias", "part-whole bias" and "embedding". Amenity misspecification will occur if the respondents incorrectly (from the standpoint of theory or policy) perceive one or more aspects of the contingent market and the good to be valued (Mitchell & Carson 1989; 246). This is considered to be a problem since individuals tend not to have ex-ante, well-defined values for many of the goods valued in CV surveys. The other biases mentioned can be viewed as special cases of amenity misspecification. In general, these biases are related to the concern about overestimation by adding up values obtained for each commodity in separate surveys to value a commodity package. By asking about individuals' WTP for a single commodity, one focuses the respondents' attention on this commodity, and they give up too much of their "total" WTP for all public goods for this specific good. This "total" WTP can be viewed as a mental account the respondents have allocated to pay for all public goods, according to psychological theory. The extreme effect of this type of bias is that the respondents state their entire mental account (for all public goods) each time they are asked about their WTP for a single public good. Recently, there have been several CV studies trying to measure, and correct for, the above-mentioned biases.

After more than 30 years of CV research, the method has passed the experimental prototype stage, but has still not reached the routine application stage. There are no general guidelines for constructing reliable CV studies, although Mitchell and Carson (1989) provide some check points for evaluating CV surveys. However, they emphasize that the presence of criteria for a good CV study may create overconfidence in those studies that meet these. Field applications should, therefore, always be combined with methodological tests. Since the CV method at first sight seems very easy to use, it is vulnerable to misuse, which can easily undermine confidence in the method. The construction and framing of a CV survey should, therefore, be carefully examined before the results from it are used for policy purposes.

In spite of the potential biases, the CV method, if properly designed, offers a unique possibility for finding the "*total* value", i.e. both use and non-use values, of changes in environmental quality. Other major advantages of the method include: the possibility of designing it to value *future* environmental changes (ex-ante analysis); the good being valued can be specified exactly to match e.g. the endpoint of a physical dose-response function, and the survey can be administered to a sample appropriate for the good being valued (whether representative of the general population or of some restricted group of people).

Among the indirect valuation techniques the TCM can calculate only the *current use* value of a recreational area, based on the existing behaviour in the market for transport services to the area. Like the TCM, HPM is based on observed behaviour in a market connected to the environmental good in question. Often differences in property prices are used to value changes in air quality or air/road traffic noise levels, and differences in wage levels are used to value occupational health risks. Neither method is well suited for measuring the value of future environmental changes. Both methods are indirect in the sense that they are based on observed behaviour in existing markets for private goods that are connected to the environmental good in question. For this connection to hold, several strict assumptions must be fulfilled. This is a major weakness of indirect approaches as opposed to CV, where a market for the environmental good is constructed directly instead of going by an "indirect route". The main advantage of indirect methods is that they are based on observed, not hypothetical, behaviour. In spite of the hypothetical nature of the CVM, it is the most comprehensive and versatile valuation technique.

For an updated, in-depth description of all these valuation techniques, see Braden and Kolstad (1991). Cummings et al. (1986) and Mitchell and Carson (1989) provide assessments of the CVM.

1.3 Objectives of this book

This book deals with the three valuation techniques CVM, TCM and HPM. These techniques were developed in the U.S.A., and the bulk of empirical applications and methodological progress has also taken place there. However, several valuation studies have also been conducted in Europe, Asia (e.g. Israel, Pakistan, India, Thailand and Taiwan), Australia and New Zealand, Africa (Kenya, Ghana, Zimbamwe, Nigeria), Latin America (Haiti, Mexico and Brazil) and Canada. The majority of these studies are, however, not well-known internationally since most of them exist only as internal working papers , and/or are not published in English.

The main aim of this book is to give an overview of European valuation studies, and the role they have played in environmental decision making in the different countries. Although the survey covers the European countries with the largest experience in environmental valuation, it is not complete. In addition to the eight European countries covered in this book (France, Germany, Switzerland, Finland, the Netherlands, Norway, Sweden and the United Kingdom), there have recently also been a few studies in Denmark, Italy and Spain. Thus, the number of European countries, where these methods are applied, is steadily increasing. To illustrate further the geographical spreading of environmental valuation techniques, reviews of the Australian and Israeli experiences are included in this volume.

With increased knowledge about the possiblities of and limits to benefit transfer, i.e. the transference of estimated environmental prices from one area to another, this pool of valuation studies might ease the task of valuing environmental effects of new policies, regulations and projects. Thus, it might become increasingly important to have updated menus of empirical valuation studies. This volume intends to serve this purpose with respect to European valuation studies.

The book is also intended to be an illustrative companion to theoretical and methodological reference books like Johansson (1987), Mitchell and Carson (1989) and Braden and Kolstad (1991), for graduate students and practitioners in the field of environmental valuation. However, several chapters of this volume, partially or fully, also deal with the methodological aspects of the currently most popular method, the CVM. In addition, the analyses of what role the results from the valuation studies have played in the decision-making process provide important signals to benefit estimation practitioners.

1.4 Organization of the book

The book consists of three parts. Part I, encompassing chapters 1 through 8, provides a country by country review of European applications of environmental valuation techniques. In all countries where valuation techniques have been applied, there has been a move from indirect methods towards the direct Contingent Valuation Method (CVM). Part II contains an overall assessment of the CVM (chapter 9), and two recent experiments on the validity of environmental "prices" calculated by this method (chapter 10 and 11). General scepticism about the validity of environmental "prices" estimated by any of the valuation techniques seems to be a major obstacle to the use of these prices by policy makers. Part III looks closer at the role valuation studies have played in environmental decision making. Chapters 12 and 13 provide separate reviews of the Australian and Israeli experience, respectively. Chapter 14 closes part III with a summary of the use of benefit estimates in environmental decision making in Europe and the U.S.

References

Braden, J.B. & C.D. Kolstad (eds.) 1991: *Measuring the demand for environmental quality. Contribution to economic analysis 198*. Elsevier Science Publishers B.V. (North-Holland), Amsterdam, 370 p.

Cummings, R.G., Brookshire, D.S. & W.D. Schultze (eds.) 1986: *Valuing environmental goods. An assessment of the Contingent valuation method*. Rowman & Allanheld Publishers, Totowa, N.J., 270 p.

Johansson, P.-O. 1989: *The economic theory and measurement of environmental benefits*. Cambridge University Press, Cambridge, 223 p.

Mitchell, R.C. & R.T. Carson 1989: *Using surveys to value public goods. The Contingent valuation method*. Resources for the future, Washington D.C. 463 p.

Chapter 2
France

FRANCOIS BONNIEUX, BRIGITTE DESAIGUES & DOMINIQUE VERMERSCH

2.1 Introduction

Even though the Contingent Valuation Method (CVM) has been widely used in most countries in Northern Europe, the two studies presented here are the first applications in France, where there has been a certain distrust in its suitability. There seem to be two main reasons for this:

1) the reluctance of the economists who consider that environmental assets cannot be assigned a monetary value (their price is infinite);
2) the absence of social traditions to include environmental constraints in the economic calculus.

Even for other valuation methods, based on the observation of behaviour, such as the travel cost method or the hedonic price method, no studies have been published recently in France, to our knowledge.

The first part of this chapter evaluates the ecological and recreational benefits of an alternative management of the waterlevel of a reservoir (Desaigues & Lesgards 1991); the second part concerns the value of sports fishing in Western France (Bonnieux et al. 1991). Both studies were carried out in 1990, and the amounts are given in 1990-French francs (FF) (Add 3.5% to convert these amounts to 1991-FF).

2.2 Ecological and recreational value of a reservoir

The study concerns the Lac de la Forêt d'Orient, a reservoir located on the Seine some 200 km upstream from Paris. The dam was built in the sixties (and opened in 1966) to regulate the flow of the Seine. In 1970, the site was recognized as a regional natural park because of the richness of its birds. The current management of the dam does, however, entail certain negative effects:

- the rise of the water level during spring interferes with the reproduction of fish and birds (ducks, waterfowls, etc); the site is considered of European importance in the field of ornithology.
- the decrease of the water level during summer and fall has a negative impact on the recreational use, making access to the water and sailing more difficult.

The study was commissioned by EDF, the national electric utility of France, and the CNRS (National Center for Scientific Research).

2.2.1 THE CONTINGENT VALUATION STUDY

Presentation of the study
The CVM was applied to measure the social costs associated with the current management of the dam and to assess the benefits from an alternative management mode: that of maintaining more nearly constant levels of water in the reservoir from April to June to improve the ecological functions, and of retarding the release of water to improve the recreational uses.

The alternative management during spring eliminates the protection from spring floods. This solution is acceptable because the probability of occurrence (24 floods in 90 years), and the cost of damage (the floods concern essentially agricultural lands) are sufficiently low. The current management assumes a variation of the level of water of 1.5 meter between April and June. The delay in water release in autumn affects mainly boating activities. Under the curent management, the level begins to decrease in July and refilling begins in October. Boating activities are affected in September.

The study was conducted in the form of personal interviews of 30 minutes on the site during the month of July (one weekend). Foreign tourists were interviewed in English (mostly Dutch and English tourists). 101 persons where interviewed on the ecological impact (maintaining a constant level of water from April to June), and 98 persons on the use impact (retarding the release of water until the end of August, or the end of September). The questionnaire was divided into three parts, the first part concerning the different uses of the site, and the frequency of visits, the second part concerning the willingness to pay (WTP) either for improving the quality of the ecosystem or for lengthening the period for recreational use, the third part concerning the socioeconomic information. Only 2 % refused to answer the questionnaire. Most of the persons interviewed had a good knowledge of the site, which facilitates the exercise of contingent valuation. Moreover, graphics and photographs were shown as visual support, to illustrate the current as well as the alternative management of the dam. A payment card which suggests different amounts starting at a low level was used to avoid the starting point bias. The respondents were also allowed to choose amounts different from the ones stated on the payment card. The payment vehicle was plausible: an entrance fee, or an extra amount added to the annual fee for fishing and boating.

The recreational population was divided into three groups according to their main activity: swimmers and hikers along the shore (the beaches are open in July and August); fishermen who can fish from March to December; boaters who can practise their activities from March to November. The first results, based on information on the frequency of visits, have permitted an estimate of the composition of the total population of visitors to the site (22 700 swimmers, 4500 boaters, and 3300 fishermen annually).

Treatment of biases
Many biases can affect the quality of the result (Mitchell Carson 1989), and the validity of the mean WTP. In this study we considered the two most important biases to be the hypothetical bias and the non-respondent bias.

a) Hypothetical bias
This bias appears when the interviewees are not familiar with the contingent market and tend to overvalue their WTP. Laboratory experiments testing for this bias (Coursey, Hovis Schulze 1987; Kealy et al. 1990; Irwin et al. 1991), have shown that people submitted to repeated valuation exercises tend to lower their WTP. Moreover, the distribution of values becomes more centered round the mean. To correct for this bias, we have assumed that the error is proportional to the stated WTP (see also the work of McClelland et al. 1991). A logarithmic transformation allows for a reduction of the bias of the mean by making the distribution of errors more normal. If we write W for the real WTP and W* for the response in the interview, this transformation is:

$$W^* = W\rho, \text{ and thus } \log W^* = \log W + \log \rho \qquad (2.1)$$
with the error term $\log \rho = \varepsilon$.

We assume that the distribution of the error is log normal, $E(\varepsilon)$ = 0 and $V(\varepsilon)$ = σ^2 and that the correct model is:

$$\log W^* = \log W + \varepsilon \qquad (2.2.)$$

This transformation is ill-defined for responses that are equal to zero (10 % for the ecological impact, 50 % for the use impact). To avoid this problem, we have modified this transformation by adding a small uniform amount to W, We have considered three different values for this amount, 10 FF, 25 FF, and 50 FF, in order to test the sensitivity of the results for this value. With 10 FF we have obtained the results with the highest R^2 and the model becomes:

$$\log (W^*+10) = \log (W+10) + \log \rho . \qquad (2.3.)$$

A more general transformation is the Box-Cox transformation of W^*. The Box-Cox transformation can be applied to the dependent variable alone or to dependent and independent variables (even with different parameters). This makes it possible to obtain error distributions that are more nearly normal. In this study it was applied only to the dependent variable $(W+10)$.

b) Non-response bias
The non-respondent bias appears when a certain percentage of the population does not answer to the questionnaire (30 to 50 % in mail surveys), or is unable or unwilling to elicit a value (often 20 to 30 % of the respondents). A zero value can reflect two possibilities: a true value of zero, or a protest bid. In order to distinguish a protest bid from a real zero value, a complementary question needs to be asked about the reason for the zero value. In our study the non-response bias concerns only the second case. To correct for this bias, we have used a tobit model, which is a regression model with censored variables. In this survey the WTP cannot be negative, one way to solve this problem, and to attach a value to the non-responses, is to use the Heckman 2 steps method. In this method the censored variables are treated as an error term, calculated by the probit model (as inverse of the Mills ratio), and then introduced in the ordinary least squares (OLS) regression model. The principal advantage of this method is that it allows for a reconstitution of the dependent variable when its value is missing.

2.2.2 ECOLOGICAL IMPACTS OF ALTERNATIVE MANAGEMENT OF THE DAM

Of the 101 persons interviewed, 76 gave a positive WTP, 21 a WTP equal to zero and 4 refused to answer. The reasons given for a refusal to pay allow for the classification of the 25 persons who did not give a positive WTP into 2 groups: those whose WTP is truly zero (10 persons), and those who would probably agree to pay, for instance, in the form of an entrance fee (15 persons who were reluctant to pay for others, or who rejected the principle of paying).

A model of discrete choice
In order to understand the factors which increase the probability of giving a positive WTP, it is interesting to build a discrete choice model. In this case the independent variable represents the probability of giving a WTP >0, or WTP $= 0$. The dependent variables are the socioeconomic characteristics of the individuals. Two functional forms were used, the logit model and the probit model. These two models give very similar results. But if we consider the residuals (the weighted sum of square residuals), the probit model seems better suited.

The independent variables of the probit model are the following:

- sex: dummy variable, 0 for men, 1 for women
- fishermen: dummy variable, 1 for fishermen, 0 otherwise
- boaters: dummy variable, 1 for boaters, 0 otherwise
- visits: the number of days of visits on the site in one year
- length of stay: 1 if less than one week, 2 if one to two weeks, 3 if more than two weeks
- substitute: dummy variable, 1 if there is, 0 otherwise
- sensitivity: dummy variable, 1 if sensitive or very sensitive, 0 otherwise
- family situation: dummy variable, 1 if married, 0 otherwise
- children: number of children
- distance origin: distance from the principal residence in km
- nationality: dummy variable, 0 if French, 1 otherwise
- age: divided into 5 classes by ascending order
- education: dummy variable, 1 for students, managerial staff, liberal professions, 0 otherwise
- revenue: divided into 6 classes in ascending order
- goal: dummy variable, 1 if the reservoir is the goal of the travel, 0 otherwise

- type of lodging: dummy variable, 1 if it is the principal or secondary residence, 0 otherwise (hotel, camping, etc.)
- distance from lodging (on the site) in km.

The results of the probit model show that the main explanatory variables are sex (women more easily give a positive WTP), sensitivity to the impact on the ecosystem, existence of a substitute (which lowers the probability), family situation, number of children, probability of giving a possitive WTP decreases with number of children), nationality (being a foreigner increases the probability of giving a positive WTP), age (young people have a higher probability of giving a positive WTP), revenue, goal, type of lodging (owners of a principal or secondary residence are less willing to give a positive value), distance from the lodging. These results are consistent with the implicit theoretical model: the probability of the willingness to pay increases with revenue and with distance. The educational variable is not significant in the model, presumably because its categories were not sufficiently detailed; it was obtained by grouping the socio-professional categories.

Estimating the mean WTP for ecological improvements

Two hypotheses were considered:

1) the zero responses *and* the non-responses are equivalent to a WTP = 0,
2) only zero responses have WTP = 0, while the non responses are replaced by "true" values as estimated from the model.

a) The first hypothesis:
Four models have been tested: the tobit model, the OLS regression, the loglinear model and the Box-Cox model. Only the most significant variables were included. Thus, the variables: boaters, substitute, family situation, education and distance were omitted. These variables were significant in explaining the probability of the willingness to pay, but not the amount of payment. The results are presented in table 2.1. The difference between the mean WTP obtained by the linear model (91FF) and by the Box-Cox transformation (66FF) can be explained by the existence of the hypothetical bias. The tobit model does not allow for correcting this bias even if it gives a better estimator. The hypothetical bias tends to overvalue the mean WTP by 30%.

Table. 2.1 Review of models for estimating mean, annual WTP (in FF) per person for ecological improvements, hypothesis 1. (β = parameters, t = t-statistic).

Variables	Tobit model		Linear model		Loglinear model		Box-Cox model	
	β	t	β	t	β	t	β	t
Sex	41.3	1.6	29.0	1.3	0.4	1.6	0.8	1.6
Boaters	-42.6	-1.5	-32.2	-1.4	-0.2	-0.9	-0.6	-1.0
Visits	1.5	2.2	1.4	2.4	0.01	1.8	0.02	2.0
Sensitivity	88.5	2.4	46.5	1.7	1.0	2.9	1.9	2.7
Children	-16.7	-1.7	-8.4	-1.1	-0.2	-1.9	-0.3	-1.8
Nationality	87.0	2.4	61.5	2.1	0.8	2.3	1.6	2.3
Age	-25.3	-2.3	-18.3	-2.1	-0.2	-2.4	-0.5	-2.4
Revenue	21.5	2.5	14.6	2.1	0.2	2.2	0.4	2.3
Goal	105.3	2.9	87.2	3.1	0.9	2.8	2.0	2.9
Lodging	-25.9	-1.0	-26.8	-1.3	-0.1	-0.5	-0.3	-0.7
Constant	-96.6	-1.5	-27.5	-0.5	2.5	4.0	3.0	2.4
R^2	0.3		0.29		0.3		0.31	
WTP (FF)	94.3		91.8		60.4		66	
σ	52.6		88.6		53.9		44.8 with $\lambda = 0.18$	

b) The second hypothesis:
This hypothesis can be considered as more plausible because for some people it is difficult to make a contingent valuation. For these persons, the model permits for the reconstitution of a nominal value, the quality of the results depending on the quality of the model. Two models have been tested: the linear and the loglinear model, both of which take into account the inverse of the Mills ratio. The main advantage of the Heckman method is to allow for the estimation of the missing dependent variables. The independent variables are different from the first hypothesis: the sex variable is no longer significant, but the distance from the lodging becomes significant. The other variables remain unchanged. The results are presented in table 2.2. The loglinear model corrected by the Mills ratio gives a high R^2 (0.66), which means that it is the best model to explain the amount of the WTP. Moreover, the error distribution is more normal and the correlation between the errors and the dependent variable is 0.33 (0.57 for the linear model).

Table 2.2 Review of models for estimating mean, annual WTP (in
FF) per person for ecological improvements, hypothesis 2.
(β = parameters, t = t-statistic).

Variables	Linear model		Loglinear model	
	β	t	β	t
Fishermen	−56.8	2.5	−0.3	1.9
Visits	1.2	2.1	0.01	1.9
Sensitivity	41.9	1.6	1.0	4.7
Children	−10.7	1.3	−0.2	2.4
Nationality	51.4	1.5	0.6	2.3
Age	−20.4	2.4	−0.3	3.9
Revenue	16.7	2.5	0.2	3.2
Goal	98.2	3.1	0.9	3.9
Lodging	−36.0	1.7	−0.2	1.2
Distance	−0.2	0.8	0.0	0.7
1/Mills ratio	78.4	3.8	1.3	8.2
Constant	0.4		2.9	
R^2	0.42		0.66	
WTP (FF)	88.5		77	
σ	78.4		68.4	
95 % confid. interval WTP	73–104		65.4–88.5	

In conclusion, according to the hypothesis concerning the non-
responses, we must retain as mean WTP, either 66F or 77F, and not
91F as an ordinary, but conservative, linear analysis would have
supposed.

2.2.3 THE USE VALUE OF AN ALTERNATIVE MANAGEMENT OF THE DAM

Of the 98 persons interviewed on this question, 44 persons gave a
positive WTP, 16 a zero WTP, and 38 did not give any response. If
we examine the reasons given for the non or zero response, the 54 persons can be separated in to two groups. 43 persons with a WTP =
0, and 11 who are not able to give a WTP (reluctant to pay for
others). A majority of persons say that they are not bothered by the
variation of the level of water, except for the boaters interviewed in
September.

A model of discrete choice

One independent variable was added to the use value, to take into account the persons interviewed in September (a dummy variable 1, if the activity took place in September). The probability that WTP = 0 is high, which explains the difference in the results if compared to the value for ecological impact. The most significant independent variables are the number of visits (which increases the probability), the sensitivity to the use impact, age (with a negative sign as for the ecological value) and revenue. The distance from lodging is no longer significant.

Estimating the mean WTP for improved opportunities for recreational use

As for the ecological improvement, two hypotheses were tested:

1) all the zero and non responses were considered to be equal to zero
2) 43 responses (of 98) were considered to be equal to zero, and 11 as non-responses which can be reconstituted by the model.

a) The first hypothesis:
The results of the four models are presented in table 2.3. The Box-Cox model gives the best adjustment, with $\lambda = 0.41$, which suggests that the hypothetical bias is more important for the use value than for the ecological value. The difference between the mean WTP obtained by the linear regression (55FF) and the Box-Cox model (25FF) is quite large (40%), and can be attributed to the existence of two distinctly different groups of users; those sensitive to the impact and those who are indifferent.

The significant independent variables are different from those in the ecological improvement case. The number of visits and their length is becoming significant, while goal and type of lodging are losing their significance.

b) The second hypothesis:
In this hypothesis we have reconstituted the WTP for 11 persons. The results are presented in table 2.4. Despite a relatively high R^2, the parameters of the explanatory variables of the linear model are less significant, except for the sensitivity or the inverse of the Mills ratio. On the contrary, the loglinear model is doubtless the best explicative model of the mean WTP. It confirms the results obtained for the ecological value. In conclusion, the mean WTP is 25F or 49F, depending on the treatment of the non-responses. This result shows the great sensitivity of the mean to the way the non-responses are treated when the probability of giving a non-positive value is high.

Table 2.3 Review of models for estimating mean, annual WTP (in FF) per person for recreational improvements, hypothesis 1. (β = parameters, t = t-statistic).

Variables	Tobit model		Linear model		Loglinear model		Box-Cox model	
	β	t	β	t	β	t	β	t
Visits	1.4	1.8	0.5	1.5	0.01	1.5	0.01	1.4
Length	−43.3	−1.6	−18.5	−1.5	−0.3	−1.8	−0.1	−1.9
Sensitivity	208.0	6.2	83.1	5.9	1.5	7.6	0.4	7.8
Family	−43.9	−1.2	−13.3	−0.8	−0.3	−1.3	−0.1	−1.4
Education	−40.2	−1.3	−15.1	−0.9	−0.5	−2.0	−0.1	−2.3
Age	−31.7	−2.2	−11.1	−1.6	−0.2	−2.3	−0.1	−2.4
Revenue	22.1	1.9	7.0	1.3	0.2	2.5	0.04	2.7
Distance	−0.3	−1.3	−0.03	−0.3	0.0	−0.9	0.0	−1.0
Constant	−38.7	−0.7	45.0	1.8	3.3	9.3	1.7	21.1
R^2	0.33		0.34		0.48		0.5	
WTP (FF)	53.9		55.3		32.2		24.7	
σ	52.7		46.7		33.2		30.3 with $\lambda = -.41$	

To conclude, the application of the CVM in valuing the recreational and patrimonial benefits induced by a modification in the management of the dam has shown that:

1) people are able to make a relation between a change in their utility function and the WTP. It is interesting to notice that the non-use (ecological) benefits are clearly more highly valued per person than the use benefits (even though one might have expected the opposite);

2) the mean WTP to be used in a cost-benefit analysis depends on the hypothesis made to treat the non-responses, and on whether or not the hypothetical bias is taken into account. If it is not, the results can be over-estimated by 30–40%.

Table 2.4 Review of models for estimating mean, annual WTP (in FF) per person for recreational improvements, hypothesis 2. (β = parameters, t = t-statistic).

Variables	Linear model		Loglinear model	
	β	t	β	t
September	17.6	1.0	0.3	2.1
Visits	0.5	1.5	0.01	2.3
Length	–6.6	–0.5	–0.1	–1.2
Sensitivity	94.7	6.1	1.6	12.2
Education	4.7	0.3	–0.2	–1.2
Age	–9.8	–1.4	–0.2	–3.9
Revenue	–1.8	–0.3	0.1	1.2
Distance origine	–0.03	–0.4	–0.01	–1.5
1/Mills ratio	40.2	3.0	1.1	9.2
Constant	37.6		3.1	
R^2	0.56		0.86	
WTP (FF)	64.3		48.8	
σ	58.5		53.8	
95 % confid. interval WTP	52.2–75.9		37.9–69.5	

2.3 Valuing game angling

This section deals only with salmon and sea-trout fishing in France. There is no commercial fishery (e.g. in river mouths with nets) so fishing is restricted to game angling in freshwater for recreational purposes only. There are relatively few people involved in these activities: 3000 for salmon and 3300 for sea-trout in 1990, but expenditures per angler are great, so game angling has significant economic impacts.

We present some results of surveys conducted on four rivers located in Western France: three predominantly for salmon (Elorn, Sée, Sélune) and one predominantly for sea-trout (Touques). 20 % of salmon anglers fish in the first three and 40 % of sea-trout anglers in fourth. On-site surveys were run during the 1990 fishing season. A common questionnaire was designed to provide background information which is summarized in the first paragraph. The following two paragraphs review the results from Contingent Valuation questions designed to value changes in the management of these two fisheries.

2.3.1 PRESENTATION OF ON-SITE SURVEYS

Information on the surveys was given in local newspapers and on T.V. As a matter of fact, the fishermen welcomed the interviewers since only two anglers (suspected of poaching) refused to answer. For salmon it was possible to compare the sample to the target population. There is no evidence of specific bias so we expect it is also true for the sea-trout sample.

The questionnaire was quite long but it was expected that the face-to-face interview would need no more than 20 minutes. However, most of the individuals wanted to add comments which are often valuable, so the interview usually took 30 minutes. It reviewed anglers' characteristics, fishing experience and effort, and expenditures. It gives sufficient information to apply the travel cost approach on micro data. Notice that the only question for which non-response is significant involves income. People were asked to locate their family income on a ladder, and 25% refused. But for the other 75%, answers are consistent with age and occupation.

Data reported in table 2.5 show differences between the two samples. Salmon anglers are older and fish for a longer time than sea-trout anglers. The value of equipment is similar, but both the length of the fishing day and the number of trips during the fishing period are greater for salmon than for sea-trout anglers. There is a significant difference in terms of behaviour which is well known. Salmon anglers are very keen and don't hesitate to spend several days at a time catching nothing; their total catch is less than 2 salmon per year! Sea-trout anglers are not so eager and visit the river for a half-day only. They are more successful in terms of fish caught: 3.5 per year, but 48% did not catch any trout! In any case, they enjoy their experience since 90% plan to come back next year.

Table 2.5 Game angling basic data

	Salmon	Sea-trout
Number of anglers 1990[1]	680	1300
Sample size	173	177
Sampling rate	.25	.14
ANGLERS' CHARACTERISTICS (average)		
Age (years)	45	40
Training (years)	15	7
Effort Number of hours per fishing day	7	5
– cost of equipment (FFFF)[2]	5560	5140
Round-trip distance (km)	162	176
Yearly total fishing fees (FF)[3]	1217	959
Cost of a fishing season (FF)[4]	8544	5759

[1] Approximation: salmon angling (Elorn, Sée and Sélune), sea-trout angling (Touques)
[2] Including reels, rods and lines.
[3] Including licence, fishing society fees, special fees for salmon and sea-trout.
[4] Including transportation costs, food, lodging, fishing and depreciation of equipment.

Game angling is expensive in terms of equipment, fees and transportation costs, and people surveyed are wealthy compared with the general French population. Round-trip distances are similar for both types of anglers and close to figures reported elsewhere, for example, 158 km to participate in angling activities in Maryland (Walsh p. 114). But salmon angling costs more than sea-trout angling. There is a difference in fees owing the higher price of the specific salmon fee. However, behaviours are significantly different since salmon anglers visit the river more often than sea-trout anglers, so transportation expenditures explain the difference in cost of a fishing season. Moreover, there are more salmon anglers who visit a substitute river than sea-trout anglers: 63 % vs. 30 %.

2.3.2 CONTINGENT VALUATION SURVEYS

On-site surveys provide background data on game angling in Western France. In order to get extra information on hypothetical questions, we conducted contingent valuation surveys. These deal with river management and address specific issues for each of the two fish species. For salmon we have considered a revision of the quota system combined with an increase in duration of the fishing season. For sea-trout angling there are new opportunities to increase the length of banks available for angling, so questions in connection with this point were asked. These two topics will be successively considered.

Salmon angling

Until 1990, the fishing season started in mid-March and closed in mid-July. This regulation of the Atlantic salmon fisheries was combined with an individual quota system. Catches were restricted, four salmon per angler before June 1st plus two after. This management scheme was implemented to improve the long-term position of the fishery. However, it is often considered as being inconsistent since it allows for the fishing of spring-salmon which are rare, and drastically limits the catches of grilses whose stock is relatively large.

In order to eliminate this drawback, it was decided for the 1991 season to postpone the closing date until mid-August, but for dryfly fishing only. However, the quota system has not been modified and the upper limit of six salmon per angler annually has been kept. The four salmon per angler limit for the first period is not drastic, because it is very difficult to catch four salmon before June. But with an increase of 25 % in the duration of the fishing period, the annual limit of six salmon could be severe. So we have designed a contingent study to assess that new regulation.

A mail survey was conducted just before the 1991 fishing season. A very simple questionnaire was sent to all the salmon anglers who gave their address in the on-site survey. The first question dealt with anglers' opinion on the quota system.

– Would you agree with a suppression of the quota system after June 1st?

Yes,   No,   Don't know   Refused

Then a payment card was used to elicit the willingness to pay of the individuals who answered positively:

– What amount on this card (or any amount in between or above) is the most you would be willing to pay for angling without catch limitation after June 1st?

In addition, an open question asked individuals to comment on fishery management and to provide suggestions. Finally, the name and address of the respondents were asked in order to link the information from the on-site and mail surveys.

Among a total of 149 mailed questionnaires, 84 were returned (i.e. a response rate of 56 %). Thirty-five agreed with a suppression of quota, 45 didn't agree and 4 didn't know. It is interesting to note that most people who answered negatively lacked information about grilses. Despite information given in the questionnaire, they think the stock is severely depleted so the fishing pressure has to be lessened. Thirty-three individuals give amounts ranging from zero (7 obs.) to 300FF (4 obs.). The average amount equals 103FF, which is very close to 25 % of the specific salmon fee. This result looks meaningful because involved anglers are willing to pay 25 % more if they can fish 25 % longer.

Sea-trout angling
Until the 1990 season, only 26 km of the Touques banks, upstream from the mouth, were devoted to recreational fishing. The building of a fish ladder could give new opportunities to increase the length of banks available for angling since sea trout will proceed 45 km further up the river. But these banks are privately owned so angling societies wish to obtain access to the river in order to increase the availability of recreational angling, and thereby improve the fishing for their members.

One possibility would be to buy a narrow corridor along the river provided enough money is collected. Thus, the CV study emphasizes this point by asking people to voluntarily contribute to a fund to buy 5 km of river banks. A questionnaire had been successfully tested on site during the last stage of the on-site survey in October 1990, when 50 individuals were asked and answered questions. Then a questionnaire was sent to each angler surveyed before October who had given his address. Ninety-seven questionnaires were mailed and 47 returned (i.e. a response rate of 48 %).

Pooling together both subsamples provides a sample size of 97. A majority of 75 anglers wish to benefit from greater facilities in order to be able to fish upstream from the fish ladder, and 51 agree to participate in a fund to buy 5 km, knowing they would be entitled to fish freely for three years. A payment card was used to assess the willingness to pay for 5 km. All give an amount greater than zero, the average amount equals 578 FF per person annually. There is an iteration in order to assess the average amount to buy an additional 5 km. Forty were willing to pay and the average amount equals 567 FF. Unfortunately the sample size was too small to run a new stage, but it is interesting to notice that the number of positive answers decreases.

If we assume the surveyed individuals to be representative of individuals angling in the Touques river, it is possible to assess an aggregate amount for extra km. For the first 5 km section, we get 26 300 FF per km per year. For the second section, the amount is smaller and equals 20 200 FF. These values make sense since the yearly rent (including restoration, cleaning up and maintenance) is 15 000 FF per km. Moreover, there are some problems with poachers who use nets to catch fish in the river mouth. Therefore, surveyed anglers were asked about their willingness to pay to hire more river-keepers. It is interesting to notice that protest answers are significant. Forty per cent of the sample refuse to pay because they already pay taxes for police control so a private body (the fishing society) should not take the role of the state. However, 50 % give positive amounts ranging from 20 FF to 500 FF per year. The average amount equals 160 FF per person annually.

2.3.3 WTP FOR SEA-TROUT ANGLING

Here we deal only with the sample of sea-trout anglers. They are faced with a dichotomous choice as they are asked to accept or reject voluntarily participation in a fund. So a discrete regression model is first considered. Then the WTP amount is taken into account, and a tobit model is specified to deal with the censored nature of the data.

Probit and logit models
If the dependent variable is a yes/no answer it is usual to try a probit or a logit model. Both have been estimated and results are reported in table 2.6 with six independent variables. Two variables, income and years of training, help to describe the anglers. Cost of equipment is a proxy for fishing effort, and catch (number of sea-trout caught during the 1989 season) is an indicator of fishing experience in the Touques river. We have defined a dummy variable to take into account substitute rivers. We have also considered the distance travelled to fish as a potential factor influencing demand.

Both models provide similar results. They perform poor statistically, but the signs of the coefficients look correct. There is good reason to believe that the demand for game angling rises with income. Thus, the positive coefficient for this variable was expected. Moreover, anglers who own many reels and rods (the average is 2.6 for each type of equipment, but 20 % own more than 5) make the greatest fishing effort. Therefore the value of equipment, which is a proxy for fishing effort, positively affects demand.

Table 2.6 Sea-trout angling demand; probit and logit models
(Asymptotic t values in parentheses).

Variables	Probit	Logit
Intercept	0.657 (1.7)	1.00 (1.4)
Substitute site (dummy)	0.318 (0.6)	0.581 (0.6)
Trip distance (km)	0.008 (1.7)	0.014 (1.6)
Cost of equipment (FF)	0.017 (0.7)	0.024 (0.5)
Catches	−0.002 (−0.3)	−0.0049 (−0.3)
Monthly income: 17 classes (increasing with income)	0.0001 (0.3)	0.0002 (0.2)
Years of training	−0.023 (−1.0)	−0.034 (−0.8)
Log likelihood	−24.95	−25.15

The positive signs for the dummy variable for substitute sites and for the distance are consistent. First, anglers who fish in substitute rivers are expected to have greater requirements in terms of fishing experience. Second, anglers living far from the Touques will stay for a week-end or for a vacation in the Touques area. For both categories, the length of banks available for angling is limited, and anglers are likely to ask for extra kilometres of banks. Therefore, these underlying explanatory variables positively affect angling demand.

The negative sign of the years of training variable requires some explanation. First, note that this variable is positively correlated with the angler's age. However, sport fishing demands great physical effort. Some of the comments support this point and indicate that senior citizens sometime move to other types of fishing. The current availability of banks fulfills their requirements. Finally, we have a negative sign for the catch variable, which is obviously inconsistent with our expectations.

Tobit model

Probit and logit models do not use all the information available. To go further, let us first consider anglers who are willing to pay a positive amount to increase angling supply. They already pay something; a licence to angling societies and specific fees. There is a game angling market, and fishing fees x_i paid by angler i are a proxy for effective fishing demand. Therefore, a positive WTP_i implicitly means a greater demand.

Let us now consider anglers who reject the deal. There is empirical evidence that some of them are unsatisfied with their fishing experience, and that others fish only a small portion of the river. The comments they make show they feel x is too much and they would like to reduce the fishing fees. Thus, for this category a negative WTP_i would be logical. However, anglers do not have the opportunity to state negative amounts.

To deal with both categories let us write:

$$x_i^* = x_1 + WTP_i \quad \text{if } WTP_i > 0$$
$$ x_i \qquad\qquad\quad \text{otherwise} \tag{2.4.}$$

For the first category, x_i^* is a Marshallian demand, whereas for the second category it is not an optimal demand. Thus, we will specify a tobit model with a specific threshold for each observation.

The tobit model uses the first category of anglers to derive what would be the optimal level of x_i^* for anglers in the second category. So the underlying logic takes into account negative WTP_i which are not observed, but which do exist.

The model was estimated by the maximum likelihood with a Newton-Raphson algorithm. Standard errors of coefficients were computed from the inverse of the observed information matrix. Results are reported in table 2.7, x_i^* being espressed in logarithm.

The results reported in table 2.6 and in table 2.7 can be compared since they are based on the same sample and the same independent variables. The tobit model seems better because all signs are consistent and t-ratios are greater. As expected, a positive correlation between catch and angling demand is obtained.

The model was used to estimate average WTP for an additional 5 km of river banks. We got 363 FF per angler per year, which is smaller than the value given above, which is based upon a simple mean. This is consistent, as the tobit model implicitly takes into account negative WTP. Therefore aggregate WTP per km and per year equals 16 500 FF and is close to the actual yearly rent (15 000 FF).

*Table 2.7 Sea-trout angling demand, tobit model
(asymptotic t values in parentheses)*

Variables	Tobit
Intercept	5.81 (17.1)
Site substitute (dummy)	0.27 (1.04)
Trip distance (km)	0.002 (2.5)
Cost of equipment (FF)	0.175 (2.2)
Catches	0.030 (2.2)
Monthly income: 17 classes (increasing with income)	0.033 (1.3)
Years of training	–0.025 (–1.9)
Log likelihood	–34.69

Some comments
We have reported some results from work in progress done in cooperation with angling societies. Some people in charge of these societies were afraid that results given above would push prices up. Thus, it will be interesting to observe the market in the future.

We think that hypothetical bias is not a serious problem in this study because there is already a market for game angling. People are not confronted with an imaginary situation, and therefore we can expect them to behave the same way in the actual market. The most difficult point concerns non-responses, which in this survey correspond to strategic behaviour. To deal with that, we intend to improve the model specification, using a generalized tobit model.

2.3 Conclusion

These studies show that the traditional scepticism vis-à-vis the CVM in France is totally unfounded. Our results are quite consistent with what has been observed in other countries. The individuals who have been interviewed, seem to have a sufficiently clear understanding of the issues to assign monetary values to environmental matters. We recommend and encourage further utilization of this method in France, especially for public projects.

References

Bonnieux, F., Boude, J.P., Guerrier C & A. Richard 1991: La pêche sportive du saumon et de la truite de mer en Basse-Normandie – Analyse économique. (Angling for salmon and sea trout in Normandie – An economic analysis). In French. *Working paper CSP,* INRA-ENSA – Rennes.

Coursey, D.L. Hovis, J.J. & W.D. Schulze 1987: On the supposed disparity between willingness to accept and willingness to pay measures of value. *Quarterly Journal of Economics,* 102, 679–690.

Desaigues, B. & V. Lesgards 1991: La valorisation des actifs naturels – un exemple d'application de la méthode d'evaluation contingente. (Valuation of natural resources – an application of the Contingent Valuation Method). In French. Working paper. Université de Bordeaux.

Irwin, J.R, McClelland, G.G & W.D. Schulze 1991: Hypothetical and real consequences to low probability risk. To be published in the Journal of Behavioral Decision Making.

Kealy, M.J., Montgomery, M. & J.F. Dovido 1990: Reliability and predictive validity of contingent values: does the nature of the good matter? *Journal of Environmental Economics and Management* 19, 244–263.

McClelland, G., Schulze, W., Waldamn, D. et al. 1991: Valuing Eastern visibility: A field test of the contingent valuation method, U.S. EPA, Cooperative agreement CR-815183-03, Washington D.C.

Mitchell, R.C. & R.T. Carson 1989: *Using surveys to value public goods: The contingent valuation method.* Resources for the Future, Washington DC. John Hopkins University Press, Baltimore.

Walsh, R.G. 1986: *Recreation economic decisions: Comparing benefits and costs.* Venture Publishing, inc. State College, Pennsylvania.

Chapter 3

Germany and Switzerland

ANSELM U. RÖMER & WERNER W. POMMEREHNE

3.1 Introduction

This chapter reviews environmental valuation studies based on the Hedonic Price Method (HPM), the Travel Cost Method (TCM) and the Contingent Valuation Method (CVM) in Germany (section 2) and in Switzerland (section 3). Finally, differences in the application of these approaches in the two countries are discussed and some thoughts devoted to future development in the use of these techniques (section 4).

3.2 The case of Germany

3.2.1 THE HEDONIC PRICE METHOD

Experiences with the HPM are briefly reported. To our knowledge, there only two studies have been undertaken so far, one by Borjans (1983) and another one by Holm-Müller et. al. (1991). Both studies investigated whether the level of noise pollution exerts a significant impact on the dwelling rent paid. However, for most of the sub-samples in both studies no such influence could be detected.

This failure, along with the reticence of other German analysts with respect to the application of the HPM, is not surprising since the gap between the assumptions about a completely competitive market and the German housing market is striking. In particular, it is much larger than the respective gap in the United States where the approach has been applied quite successfully since the late sixties. Two differences between the German and the American situation are apparent:

(i) The German rental market is highly regulated. Price increases are limited by law to a certain percentage of the preceding year's price and the rental price for comparable flats. Given the substantial excess demand, the observed price may deviate significantly from a free market equilibrium price.

(ii) The mobility of the average German family is much lower than in the United States. This low mobility clashes with the requirement of a continuous evaluation of the environmental quality associated with flats and the preparedness to react to changing quality by moving out.

Nevertheless, we would like to emphasize that even in Germany the HPM may be successfully applied. Basing the hedonic approach on a disequilibrium model using house-selling prices (instead of dwelling rents), and applying the analysis to one (relatively homogeneous) community, it should be possible to obtain implicit prices of the respective environmental improvements.

3.2.2 THE TRAVEL COST METHOD

We are aware of only one application of the TCM. As a part of a larger study, Ewers and Schulz (1981) tried to quantify the recreational benefits resulting from a potential water quality improvement of the Lake Tegel in the city of Berlin (West). The following nine activities were analysed: walking, swimming, shipping (on commercial boats), surfing, rowing, fishing, sailing, boating (on private boats) and waterskiing. For each of these activities the resulting benefit was assumed to exceed the "travel cost", consisting of the monetary travel cost, the opportunity cost of time, and the additional expenses linked to the specific recreational activity. The authors acknowledged the crucial problem of valuing the opportunity cost of time and considered different opportunity wage rates, ranging from 1 to 7 German marks (DM) per hour. The resulting total benefit – as an aggregate of all recreation categories and of all users – ranges between 37 and 60 million DM per annum, with 51 millon DM as the most credible estimate in the authors' view. Since this level of benefit was assumed to be maintained if stringent ecological restoration of the lake is undertaken, the question is how large the decline in visitation rate would be if there were no restoration. In order to get an estimate of this lower use frequency, the authors relied on expert statements (rather than on individual preferences) and calculated some more or less arbitrary percentage numbers of individuals who would still use the lake for recreational purposes. Depending on the degree of deterioration, the benefit would shrink from 51 million DM to 22 million DM per annum (for the most credible estimate).

Finally, this value was incorporated into a total benefit calculation that also considered potential benefits from non-recreational sources such as drinking-water and professional fishery. For this overall total, a sensitivity analysis with respect to a number of parameters was performed and benefit-cost ratios (referring to the total cost to restore the lake) were computed. Taking into account many uncertainties, the authors employed a min-max strategy to estimate the benefit. In the standard as well as in the maximum variant the benefit-cost ratios exceed one in all cases. The minimum variant produces a negative net present value of the measure, i.e. the benefit-cost ratio ranges between 0.6 and 0.04.

All facts considered, the study is rather well done and contains a lot of information. The extensive use of sensitivity analysis also allows the decision maker to study the impact of certain key assumptions. Even though the analysis contains many elements of expert judgement, it is one of the first German studies which considers (at least partially) revealed individual preferences.

Little can be said about the impact of this study on the political process. The direct impact probably has not been significant, since the whole restoration program for the lake had already been agreed upon before the study was performed. However, the possibility of indirect impacts of the study, e.g. on similar decision processes concerning other lakes, should be pointed out even though the empirical results may not be easily transferable to other problems.

3.2.3 THE CONTINGENT VALUATION METHOD

There have been two early applications of the survey technique to measure the individual willingness-to-pay (WTP). The first one covered the benefits of parks in the city of Berlin (Mierheim 1974), the second focussed on the value of improved air quality in the city of Wetzlar (Jordan 1976). However, both studies failed to create a well structured contingent market situation. Therefore, the interpretation of the results is problematic.

The first study that met most of the requirements of a contin-gent market was the study by Schulz (1985). He tried to quantify the individual valuation for a number of specified air quality changes in the city of Berlin (West):

- prevention of a deterioration to very badly polluted air with more or less continuous smog alarm,
- improvement to average city air quality with no smog alarm,

- improvement to mediocre polluted air quality as it is found in smaller cities, and
- improvements to hardly polluted air quality as it is found in holiday resorts.

The study yielded some interesting results. The relatively high response rate of nearly 50% in this mail survey of the general population is quite noteworthy. Furthermore, only a few respondents (about 4%) were not willing or able to answer the valuation questions. Thus, respondents were not generally put off when they were asked to value the environmental commodities in monetary terms.

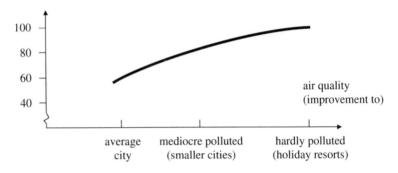

Figure 3.1 Monetary valuation of air quality improvement in the city of Berlin (West) 1983, in DM per month.
Source: Schulz (1985)

Figure 3.1 illustrates the main results of the study. The average monetary valuation for air quality improvement is always positive and it increases at a decreasing rate as the air quality improves. This result meets the theoretical expectations. Furthermore, the mean values of WTP elicited are plausible and comparable to those revealed in U.S. studies.

On the basis of this result, a univariate regression model was estimated, which contained the age of the respondents as the only explanatory variable. Schulz also computed the aggregate monetary benefit for all West Berlin citizens for the various degrees of air quality improvement. The estimated annual total benefit ranges from 4 billion DM for an air quality of a holiday resort to 1.75 billion DM for the current air quality (measured as WTP to avoid a further deterioration). These figures were not only widely reported in the press, but also provided the basis for a nationwide calculation of the respective benefits. Although this calculation is based on very simplistic assumptions (for instance, an average air quality for the whole country is assumed to represent the status quo), the figures received considerable public attention. This is not too surprising since those who were engaged in advancing air quality improvements were provided with some quantitative estimates of the respective benefits, i.e. they could substantiate their arguments in the political process.

A further impact of this study and the one by Ewers and Schulz (1981) could be seen in the fact that Schulz was promoted to the Federal Environmental Agency where he is now responsible for "economic environmental questions". Under his auspices, the agency and the secretary of the environment jointly launched a major project "Benefits of Environmental Protection – Cost of Environmental Pollution" whose preliminary results were published in September 1991. With respect to the benefit side, five major studies were initiated, all of them targeting to produce a nationwide benefit estimate. These studies are summarized below.

(1) The study of Hampicke et al. (1991) covers the difficult question of how to value the preservation of species and biotopes. Their generally carefully elaborated questionnaire contains a number of interesting features since various contingent designs were used. Some of their major findings are:

- Respondents were willing to pay more for the general preservation of species and biotopes if they were told that there is a general payment obligation.
- The mean total resource value of 22 DM per month was twice as high as the existence value for a measure that preserves species.
- Citizens preferred to deliver the payment to a private foundation (controlled by an environmental protection initiative) rather than to a public sector agency. For instance, when it was stated that a public sector agency (instead of a private foundation) would receive the money, the mean WTP of the non-zero bidders decreased from 19 to 12 DM, and the share of the zero bidders increased from 15 % to 31 %.
- Offering a choice among three programmes, which provided different degrees of protection for the species, the citizens preferred the most far-reaching one and expressed the highest WTP for it. Unfortunately, the authors detached the preference revelation from the payment question. This led to the ambigous

result that 77 % of the respondents favoured the far-reaching program, whereas only 57 % were prepared to bear the respective cost.

(2) Weinberger et al. (1991) try to measure the value of noise reduction. Using a mail survey, they elicited individuals' WTP to move to a quieter flat where hardly any noise exists and to a flat where there is little noise, corresponding to noise levels of 40 dB, (decibels) and 55 dB respectively. Since the actual noise situation of each participant was known, the monthly WTP could be derived for different initial noise levels. The respective WTP per household ranged from 3 to 69 DM for complete noise elimination and from 2 to 47 DM for a reduction to little noise. The second range of values for the smaller improvement is lower than the first, but this fact does not underline the internal consistency of the obtained results, since both values are not generated independently. Nevertheless, the results correspond well to the theoretical expectation that households exposed to higher noise levels value a noise reduction higher than households exposed to lower noise levels. The marginal WTP for noise reduction by one unit (dB) amounts to 1.97 DM per month. 30 DM per month per household (or 22 billion DM per year for all households) were computed to reflect the average benefit from achieving a situation where there is hardly any noise. Compared to the valuations elicited by Pommerehne (1988) for Basle and by Iten (1990) for Zurich, who found that the average WTP amounted to 70 Swiss francs (SFr) and 120 SFr per month, respectively (for a similar sized noise reduction), the benefit estimates of Weinberger et al. may seem, prima facie, too low. However, taking into account that both, Zurich and Basle, are cities with a high average noise level, the estimates of Weinberger et al. may not be too conservative.

(3) The study by Holm-Müller et al. (1991) seeks to determine the demand for environmental quality. Apart from the already described attempt to measure the benefit of noise reduction with the help of the HPM, they employed a sophisticated budget-game approach and a contingent valuation analysis.

The budget-game consisted of two phases. Phase 1 revealed the relative evaluation of different environmental goods. For this purpose a fixed environmental budget (for each participant) had to be rearranged to maximize individual utility of improved air quality, surface-water quality and reduced noise. Corresponding budget shifts were linked to well-defined environmental quality changes. The main result was that participants always wanted air and water quality to be improved at the expense of a reduction in the noise budget. In addition, the majority preferred air quality improvements to surface-water quality improvements.

In the second phase, the environmental budget was no longer fixed, but participants could decide about trade offs to their private budget. The primary target consisted in capturing the median WTP. Only six of more than 200 participants wanted to improve their private budget at the expense of environmental quality. Even with increasing cost (a higher tax burden/higher consumer prices) for initial environmental improvements, participants preferred to return to the status quo, than to "sell" environmental quality. The observed asymmetry between willingness to pay and willingness to accept matches well with other results documented in the literature. (See Cummings, Brookshire and Schulz (1986), table 3.2 and, including more recent studies, Römer (1991), table 3).

Table 3.1. provides some of the main results of Holm-Müller et al. (1991). The first row in the table indicates that marginal air quality improvement (of one unit according to a well defined quality index) ranks first, followed by surface-water quality improvement, while noise reduction is valued least. The relatively large spans for each commodity reflect different conditions at the locations chosen for the experiments and a high variance in WTP within the subsamples.

Table 3.1 Main results of the budget game of Holm-Müller et al. (1991) in DM per month

	Air	Surface water	Noise	Total
Marginal WTP (median)	75–190	35–110	10–20	–
Mean maximum WTP for all commodities	99	44	1	144
Mean maximum WTP for a single commodity	111	59	10	180

The mean maximum WTP for a change to the best environmental quality for all three areas (row 2) is lower than the maximum WTP for a single environmental commodity (row 3) which highlights the problem of consistent aggregation of WTPs elicited for different environmental commodities.

The authors also conducted a standardized CV survey, based on the results of the budget game. In 3800 personal interviews, they questioned a representative sample of the German population. Valuation objects included an improvement of the three environmental commodities used in the budget game as well as accessibility to the closest recreational area, improvement of the drinking water quality and preservation of species. Finally, all WTPs were added and participants got the chance to adapt the stated WTPs.

Table 3.2 Main results of the survey of Holm-Müller et al. (1991)

	Air	Surface water	Noise	Recreational area	Drinking water	Preservation of species
Mean wtp[a]	9.4	8.0	4.6	2.6	4.3	16.1
zero wtp[b]	36.7	40.5	57.1	73.5	41.7	31.3
best quality[c]	37.6	34.6	48.0	48.1	58.8	–
Best or second-best quality	69.6	61.5	78.3	71.0	88.4	–

[a] in DM per month
[b] % of all participants (based on the sample of those who put the status quo quality not into the best category) who were not willing to state a positive bid.
[c] % of all participants who put the status quo quality into the best category.

Some of the main outcomes of the survey are documented in table 3.2:

– The highest mean WTP is associated with the preservation of species, followed by that for air quality improvement, while an improvement in the accessibility to a recreational area is valued lowest. However, the high valuation of the preservation of species may simply result from the survey design. While all other improvements were offered in a stepwise fashion, the preservation of flora and fauna was described as an all-or-nothing choice. It can also be questioned whether the sharp decline in the mean WTP for the first four commodities may simply reflect order effects, i.e. participants may have been fed up being asked for their WTP again and again. Even though the higher amounts for the last two commodities are not in line with this hypothesis, a simple change of the question order in some subsample would have been instructive.

– A high percentage of the participants stated a WTP of zero for an improvement of one quality step for the respective environmental commodity. The maximum percentage of zero bidders can be found for improved accessibility to a recreational area, while the preservation of species shows the lowest – but in absolute terms still high – percentage of zero bidders. This may indicate an extremely high protest rate for respondents who refuse to accept the contingent scenario, and casts severe doubts on the validity and reliability of the whole survey. Unlike current standard practice of questioning these respondents concerning their motives, no such analysis is undertaken in this study. Implicitly, the authors seem to accept the zero answers as a reflection of true willingness to pay.

– Furthermore, more than 60 % of all participants regarded the status quo quality of the local environmental situation as belonging to the best or second best category according to a given quality index. Thus, the impression arises that environmental quality improvement is an issue only for a minority. However, this view contradicts sharply other survey results (see e.g. Allbus 1989 or Mackscheidt 1986) and may indicate an inadequate choice of categories.

It is our personal impression that the survey figures elicited by Holm-Müller et al. – for the reasons outlined above – should be treated very cautiously.

(4) Schluchter et al. (1991) try to quantify the psychological cost of environmental disamenities. About 5000 participants were questioned with the help of a computer interview performed at trade fairs. In the first part, individuals' well-being with respect to a number of environmental disamenities was evaluated, each on a scale. The sum of the scale values of the respective participant should indicate to each interviewee his or her personal psycho-social cost of the disamenities. A halving of these costs was then offered and the monthly WTP was elicited. Furthermore, the WTP for complete elimination of all environmental disamenities was obtained. After the raw data had been corrected for starting points biases, the mean WTP amounted to 123 DM per month for a significant reduction and to 176 DM for complete elimination of these disamenities. In order to calculate a yearly total benefit figure for all German households, mean WTPs are merely multiplied by 12 times the number of households, yielding a total benefit of approximately 40 billion DM

for a significant reduction and of 57 billion DM for complete elimination of the disamenities. Basing this procedure on computer interviews performed at trade fairs, is likely to cause a severe sample selection bias. Nevertheless, this study covers an interesting benefit category which in economics has often been neglected. However, little is known about the applicability of the CVM to a commodity such as psycho-social cost, which by its very nature cannot be clearly defined. Thus, it would be of crucial importance to check the internal consistency of the answers, i.e. to get an idea how individuals perceive the contingent commodities. In particular, one might ask what the halving of the psyco-social cost means to the respondents. May respondents not simply adapt to the improvement, i.e. use the gained psychic capacities to focus on other environmental problems which had been neglected before? And what is the relation between the traditional use benefits and the psychic benefits investigated by Schluchter et al.? Can both benefit categories be separated at all?

Finally, the study of Klokow and Mathes (1991), tries to quantify the negative impact on individual utility of reduced recreation value of the natural environment, caused by pollution. Yet, it does not meet even the most rudimertary requirements of a contingent market. Therefore, it will not be considered any further.

A different approach is followed in our study (Römer & Pommerehne 1991), which focuses on two methodological questions of the CVM. First, the study investigates whether the CVM can be applied to the most difficult problem of valuing a reduction of environmental risks, a question that so far has been answered more or less pessimistically in the standard literature (see Cummings, Brookshire Schulze 1986, p. 230). Second, the study questions the implicit assumption underlying all CV studies, that the only way to achieve the offered environmental improvement exists in stating WTP. In our study we argue that often related activities on private and political markets often exist, which will offer alternative means to achieve the environmental improvement. These activities may well influence individuals' behaviour, i.e. the WTP revealed in the contingent scenario. Within a survey among citizens of Berlin (West) that focuses on the reduction of the well-documented hazardous waste risk, the above mentioned questions were adressed. Participants were told that without governmental action a certain number of citizens is expected to die within the next ten years (base-line risk). Referring to this status quo, the WTP for two subsequent risk and the risk reductions was elicited. The sample was split in order to test the impact of the size of the base-line risk reductions offered. The specific risk figures are noted in table 3.3. The survey was administered to 166 participants as a personal interview, half of whom were allocated to one of the subsamples.

Table 3.3 Monthly option price bids for risk reductions for a time period of 10 years in DM per person

Subsamples	Risk reductions	Mean bid
A First reduction	200 to 100 expected fatalities	28.3
A Second reduction	100 to 50 expected fatalities	10.3
B First reduction	1000 to 200 expected fatalities	37.1
B Second reduction	200 to 100 expected fatalities	10.8

Source: Römer and Pommerehne 1991

Table 3.3 reveals that, on average, the respondents answered the valuation question as one would expect. All risk reductions have been valued positively, and the second and smaller risk reduction in each subsample was valued less than the first one. Moreover, the first risk reduction in subsample A has independently been valued lower than the first risk reduction in subsample B (all differences turn out to be statistically significant). Finally, in a multiple regression analysis more than a third of the variance of the individual bids can be explained, which clearly demonstrates that the respondents' valuations were not completely incidental. Thus, we find little evidence that a risks reduction cannot be evaluated with the CVM.

The regression analysis also reveals that a number of activities in related private and political markets significantly influence the stated WTP. This holds for the considered private averting activity (substituting public tap water for bottled water, thus avoiding the risk of consuming contaminated ground water) as well as for a number of activities aiming at a public risk reduction, such as complaints about the disamenity or the support of a political party for environmental reasons. The interactions between the stated bid and the activities outside the contingent market clearly demonstrate that the partial analytic view is inadequate since it focuses on the contingent market as the only means to gain an environmental improvement. Instead, a broader perspective is required (for details see Römer 1932).

3.3 The case of Switzerland

3.3.1 THE HEDONIC PRICE METHOD

Three hedonic price studies have been undertaken in Switzerland, all of them with respect to the problem of road traffic noise. Pommerehne (1988) surveyed the housing market of Basle, Iten (1990) that of the city of Zurich, and Grosclaude et al. (1991) that of the city of Neuchâtel. Unlike the German cases, all studies point out the significant impact of road traffic noise on the rental price suggested by the hedonic theory. Table 3.4 compares the estimated hedonic prices for a noise reduction by one unit (dB).

Table 3.4 Percentage increase of the monthly dwelling rent for a road traffic noise reduction by one unit (dB)

Author	City	Percentage increase
Pommerehne (1988)	Basle	1.26
Iten (1990)	Zurich	0.90
Grosclaude et al. (1991)	Neuchâtel	0.91

These results show a consistent pattern, since in all studies the reduction of road traffic noise by one unit is – ceteris paribus – related to an increase of the monthly dwelling rent of about one percent. In addition, these estimates are quite similar to the results of respective U.S. studies (see Pommerehne 1987). In a number of American cities, price increases range from 0.65 % to 1.33 % (for each reduction by one unit of dB), with a mean of 0.99 %. Furthermore, all Swiss studies found out that the rent increase due to marginal noise reduction rose analogou to the noise level of the status quo. The same applies to an aircraft noise study for the city of Basle undertaken by Pommerehne.

Iten (1990) also considered the impact of air pollution on housing prices. He found that a one percent increase in air pollution leads to a price depreciation of 0.05 to 0.60 percent. Again, this result is compatible with estimates for the U.S., yielding a range between 0.06 and 0.50 percent (Pommerehne Römer 1992, table 2).

3.3.2 THE TRAVEL COST METHOD

Two carefully done studies used the TCM to estimate the recreational use benefit of a nearby forest. Schelbert et al. (1988) evaluated a specific part of the Zurichberg forest and Nielsen (1992) the respective benefit of the San Bernardo forest in Ticino.

For the Zurichberg forest, the average travel cost of an individual amounted to 3.6 SFr per visit or 325 SFr per user per year, yielding a total benefit of 700 SFr and a net benefit of 375 SFr per user per year. While Schelbert et al. took into account only travel cost, Nielsen computed the use value based on three components. She added the mean opportunity cost of time spent in the forest – on average 17 SFr – and the maximum amount individuals would be willing to pay as an entrance fee without reducing the frequency of their visits to the mean travel cost of 5 SFr per visit. The WTP component had been elicited with the help of a CV survey and amounted on average to 3 SFr. Thus, the cotal cost an average individual would be prepared to bear for his/her visit amounted to 25 SFr. These costs per visit give a total annual benefit of the forests for each user of 4250 SFr, with a net surplus of 3500 SFr. It is not too surprising that Nielsen's estimates by far exceed those of Schelbert et al., since she included two additional (perhaps disputable) opportunity cost categories into her model.

3.3.3 THE CONTINGENT VALUATION METHOD

Both of the above mentioned studies also used the CVM. The study by Schelbert et al. (1988) validated the result obtained by the TCM: They elicited an average WTP of 3.30 SFr per user per visit and of 430 SFr per person per year as use value of the Zurichberg forest. This accords well with the net surplus of 375 SFr per user per year computed with the TCM. Furthermore, the study applied the CVM to quantify the non-use benefits associated with the forest. In order to reveal these benefits, the participants' preparedness to join a forest conservation interest group, their voluntary financial contributions and their support for this group by working free of charge, were investigated. In order to get a conservative estimate, only one (the larger) of the two monetary values was used as an estimate of the non-use value. An average non-use value of 120 SFr per user per year was elicited. Thus, the average total resource value consisting of the total use benefit of 700 SFr plus the non-use value of 120 SFr amounts to 820 SFr per user per year.

Nielsen (1992) elicited a similar mean WTP of 3 SFr per user per visit for the San-Bernardo forest. However, as has been mentioned before, in her travel cost model she used this amount as an additional opportunity cost category. Besides, she also used the CVM to estimate the non-use value of the forest. Trying to measure this value, survey respondents were asked for their annual WTP to avoid a serious deterioration of the forest condition (a mean value of 220 SFr), a complete ecological breakdown (470 SFr), as well as for their yearly WTP to achieve an improvement of the forest condition (170 SFr). Although the percentage of zero bidders varied from 40 to 80%, the calculation of the mean WTP was based on the assumption that all of the bids were true zero bids. Thus, the average non-zero bid must have been quite high, ranging between 360 and 850 SFr. The question remains whether this result implies that the participants offering positive bids were not able to differentiate between use and non-use values. Moreover, one may ask whether the addition of the use and non-use values would have led to an overestimation of the total resource value within both studies. In order to check for this possibility, it would have been interesting to elicit the WTP of non-forest users for the non-use values, or to elicit the valuation of the users for the preservation of different forests from those actually visited.

Two other CV studies were performed, partly to validate the results of the HPM. Pommerehne (1988) surveyed the same households that formed the basis of his hedonic regression analysis for Basle and captured their WTP for a 50% reduction of the road traffic noise. The obtained results are not only very similar (an average of 81 SFr per household per month computed with the HPM versus an average of 75 SFr elicited applying the CVM), but also deviate as is expected theoretically (with the differential being statistically significant at the 95% confidence level). However, for aircraft noise the results are not that favourable. Here, the average value of 22.3 SFr obtained through the HPM is smaller than the mean WTP of 32.3 SFr revealed on the basis of the CVM. Besides the specific reasons for this deviation outlined in Pommerehne (1988), these results may not contradict theory if one allows plausible boundaries of accuracy for both estimates.

Iten (1990) employed a special form of the CVM – the conjoint analysis – to validate his HP estimates for traffic noise reduction and air quality improvement. Again, the HP and CV estimates of a 50% reduction in road traffic noise and a 50% improvement in air quality correspond closely. The HPM yielded an average monthly value of 180 SFr per household, whereas the conjoint analysis elicited 200 SFr, in each case considering households of the middle income group. Under reasonable boundaries of accuracy, these results still may be in line with theory.

To sum up: the degree of coincidence between the results of different methods to estimate the demand for an environmental good in the reported studies is rather striking. Thus, it provides forceful evidence that the proper valuation of environmental commodities is not arbitrary or meaningless, but is based on sound microeconomic theory. The techniques employed are able to reveal valuable and somewhat precise information about individual preferences concerning "free" (since unpriced) environmental amenities, which in the meantime have become scarce.

3.6 Some comparative remarks

After having reported in some detail about benefit studies in Germany and Switzerland, the question arises as to the similarities and differences that can be found with respect to the studies in the two countries.

Looking at the past, some early German studies can be found up to the mid-eighties, followed by a longer period of stagnation and ending with the release of the five studies commissioned by the environmental agency. Switzerland needed more than a decade longer before the first benefit study was launched, but ever since then new studies have been published quite regularly and – considering the small size of the country – with a surprising high frequency. With respect to the relative importance of each approach, we notice a strongly increased use of CV studies in Germany, while all three methods have been equally applied in Switzerland.

In respect to the institutional environment in Switzerland, all studies were performed by researchers working at university instututes. This does not apply for the German studies by Holm-Müller et al., Schluchter et al. and Klokow and Mathes. Moreover, it has to be emphasized that Swiss researchers were able to receive funding from a variety of institutions, while in Germany the environmental agency has gradually become the monopolistic sponsor. This possibly had some impact on the target, the construction and the performance of the benefit studies.

With respect to the target, Swiss studies usually concentrate on a single environmental commodity, which has already been thoroughly investigated by U.S. studies, while some of the more recent German studies are very extensive, covering several environmental amenities (e.g. Holm-Müller) or – as in the case of Schluchter – "amenities" that have not been considered so far. Although there is no doubt that such a procedure per se has some merit, it causes some problems if the studies are supposed to produce nationwide benefit estimates. Focusing on a number of amenities or on a single but still unresearched commodity requires a sophisticated research design that allows multiple internal consistency tests, e.g. tests which are based on split samples. In contrast, the requirement to produce nationwide benefit estimates, forces the researcher to abstain from such a procedure and to distribute his sample across the country in order to take into account the major regional differences concerning the environmental commodities and the differences in the key social characteristics of the respondents.

In contrast, the design of all Swiss studies is oriented by the requirement to reveal the benefits for a specific environmental commodity in clearly defined and, consequently, relatively homogeneous regions. This not only enables Swiss researchers to use a more detailed and profound research design but also to elaborate stronger links between the empirical work and economic theory.

Consequently, the main emphasis within the empirical procedure in Switzerland is to provide evidence of the reliability and the internal (and if possible also external) validity of the generated data. The fact that all the work is performed in an academic environment, where criticism is a virtue, may also support this orientation of the research design. In contrast, the German environmental agency may not be particularly interested in ongoing academic disputes but may look for some quantitative figures (however solid these figures may be) in order to substantiate their demand for increased environmental protection. Thus, it is no surprise that studies sponsored by the agency provide only limited evidence of the reliability and validity of the data in use. To give an example: apart from our own research, none of the CV studies has ever used multiple regression analysis to explain the individual bids, even though this procedure enables the researcher to test for the reliability and validity of the data as has been highly recommended by Mitchell and Carson (1989), whose book – ironically – is cited in most of these studies. Again, in the Swiss studies – oriented towards American standards – most cases include multiple regression analysis.

The German and Swiss experience with respect to benefit studies has differed in many aspects. However, if one were forced to reduce the comparison to a single issue it might be said that Swiss research has been science oriented while German research has been policy oriented.

The question arises whether this line of development will continue in the future. As long as the institutional environment remains unchanged this may well be the case. However, the Council of Advisors of the project "Benefit of Environmental Protection – Cost of Environmental Pollution" in their evaluation of the studies proposed a careful reorientation towards regionally limited benefit studies (Endres et al. 1991 p. 94). This would undoubtedly enable the researcher to measure benefits on a more solid ground and to advance the basic development of the estimation methods which in our view has not yet been completed. Such a reorientation may not only improve the quality of the results, but also increase their acceptance within the politico-administrative decision-making process.

References

Allbus 1988: *Allgemeine Bevölkerungsumfrage der Sozialwissenschaften* (General Population Survey of the Social Sciences) 1989 ed. by the Zentralarchiv für empirische Sozialforschung, University of Cologne in cooperation with ZUMA Mannheim, ZA. No. 1670, Cologne, 412 p.

Borjans, R. 1983: Immobilienpreise als Indikatoren der Umweltbelastung durch den städtischen Kraftverkehr (Real Estate Prices as Indicators of Environmental Pollution Caused by Urban Traffic). Verkehrsverlag Fischer, Düsseldorf, 310 p.

Cummings, R.G., Brookshire, D.S. & W.D. Schulze 1986: *Valuing Environmental Goods. An Assessment of the Contingent Valuation Method.* Rowman and Allanheld, Totowa N.J., 270 p.

Endres, A., Jarre, J. P. Klemmer & K. Zimmermann 1991: *Der Nutzen des Umweltschutzes* (The Benefit of Environmental Protection). Ed. by the Bundesumweltministerium (Secretary of the Environment). Bonn, 152 p.

Ewers, H.J. & W. Schulz 1981: *Die monetären Nutzen gewässergüteverbessernder Maß-nahmen – dargestellt am Beispiel des Tegler Sees in Berlin* (The Monetary Benefits of Water Quality Improving Measures – Demonstrated by the Example of the Lake Tegel in Berlin). Duncker und Humblot, Berlin, 358 p.

Grosclaude, P., Soguel, N. & M.A. Stritt 1991: L'évaluation des nuisances du trafic routier en ville de Neuchâtel (An Evaluation of the Road Traffic Noise in the City of Neuchâtel). Paper Prepared for the Conference "Economy and the Environment in the 90's", August 1991, Neuchâtel.

Hampicke, U, Tampe, K. Kiemstedt, H. Horlitz, Th. Walters, U. & D. Timp 1991: Die volkswirtschaftliche Bedeutung des Arten- und Biotopschwundes in der Bundesrepublik Deutschland (The Economic Importance of Preserving Species and Biotopes in the Federal Republic of Germany). *Berichte des Bundesumweltamtes* 3/91, Erich Schmidt Verlag, Berlin, 654 p.

Holm-Müller, K., Hansen, H. Klockman, M. & P. Luther 1991: Die Nachfrage nach Umweltqualität in der Bundesrepublik Deutschland (The Demand for Environmental Quality in the Federal Republic of Germany). *Berichte des Umweltbundesamtes* 4/91, Erich Schmidt Verlag, Berlin, 346 p.

Iten, R. 1990: Die mikroökonomische Bewertung von Veränderungen der Umweltqualität. Dargestellt am Beispiel der Stadt Zürich (The Microeconomic Valuation of Changes of the Environmental Quality. Demonstrated at the Example of the City of Zurich). In: *Schriftenreihe des Instituts für empirische Wirtschaftsforschung der Universität Zurich,* Bd. 20, Schellenberg, Winterhur, 142 p.

Jordan, E. 1976: Empirische Aspekte der Messung und Bewertung von Umweltschäden auss ökonomischer Sicht (Empirical Aspects of the Measurement and Evaluation of Envvironmental Damages from an Economic Perspective). PhD thesis, University of Dortmund, Dortmund, 178p.

Klokow S. & U. Mathes 1991: *Umweltbedingte Folgekosten im Bereich Freizeit und Erholung.* (Environmental Follow-Up-Costs in the Area of Leisure and Recreation). Texte des Umweltsbundesamtes, Berlin, 365 p.

Mackscheidt, K. 1986: Präferenzen für öffentliche Güterangebote. (Preferences for the Supply of Public Goods). In: Wille, E. (ed.): *Konkrete Probleme öffentlicher Planung. Grundlegende Aspekte der Zielbildung, Effizienz und Kontrolle* (Specific Problems of Public Planning: Basic Aspects of the Formation of Targets, Efficiency and Control). Peter Lang, Frankfurt, 2–24.

Mierheim, H. 1974: Nutzen-Kosten Analysen öffentlicher Grünanlagen im innerstädtischen Bereich. Eine Untersuchung über die Anwendbarkeit am Beispiel Berlin-West (Benefit-Cost Analysis of Public Parks in Inner City Areas. An Evaluation of its Applicability Concerning the Example of Berlin-West). PhD thesis, Technical University of Berlin, Berlin, 256p.

Mitchell, R.C. & R.T. Carson 1989: *Using Surveys to Value Public Goods: The Contingent Valuation Method.* Resources for the Future, John Hopkins University Press, Washington D.C., 463 p.

Nielsen, C. 1992: Der Wert stadtnaher Wälder als Erholungsraum: Eine ökonomische Analyse am Beispiel von Lugano (The Value of Nearby Forests as Recreational Areas: An Economic Analysis Taking as an Example Lugano). Ph. Dissertation, University of Zurich, forthcoming.

Pommerehne, W.W. 1987: *Präferenzen für öffentliche Güter* (Preferences for Public Goods). Mohr, Tübingen, 290 p.

Pommerehne, W.W. 1988: Measuring Environmental Benefits: A Comparison of Hedonic Technique and Contingent Valuation. In: Bös, D; M. Rose & C. Seidl (eds.): *Welfare and Efficiency in Public Economics.* Springer, Heidelberg, 363–400.

Pommerehne, W.W. & A.U. Römer 1992: Ansätze zur Erfassung der Präferenzen für öffentliche Güter, (Approaches to Measure Preferences for Public Goods). In: *Jahrbuch für Sozialwissenschaften,* (forthcoming)

Römer, A.U. 1991: Der kontingente Bewertungsansatz. Eine geeignete Methode zur Bewertung umweltverbessernder Maßnahmen? (The Contingent Valuation Approach: An Adequate Method to Value Measures Aimed at Improving the Environment?). *Zeitschrift für Umweltpolitik und Umweltrecht/Journal of Environmental Policy and Law* 11, 411–456.

Römer, A.U. & W.W. Pommerehne 1991: Revealing Preferences for the Reductions of Public Risks: An Application of the CV Approach. Paper Prepared for the Annual Meeting of the European Association of Environmental and Resource Economists, June 1991, Stockholm. Manuscript, University of Saarbrücken.

Schelbert, H, Lang, T. Buse. I. Henzmann, J. Maggi, R. Iten, R. & C. Nielsen 1988: *Wertvolle Umwelt* (Precious Environment). ed. by the Zürcher Kantonalbank, 90 p.

Schluchter, W., Elger, U. & H. Hönigsberger 1991: *Die psychologischen Kosten der Umweltverschmutzung* (The Psychological Costs of Environmental Pollution). Texte des Umweltbundesamtes, Berlin, 204 p.

Schulz, W. 1985: Der monetäre Wert besserer Luft: Eine empirische Analyse individueller Zahlungsbereitschaften und ihrer Determinanten auf der Basis von Repräsentativumfragen (The Monetary Value of Improved Air Quality. An Empirical Analysis of Individual Willingsness to Pay and Its Determinants Based on Representative Surveys). *Europäische Hochschulschriften,* Reihe V, Peter Lang, Frankfurt, 380 p.

Weinberger, M.; G. Thomassen & R. Willecke 1991: Kosten des Lärms in der Bundesrepublik Deutschland (The Cost of Noise in the Federal Republic of Germany). Berichte des Bundesumweltamtes 9/1991, Erich Schmidt Verlag, Berlin, 246p.

Chapter 4
Finland

ERKKI MÄNTYMAA, VILLE OVASKAINEN & TUIJA SIEVÄNEN

4.1 Overview of valuation research in Finland

Research into the valuation of environmental benefits in Finland first began at quite a late stage. Compared to many other European countries, Finland is fairly sparsely inhabited. The country is rich in waterways and forest resources. Many environmental problems have not been considered as serious as in many other countries. It is only recently that the public and the political decision makers have started to ask for more information about the environmental values.

The earliest studies in this field were carried out in the late 1970s and early 1980s by scientists whose background was in the technological sciences. These studies (e.g. Kyber 1981) have mostly been used in the judicature to evaluate the environmental impacts of e.g. pulp and paper industries and hydropower plants. The method used was similar to the Hedonic Price (HP) approach, but most of the analyses were not explicitly based on economic theory.

The first real HP study was Falcke (1982), who used data from the USA. The demand for improved water quality was estimated in 17 sites. The study was based on the notion that the net benefits from an improved water resource varied inversely with the property's distance from the shore.

The first Finnish studies using the Contingent Valuation Method (CVM) were carried out in the late 1980s. One of the first (Sipponen 1987) was concerned with the value of recreational fishing in Central Finland. From an economic point of view, the study was theoretically quite weak.

Two Contingent Valuation (CV) studies were completed last year. Sievänen et al. (1991) discuss the alternative tools for measuring the monetary value of outdoor recreation, and how socioeconomic variables influence the valuation. Ovaskainen et al. (1991) report on an experiment where the total hunting value of grouse was measured using the CVM.

Naskali (1991) has started his CV research with a theoretical analysis of the concept of existence value of wilderness preservation. He plans to apply his theoretical findings in an empirical study on economic values and management of wilderness resources. Moisseinen (1991) is also interested in existence values. She is going to estimate option prices and existence values of the Saimaa seal using a CV framework. The Saimaa seal (Phoca hispida saimensis) lives only in Lake Saimaa in Finland, and the population is endangered.

Mäntymaa (1991) uses CV surveys to estimate the economic value of the water quality changes. Heiskanen et al. (1992) try to test for part-whole bias of CVM by asking for people's WTP for the preservation of different environmental goods: the environment as a whole, the eleven great lakes, and one specific lake in Finland. They use the discrete choice technique, i.e. different samples of people are asked to answer "yes" or "no" to different preselected amounts, and they include the alternative of "indifferent" in the CV question.

Aakkula (1991) is trying to analyse the potential for scenic agriculture in Finland by valuing the agricultural landscape by means of CVM. Scenic agriculture is a potential alternative of agricultural policy if production has to be reduced because of the current excess supply.

This list of completed and ongoing projects shows that the interest in CV research in Finland is growing. Three Finnish CV studies, Sievänen et al. (1991), Ovaskainen et al. (1991) and Mäntymaa (1991), will be reviewed below.

4.2. Review of contingent valuation studies in Finland

4.2.1 VALUATION OF OUTDOOR RECREATION

Forest recreation in Finland, as in all Scandinavian countries, is traditionally based on everyman's right, i.e. a common right of free access to all natural, undeveloped areas. According to everyman's right, people are free to walk, ski, ride, bicycle, swim, boat, pick berries, mushrooms and flowers, take drinking water and camp occasionally on land regardless of ownership. In an economic sense, it is an externality of an institutional nature.

Participation rate in outdoor activities is high (85 per cent of population) in Finland, and the frequency of visits is 1–2 times per week on average.

In all Scandinavian countries, the government provides many public services and goods free of charge, or subsidizes the production and supply of certain goods and services. Many leisure services, especially those of outdoor recreation, belong to the services which are available on equal terms to all people for little or no outlay. Very little economic analysis has been involved in the decision-making process concerning these services.

Previously abundant environmental goods have become scarce. Valuation of environmental goods is considered necessary for environmental policy making. The valuation of outdoor recreation, in which use of land and many other resources are traditionally free of charge, has become important. The pursued land-use policy, as well as the expenses of managing recreational resources, needs to be justified in economic terms.

Pouta (1990) and Sievänen et al. (1991) performed the first study valuing forest recreation in Finland. Both the Travel Cost Method (TCM) and the Contingent Valuation Method (CVM) were used. To a great extent the study was an experiment. The institutional restrictions made the design of the CV questions complicated. Thus, the study should be considered as an experiment. The data (406 participants) were collected as in-person interviews at the recreation site, which was a regional recreation area close to Helsinki.

All respondents were asked to answer all valuation questions.

The study examines the suitability of the CV approach to Finnish conditions, where people are not used to paying for recreation. The study discusses alternative ways of framing questions for valuing recreation visits, and analyses the effects of socioeconomic variables on the valuation estimates. The most serious measurement problems concern the hypothetical nature of the CVM and the potential protesting behaviour among the participants (Cummings et al. 1986). In this case, the latter is related to assuming that the everyman's right is not valid, which we do when people are asked to pay to get access to forest areas.

Three different kinds of CVM questions were asked. A conventional question focusing on the willingness to pay (WTP) for entrance (CVM-entrance, curve A in figure 4.1) to the recreation area was the main tool of measurement. A scale from 5 FIM to 300 FIM was used (payment card-technique). Two other questions, one concerning WTP for travelling (CVM-travelling, curve C in figure 4.1) to the recreation site and one on the value of a recreation visit (CVM-attitude, curve B in figure 4.1) related to values of other leisure activities, were developed in order to make the WTP questions less hypothehtical. The "attitude" value-question asked the respondent to compare the value of recreation visits to other leisure activities familiar to him/her. The question was: "Compare outdoor recreation with leisure activities incurring charges. Which activity would you consider to be of equal value to your visit to this recreation area?" A payment card with a scale from 10 FIM to 300 FIM was used.

In table 4.1, the recreation values processed by different measures are described (means, medians and standard deviations).

WTP stated as entrance fees was fairly low. One may assume that many respondents arrived at their WTP by relating a "forest fee" to, for example, a swimming hall fee, which is a familiar, and in many ways, comparable public service fee. People are not prepared to cover all costs of recreation services by entrance fees as they already pay taxes (which they expect to be used for such purposes). The respondents expect society to subsidize recreation services, and therefore they underestimate their bids compared to their "real value" of a recreation visit. This kind of bias could probably be reduced by providing the respondents with more information (Cummings et al. 1986).

Table 4.1. Mean WTP (FIM) for a visit to a forest recreation area estimated by different valuation methods

Valuation method	Median[1]	Mean	sd	Min[2]	Max
– CVM					
– Entrance fee	10	12	12	0	80
– Travel	10–20	16	14	0	>60
– Attitude	86	101	77	10	227
– TCM	20	24	15		

[1] Mean and median are not descriptive because the distribution did not culminate
[2] Min and max values were given in a scale of a payment card

A basis for the value of one visit to the recreational area was calculated from the direct travel costs of the actual visit (Travel Cost Method (TCM), curve D in figure 9.1). As the means of transportation and the distance from the visitor's residence to the area were known, the travel costs could be estimated. The distance was considered to be a continuous factor, and the demand curve was estimated on the basis of travel costs of individuals which represent the portion of visiting population coming from the same distance. The average number of visits per year and visitor in this area was eight. This kind of individual approach of TCM to calculate the recreation value is considered to be relevant in areas which are located close to the visitors and which are frequently visited by respondents (Walsh 1986, 217). The question of maximum WTP for travelling to the recreation site assumes that the area is located further away, and that there are no equal recreation opportunities closer to home. When the difference between the average actual travel cost and the average willingness to pay for travelling were calculated, the WTP value exceeded the actual travel cost.

An interesting experiment in this study was the attempt to relate the value of a forest recreation visit to the market prices of some leisure services or goods (swimming hall fee, concert ticket, book or cost of an evening out at a restaurant). The idea was to ask about the value of a recreational visit by comparing it with the cost of services for which people are used to pay something for. The aim was not to elicit the value of the forest experience itself, but to capture the psychological value of the visit (for the psychological value and the CVM, see Ajzen and Peterson 1988).

Our understanding of this kind of question is that we measured people's attitudes towards outdoor recreation rather than the value of a recreational visit to the particular recreation site. While people subjectively appreciate forest recreation, it seems as though they are not willing to pay the amounts stated as their "attitude" value.

The average number of visits per visitor in this area and the frequency of participation in outdoor activities in general were high among the visitors (3–4 times per week by half of the visitors). The high bids for one visit are not realistic if the total number of visits is considered. The visitors' budget constraints do not allow the values expressed by "attitude" value to be realized.

Figure 4.1 shows that the recreational values gained by the TCM and "CVM – Travel" and "CVM-entrance fee" do not differ much. This indicates that both the TC and CV versions seem to work in the valuation of recreational opportunities. The "CVM-Attitude" value differs dramatically from the others. One may suppose that the WTP for travelling and entrance involve some underestimation due to strategic or protest behaviour bias, while the "attitude" value expresses the importance of the forest visit in monetary terms, even if this is an overestimate. Thus, the "real" value of a recreational visit is probably somewhere between the "attitude" value and WTP for entrance fee and travelling.

Willingness to pay (FIM) per visit

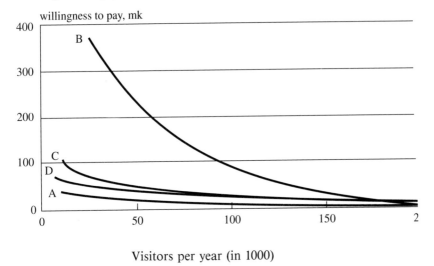

Visitors per year (in 1000)

Valuation techniques:
A CVM – Entrance fee   B CVM – Attitude
C CVM – Travel   D Travel Cost Method (TCM)

Figure 4.1 Demand curves for recreational visits to a forest area, esti-
mated from different environmental valuation techniques

The WTP for entrance and the "attitude" value were closely related
according to a Chi Square test. The same was true of the WTP for
travelling and WTP for entrance. This means that respondents tend
to behave consistently by choosing either low or high bids from the
offered payment card scales representing different kindss of measurements, e.g. CV – questions. When Spearman correlations were calculated between these different measures, the relationships are significant though the correlations are low. This means that the different
measurements tend to create their own value levels. However, the
distributions are similar except for the attitude value which differs
from other measurements. This also supports the conclusion that the
"attitude" value question is not comparable to the other WTP questions, but expresses the high level of importance that Finnish people
place on outdoor recreation.

Some socioeconomic factors were also regressed towards the WTP estimates. Age showed a significant, negative relationship with both the WTP for entrance and the "attitude" value. Older people were less willing to pay for entrance, and they expressed lower attitude values for the outdoor recreation visit in the forest.

4.2.2 THE BENEFITS OF MANAGING FORESTS FOR GROUSE HABITATS

Savolainen (1990) and Ovaskainen et al. (1991) studied the economics of the multiple use of forests focusing on hunting values. The total hunting value of grouse was measured using the Contingent Valuation Method (CVM). Specifically, the study attempted to estimate the benefits of managing forests for grouse habitats.

The background for the study was the interest in, and development of, multiple-use forestry at the Evo College of Forestry. This work has aimed at developing forest management schedules that provide favourable habitats for grouse populations. While the ecological requirements of each species (the capercaillie, black grouse and hazelhen) are known, the economic feasibility of adopting the adjusted management practices was not.

The benefits can be taken to be represented by the increment in the total hunting value of the game stock attributable to the habitat change. However, this is not readily measurable. Hunting rights in Finland are held by the landowner. Others may hunt by joining hunting clubs that hire the hunting rights to specific areas. For public lands, hunting permits are sold by the Forest Districts of the National Board of Forestry. The prices of hunting permits are only a minor part of hunting costs. Also, the value of meat obtained is only a minor part of the total value of hunting. To find the socially optimal price of hunting, the recreational value of hunting must be included.

Therefore, the hunting value of three common grouse species was studied in a survey. On the cost side, the timber opportunity cost of the management adjustments was calculated for one case. Accordingly, the aim of the study was two-fold: to gain experience in the use of the CVM in Finland and attempt to use a cost-benefit analysis of the proposed adjustments in forest management.

A questionnaire was first sent to all members of the local game management association in Lammi, where the Evo College of Forestry in southern Finland is situated. For supplementary and comparative data, the survey was repeated in collaboration with the National Board of Forestry in the Forest District of Keski-Pohja, Ostrobothnia. The population of hunters was identified as the buyers of the annual hunting permit for the region. It should be noted that the data represent case studies in two limited regions rather than representative samples over all Finland. Also, the survey in Lammi includes potential hunters' WTP for the option to hunt grouse, while for Keski-Pohja, all respondents can be taken to be actual users.

To measure the benefits of managing forests in special ways for improved grouse habitats, the ultimate interest was on the incremental hunting value attributable to the resulting change in the stock of grouse. Therefore, we asked for the maximum WTP for hunting in the area at different grouse stock levels, all other factors been equal.

The hunters were asked about their maximum WTP for the hunting experience as a whole using an open-ended formulation that resembles the payment card technique. The basic WTP question was formulated as follows:

Suppose you go hunting in the same area as you do today, the stock of grouse remains the same, etc. Imagine that your total hunting costs would increase. *What is the maximum total cost of grouse hunting per year that you would be prepared to pay rather than quit hunting?*

Next, the respondents were asked to assume that the stock of grouse would be twice as large as currently or only half the current level, and the question was repeated. In the Lammi questionnaire, an additional question asked about the WTP assuming that capercaillie would become abundant enough to be hunted (not allowed currently). Also, the respondents were asked about their actual hunting costs (travel costs, cost of hunting permits, etc). The main results are reported in *Table 4.2*.

For Lammi, the actual hunters' mean WTP in 1988 hardly exceeded the mean actual hunting costs (FIM 600). This suggests that practically no consumer surplus accrued at the current stock level. Other hunters who did not actually hunt grouse in the region in 1988 reported a mean WTP of almost 3/4 of the actual hunters' WTP. While somewhat surprising, the small difference is not illogical given the currently poor stock of grouse in southern Finland.

For Keski-Pohja, the data was analysed in separate subgroups for local and "tourist" hunters i.e. living less and more than 100 km from the site, respectively. In both groups, the reported mean WTP for hunting was more than twice as high as that of actual hunters in Lammi. Despite higher hunting costs (FIM 930 and 1217), the net hunting values (consumer surplus) would remain positive even if the stock would decline. Given that the stock of grouse in Keski-Pohja is significantly stronger than in southern Finland, the results are as expected.

Table 4.2, Mean WTP for grouse hunting (FIM/year/hunter) by region and subgroup at varied stock levels (median WTP and standard deviation are also stated for the current stoch level)

Stock of grouse	Lammi		Keski-Pohja	
	Actual grouse hunters	Other (potential) hunters	Local hunters	"Tourist" hunters
1/2 of current	462	347	1225	1411
Same as current	604	446	1370	1650
median	(750)	(250)	(750)	(1250)
std. dev.	(449)	(414)	(1454)	(1452)
2 times current	786	591	1550	1826

In response to a hypothetical increase in the stock of grouse, the reported WTP for hunting clearly increased in both regions as well as both subgroups within each region. A stock decline seemed to induce a greater relative change than an equal relative improvement, and relative changes were greater for Lammi than Keski-Pohja. The results seem logical, as one may expect that the total hunting value grows at a diminishing rate with game density. However, the difference in WTP between the regions can not be explained completely by differences in the stock.

The total gross vs. net values of hunting were obtained as a product of the mean WTP vs. consumer surplus and number of hunters by subgroups. Breaking the total hunting value into "recreational" and "meat" parts showed that the total value is vastly dominated by recreational values (almost 90 %). On the other hand, the hunting values per hectare of forest land are marginal compared to the commercial timber value of forests.

The WTP measures in this study appear consistent. For example, the mean reported WTP of potential grouse hunters remained well below the actual grouse hunters' mean WTP, as well as their actual costs. With respect to the level of the grouse stock, the measures also behave consistently both within and between the regions.

On the other hand, the experiment stresses that for the CVM to work well, the goods considered must be familiar to the respondents. In Keski-Pohja, almost all respondents had actually hunted grouse and the response rate was as high as 90 %. In Lammi, many who had not actually hunted grouse failed to answer, while all actual hunters responded. Also, the individual bids and measures for mean WTP share some properties common in CV studies (e.g. Cummings et al.

1986). The frequency distribution was rather skewed towards the lowest classes, with the median usually lower than the mean, and there was a long tail on the distribution. Also the standard deviation of the bids was high compared to the mean (Table 4.2).

The results of the CV study were applied in a subsequent cost-benefit analysis. Adjustments in forest management for favourable wildlife habitats are likely to incur costs in terms of reduced timber revenues. To examine the economic justification of the adjusted management schedules, opportunity costs of such adjustments (calculated as reductions in the net timber revenues compared to the revenves from the conventional management schedules) was compared to the benefits of improved grouse habitats. The undiscounted net revenues per hectare were equal to or somewhat higher than those from the conventional schedules. For the black grouse and hazelhen habitats, the discounted annual equivalent opportunity costs were negligible compared to mean annual timber revenues. The capercaillie habitat, in contrast, implies a significant opportunity cost.

To estimate the aggregate opportunity costs, the "grouse adjusted" management programmes were assumed to be applied on all suitable forest lands in Lammi. It is reasonable to assume that the programme over time would lead to a doubling of the grouse populations, which is similar to the commodity specification as used in the contingent valuation study in Lammi. Thus, its benefits are represented by the increase in the net hunting value compared to the current stock level.

The results suggest that the economic feasibility of the black grouse and hazelhen habitats is no problem at all, as the profitability of the schedules does not really differ from the conventional ones. From the cost-benefit analysis of the capercaillie habitats, however, the adjusted forest management schedule can not be recommended, since the opportunity costs of extended timber rotations clearly outweighs the incremental hunting benefits.

4.2.3 MEASUREMENT OF THE ENVIRONMENTAL BENEFITS OF A LAKE

Earlier in this chapter, we discussed the everyman's right to the recreational use of undeveloped areas and its influence on environmental valuation studies. Another potential bias in the CV studies is related to the "polluter pays" principle. Many people think that polluters, e.g. the public sector or industry, are liable to pay the protection costs. Therefore it can be difficult to create understandable CV questions that people would be willing and able to answer correctly.

One of the ongoing valuation studies (Mäntymaa 1991) concerns Lake Oulujärvi which is the fourth largest lake in Finland. It is important to estimate environmental benefits of the lake as several large scale projects have been planned, which might have far-reaching impacts on the future environment of the lake. These projects include a large pulp factory on the eastern side of the lake, a main road across the lake, and several tourist centres around it. There is an allocation problem between these projects as well as between the projects and the environmental protection.

The purpose of the research is to put a value on the quality of the environment attached to a lake in monetary terms. The CVM is used to measure the importance of water quality to actual users, potential users and non-users.

Data for the study have been collected by in-person interviews. The survey sample consists of about 350 individuals living around Lake Oulujärvi.

The study design has three specific features:

1. Free selection of the reference level of water quality
2. Bidding tree technique
3. Segmentation of the research population according to interest groups

Water quality reference level
The levels of water quality are described by a five grade scale. The best possible level is "excellent", and the next are "good", "satisfactory" and "passing". The worst level of water quality is "unsuitable". The meanings of these concepts have been explained to the respondents. Before the willingness-to-pay (WTP) question, the respondent has to suggest his/her own estimate of the current water quality. In the valuation questions the chosen quality is used as the reference level.

Each of the respondents has been asked the WTP questions in the two ways. If the respondent considers the quality of water to be, for example, "satisfactory", the questions become.

1. How much would your household be willing to pay each year to improve the water quality from the "satisfactory" level to the "good" level?
2. How much would your household be willing to pay each year to keep the water quality from diminishing from the "good" level to one grade worse (the "passing" level)?

This kind of question has two advantages. First, when we ask one step up and one step down from the reference point, we can get two marginal WTP bids. Using these, we can estimate the shape of the demand curve for water quality. If the assumption of diminishing marginal utilities is valid, the first marginal WTP bid should be smaller than the second.

The second advantage follows from the free selection of water quality. Respondents choose their own quality level corresponding to their interests and the area of the lake where they usually visit. This kind of procedure gives more reference points for the demand curve than using only one level of quality given by the interviewer (cf. Smith & Desvousges 1986).

If the response was a zero bid, or the respondent could not answer the questions or refused to answer at all, he/she was asked an additional question, i.e. a willingness-to-accept question:

How much should your household be compensated each year, if the water quality was reduced from the present level to one grade worse?

The bidding tree technique
The second feature of the study was to apply two versions of the CVM. One is the conventional continuous valuation question, which asks directly about the respondents' WTP. As the other, a new elicitation method, the bidding tree technique, was developed. This technique seeks to combine some desirable features of the most widely used elicitation methods, the bidding game and the payment card, while avoiding some of their weaknesses. The hypothesis is that people can answer the bidding tree question more easily than the direct valuation question.

The bidding tree technique uses cards, comparable to payment cards, but involves three bidding rounds before the final answer is reached. In the first round the interviewer gives the respondent a card with two large ranges of bids. The individual is then asked to select a value range. According to the respondent's stated WTP range, the interviewer selects a new card with narrower ranges and shows it to the respondent. After the third round, the range is "narrow enough" for the final choice. The respondent is now, through a direct question, asked to state his/her WTP as a specific amount.

Interest grouping
To control and test the validity of the method, i.e. whether people can understand the WTP questions and give valid answers, the population was divided into three interest groups.

In theory, WTP values vary among individuals of a given income level. It can be assumed that WTP for protection of an environmental resource, e.g. a lake, depends on the benefits and costs that individuals attach to the protection. For example, fishermen and owners of summer cottages suffer most from the pollution of a lake, while potential sellers of timber can expect to suffer from the large environmental protection investments of the pulp factory.

In this study, the aim is to find the range in which the WTP for environmental benefits varies between different interest groups. The sample of the survey has been formed with some subsamples in which the WTP can be expected to differ from one another. As a "control group" we have used a random sample of people who have no special interests in the lake.

If the users of an environmental commodity are willing to pay more for high quality of the commodity than non-users and those who could receive some disadvantages from the protection of the commodity, the results will support the validity of the CV survey. Preliminary results show that the average WTP to avoid one level poorer water quality was 930, 764 and 464 1990-FIM per person annually for users, the general public (non-users) and forest owners, respectively. This seems to be consistent with the expectations.

4.3 The main implementation issues

4.3.1 URBAN AND NATIONAL LAND USE ISSUES

The many problems in land use policy and natural resource allocation require that the environmental valuation methods are developed to make the non-material and intangible values of natural resources and environment commensurate with material values. Many issues of land use planning, both at national, regional and local levels indicate these problems.

Land use planning of urban areas is a good example. In the process of allocating natural and undeveloped land for different purposes, the ways of use that show high value in monetary terms such as housing and industrial development are often preferred to the uses such as recreation of which there is no monetary evaluation. The effect of decisions made in land use planning are longlasting, often almost irreversible. The admistrators and city planners who work in the field of recreation see that the only way to show the importance of recreational areas in the urban environment is to try to measure the monetary value of recreational use.

At the national level, the same allocation and land use planning problems concern forest areas, peatland areas and water areas when decisions are made between commercial uses – timber production, use of peat or hydro power as a source of energy or lake as a recipient of waste water – and nature conservation and environmental protection. The environmental valuation methods could be used in the context of evaluating and comparing the different environmental protection and nature conservation programs.

4.3.2 ADMINISTRATIVE NEEDS – ACCOUNTABILITY OF PUBLIC AGENCIES

Many public agencies managing public lands and other resources in Finland are facing the demand of accountability, which is a new situation to the organizations. This means that many of the investments to produce services and facilities for public benefit, e.g. the multiple use of public forests, are to be compared with output, mainly as direct income. There are not user fees for the recreational services on public lands. Only fishing and hunting permits and camping fees in well-developed recreational areas are charged. For example the National Board of Forestry has to show that inputs to unpriced recreation services or nature conservation provide measurable income or benefits. Also, there is a need to develop methods to include environmental and intangible values to property balance assessments to evaluate the short vs. long-term implications of alternative decisions. For example, it is easy to show a large short-term profit by heavy timber cutting, but the potential reduction in the quality of environment should also be considered.

4.3.3 DEVELOPING FOREST MANAGEMENT SCHEDULES

Forest management schedules which consider multifunctional uses of forest resources such as the demands of the wildlife habitats or recreation needs are to be tested for economic feasibility. In many cases, the alternative management methods produce economic, ethical, esthetical and recreational benefits, which make their total value a lot greater than the monetary value of timber production alone.

There are hints of change in attitudes also in the forestry practices. The forest management directives that recently have been developed in many organizations pay more attention to multiple use issues. Economic studies which may show that the suggested alternative management schedules are not necessarily less productive for timber

production than conventional ones allow more freedom of choice to
forestry practices.

4.3.4 WATER MANAGEMENT ISSUES

According to the Water law (i.e. a law related to waterways and water
management), the total benefits should exceed the disadvantages
(including social costs) of all projects affecting water ways. In the
past, the court which administers the permissions to water projects
has paid attention only to private interests. After the new law of
1987, public interests should also be considered.

The interest in the monetary valuation methods, instead of verbal
descriptions of advantages and disadvantages, is growing in the Finnish court of justice. Advanced scientific information could become
a permanent part of the judicature.

4.3.5 DEVELOPMENT OF NATURAL RESOURCE
ACCOUNTING

An important challenge for the implementation of environmental
valuation studies is the Natural Resources Accounting system. In the
statistics, the material stocks and flows of natural resources are already calculated, but the many non-material benefits of the environment are not considered. For example, forest resources include only
the wood resources but not other aspects of the forest ecosystem.
Also, in this kind of statistics, money is the most important and most
often the only commensurate measure for comparison.

The potential use and development of natural resource accounting
as an instrument of planning and decision making depends essentially on the availability of basic data on natural resources, and different stages of resource use. Here, methods that add environmental
and non-material values to the framework of natural resource accounting are valuable.

References

Aakkula, J. 1991: Maisemamaatalouden mahdollisuudet Suomessa (The potentiality
of scenic agriculture in Finland – The value of agricultural landscape estimated by
means of WTP and WTA). In Finnish. Paper presented at Workshop on resource
and environmental economics, March 4–5, 1991, Oulu, Finland, 5 p. (unpublished).
Ajzen, I. & G. Peterson 1988: Contingent Value measurements: The price of everything and the value of nothing? In Peterson, G., Driver, B. & R. Gregory (eds.)

Amenity resource valuation. Integrating economics with other disciplines. Venture Publishing, Inc., 65-76 p.

Cummings, R.G., Bookshire, D.S. & W.D. Schulze 1986: *Valuing environmental goods. An assessment of the Contingent Valuation Method.* Rowman & Allanheld, Totowa, New Jersey, 270 p.

Falcke, C.O. 1982: Water quality and property prices: An econometric analysis of environmental benefits. Societas Scientiarum Fennica, Commentationes Scientiarum Socialium 18: 1982, Helsinki, 189 p.

Heiskanen, H., Mäntymaa, E. & R. Svento 1992: Valuing public goods: The purchase of environmental quality. Paper presented at XIV Annual Symposium of Finnish Economists, February 10-11, 1992, Oulu, Finland, 15 p. (unpublished).

Kyber, M. 1981: Vesistön likaantumisen virkistyskäytölle aiheuttamat haitat ja niiden arviointi katselmustoimituksessa (Impacts for recreational use of waterways caused by pollution and their evaluation in the inspection of scene). In Finnish. *Technical Research Centre of Finland, Research notes 23:* 1981. Espoo, 90 p.

Mäntymaa, E. 1991: Some new ideas and preliminary results for using the CVM in measuring the environmental benefits of a lake. Paper presented at Autumn Workshop in Environmental Economics in Venice, September 29 – October 5, 1991, 17 p. (unpublished).

Moisseinen, E. 1991: Arvon norppakin ansaitsee? Contingent Valuation-menetelmä optiohinnan ja olemassaoloarvon estimoinnissa (Estimation of option prices and existence values in a CV framework). In Finnish. Paper presented at Workshop on resource and environmental economics, December 9-10, 1991, Hailuoto, Finland, 5 p. (unpublished).

Naskali, A. 1991: The concept of existence value and wilderness preservation. In Solberg, B. (ed.) Proceedings of the Biennial Meeting of the Scandinavian Society of Forest Economics, April 10-13, 1991, Gausdal, Norway.

Ovaskainen, V., Savolainen, H. & Sievänen, T. 1991: The benefits of managing forests for grouse habitats: A Contingent Valuation Experiment. Paper presented at Biennial Meeting of the Scandinavian Society of Forest Economics, April 10-13, 1991, Gausdal, Norway. Scandinavian Forest Economics 32, 12

Pouta, E. 1990: Ulkoilualueen virkistyshyötyjen taloudellinen arviointi (Economic evaluation of recreational benefits). In Finnish. University of Helsinki, Department of Social Economics of Forestry, M.Sc. Thesis, 88 p. (unpublished).

Savolainen, H. 1990: Metsäkanalintujen huomioon ottaminen metsän kasvatuksessa. Hyödyt ja kustannukset (Considering grouse populations in forest management. Benefits and costs). In Finnish. University of Helsinki, Department of Social Economics of Forestry, M.Sc. Thesis, 85 p. (unpublished).

Sievänen, T., Pouta, E. & V. Ovaskainen 1991: Problems of measuring recreation value given everyman's rights. In Solberg, B. (ed.) Proceedings og the Biennial Meeting of the Scandinavian Society of Forest Economics, April 10-13, 1991, Gausdal, Norway. Scandinavian Forest Economics 32, 13 p.

Sipponen, M. 1987: Keskisuomalaisten kotitarve- ja virkistyskalastuksesta ja sen arvosta v. 1981 erityisesti vesioikeudellisen intressivertailun kannalta. (On fishing for household and recreational of people living in Central Finland and on its value especially from the point of view of water rights judicature). In Finnish. *University of Jyväskylä, Department of biology, Research notes 48,* Jyväskylä, 143 p.

Smith, V.K. & W.H. Desvousges 1986: *Measuring water quality benefits.* Kluwer-Nijhoff Publishing, Boston, USA, 327 p.

Walsh, R.C. 1986: *Recreation Economic Decisions: Comparing Benefits and Costs.* Venture Publishing, Inc., 637 p.

Chapter 5
The Netherlands

RUUD HOEVENAGEL, ONNO KUIK & FRANS OOSTERHUIS

5.1 Introduction

The monetary valuation of environmental change has a relatively long history in the Netherlands. As early as 1973, individuals were asked for their compensation for accepting aircraft noise (Jansen and Opschoor, 1973). This study was the first to apply an in-person survey based on the Contingent Valuation method in the Netherlands, and, indeed, in Europe. In 1974, an assessment was made of the monetary damage due to air pollution in the Netherlands (Jansen et al., 1974). Part of this assessment used the Hedonic Price method to value the monetary impact of air pollution (using a measure of stench) on living conditions.

In this early period, the monetary value of various outdoor recreation sites was estimated by using Travel Costs models. For a discussion of Travel Cost applications of that time, see Bouma (1974). Another approach to value natural amenities – the Shadow Project method – was developed by Klaassen and Botterweg (1974).

However, despite these early activities, the practical usefulness of monetary estimates in public decision-making was doubted. The main obstacles were: methodological weaknesses of the methods used, and a lack of reliable data (Opschoor, 1987). One of the Dutch pioneers of environmental valuation concluded in 1974 that monetary valuations of environmental damage were shaky to such an extent that they were unfit as the sole basis for policy decisions (Opschoor 1974).

In the early 1980s, the interest in valuation research was stimulated by the theoretical and practical developments in the United States. The environmental department of the Dutch Government issued a small research project assessing the possibilities of monetary valuation of the benefits of environmental policies in some main policy areas. The approaches used in this project were rather less imaginative than the approaches that were tried out in the early 1970s. The various studies used dose-response relationships (based on the literature or "assumed") to quantify the impacts of policies. These estimated impacts were then valued with unit values, based on market prices or "shadow" prices (for example, entrance fees for swimming pools were used as a "shadow" price to value swimming in fresh water). Impacts which were valued included: materials corrosion, crop damage, noise damage, freshwater-based recreation (swimming and angling), fishery and navigation damage. The studies used what Pearce and Markandya (1989) call the "indirect" valuation procedures.

In a recent assessment of the valuation studies of this period, Kuik et al. (1991) argue that the extreme cautiousness with which impacts were valued led to large downward biases in the valuation. The studies lack both "completeness", that is, important damage categories were not valued (e.g. sensitive ecosystems, human health), and "comprehensiveness", that is, only use values were included and no non-use values (existence, bequest values).

The results of the studies were published in the Environmental Programme of the Netherlands 1986–1990 (Anon 1985). Together with estimates of some other studies (including the estimate of health damage effects of air pollution from the 1974 study of Jansen et al.), the total monetary value of environmental damage in The Netherlands was estimated to be *at least* 2 to 3.8 billion Dutch guilder (DFL) per year or 0.6 to 1.1 % of national income. After this publication, government interest in monetary valuation seems to have faded. For example, later environmental programmes did not include this or any other monetary estimate of environmental damage.

In the 1980s, little use was made of "direct" valuation procedures (Pearce and Markandya, 1989), such as the Hedonic Price and Travel Cost methods. Only the Contingent Valuation method was occasionally used, and gained increasing acceptance, albeit, it must be added, in academic circles only.

5.2 Case studies

This section describes the contingent valuation (CV) studies that have been carried out in the Netherlands. Design, results and implications of each CV study will be examined. The amounts stated refer to the year of study, and are stated in Dutch Guilder (DFL).

5.2.1 VALUATION OF DAMAGE DUE TO AIRCRAFT NOISE

Design

Jansen and Opschoor (1973) carried out an in-person survey among 600 home-owners in three Dutch cities. This study tried to measure the social costs of aircraft noise on the basis of contingent valuation questions. However, we prefer to call this survey a "CV-like" study, as several aspects, now considered to be important, were missing in the questionnaire. These aspects include a careful description of the contingent market, of the used payment vehicle, etc. On the other hand, this study was the first to ask individuals directly, using house prices, for the amount of money which would just compensate them for the noise nuisance suffered, and make them as well off as they were before. Hence, this study was one of the first that used a "willingness to accept" (WTA) format. The questions which revealed respondents' WTP amounts were (roughly):

"Suppose a broker has found a new house for you in another area, a house that meets all your wishes. What would you be willing to pay for this house?"

"Now, suppose this house was just sold. However, the broker has a couple of other houses available which are identical to the above-mentioned house, with only one exception: the houses are located near an airport which will give you some noise nuisance. How much cheaper should this house be before you would be willing to buy it?"

Results

Probably the most interesting result of this study was that many respondents, more than 50% (!), gave as an answer "for no price would I buy such a house". Although such answers are not unusual for questionnaires asking for respondents' WTA amounts, this large percentage makes it very troublesome to interpret the results of the study.

Implications

The results of this study should have been used in the Cost-Benefit Analysis aimed at deciding whether to construct and where to situate a second Dutch national airport. Such an analysis, however, never took place. Due to the oil crises, the idea of building a second Dutch national airport was cancelled.

5.2.2 VALUATION OF THE VITALITY OF DUTCH FORESTS
AND HEATH

Design
Van der Linden and Oosterhuis (1987) carried out an in-person survey in 1987 among a sample of 499 Dutch (heads of) households. The central question in this survey was what the Dutch population would be willing to pay (WTP) to prevent further deterioration of the Dutch forests and heath. More specifically, the choice was between a situation in which, by the year 2010, 80% of the forests would be "nonvital" and 90% of the heath would have turned into grass, on the one hand, and maintenance of the present situation, in which the damage is still rather limited, on the other.

The questionnaire was structured as follows: First, general questions were asked concerning knowledge and opinion about environmental problems in general, and acid rain in particular. Next, there were a series of questions which should make the respondent aware of the functions forests perform for society and for themselves. After this, the hypothetical change was described. The "damaged" situation was illustrated by four colour photographs. Respondents were then asked to evaluate the consequences of the proposed change qualitatively, in relationship to the functions of forest and heath they perceived. A separate question was intended to raise their consciousness of both user and non-user values. Following this, it was stated that additional measures would be necessary to prevent the defined deterioration. Respondents were told that everybody would have to pay, since enterprises would account for the extra costs in the prices of their products".

Hence, the payment vehicle used was "higher prices for all kinds of products".

Then they were asked how much they were willing to pay to prevent the "damaged" scenario becoming reality. To avoid a high nonresponserate, a short bidding game was used, but the final bid was asked as an open question. Finally, some general questions were asked about car ownership, pressure group membership, political preference and socio-demographic characteristics.

Results
The mean willingness to pay appeared to be DFL 22.83 a month. This amounts to about 1.5 billion DFL per year for all Dutch households. It is interesting to compare the aggregated WTP amount with the estimated loss of timber production. In the same study, the authors calculated this amount as 13.1 million DFL a year.

Implications

Although the study was funded by the Ministry of Housing, Physical Planning and Environmental Management, there have not been any governmental implications of this study. However, it should be noted that this study increased the interest in the CV method in tThe Netherlands.

5.2.3 VALUING A CLEAN ENVIRONMENT

Design

Hoevenagel and Verbruggen (1989) conducted a mail survey in 1989 among a sample of 799 Dutch (heads of) households. The central question in this study was what the Dutch population would be willing to pay to obtain a clean environment in the year 2015. More specifically, the choice was between a situation in which, by the year 2015, the environment would have further deteriorated (this situation was expected to occur if no additional environmental measures were taken), and a situation in which, by the year 2015, the environment would be "clean" (the result of a stringent environmental policy).

After asking four general questions, both situations were described. They were represented by a mixture of seven (inter)national environmental issues: the greenhouse-effect, depletion of the ozone-layer, deforestation, the acid rain problem, water quality in Dutch rivers, the pig manure problem, and air pollution in Dutch cities. All seven problems were described by their most important effects, using very simple wordings. Following these descriptions, it was stated that a stringent policy would be necessary to obtain a clean environment in 2015. Respondents were told that some of the measures would be executed abroad, since some of the problems are international. For the Dutch part, however, everybody would have to "chip in", as enterprises would account for the extra costs in their products. In order to elicit the respondents' WTP amounts, an open-ended question was used, preceded by a short bidding game.

Results

This study showed a non response rate of 68 %, which is high for a mail CV questionnaire. Moreover, almost 70 % of the respondents stated as their maximum WTP amount a "bidding game amount". The sample mean WTP amount appeared to be DFL 59 a month. Because the sample was not representative for the Dutch population (too many highly-educated persons), this figure was reweighted on the basis of education level. The weighted mean WTP amount appeared to be DFL 43 a month.

Implications
The results have been published on the front-page of several Dutch newspapers. It was seen as another proof of the fact that Dutch households were willing to pay for cleaning the environment.

5.2.4 A METHODOLOGICAL STUDY AIMED AT REDUCING VARIOUS POTENTIAL CV BIASES

Design
Hoevenagel (1993) aims at providing recommendations to minimize the various potential biases surrounding the CV method. Whereas many potential CV biases can be reduced by careful design, others contain serious problems with regard to the validity of the CV method. This study is oriented towards the latter, concentrating on part-whole and anchoring biases.

The study consists of several CV experiments. For example, the above-mentioned survey (Hoevenagel and Verbruggen, 1989) was part of an experiment that tested for the effects of three descriptions of the good, "a clean environment", on WTP amounts. Another experiment looked at starting-point bias in combination with sequence bias and part-whole bias.

Results and implications
The results of this study will be published in a Ph.D. thesis in 1993. Until then, the implications of this study can only be guessed at. Hopefully, it will give rise to a better understanding of the scope and limitations of the CV method.

5.3 Prospects of valuation research in the Netherlands

A recent assessment of the position of environmental economics in the Netherlands (Opschoor et al. 1991) concludes that there seems to be a large gap between the interest of Dutch economic researchers into the subject of valuation (which is relatively large) and the demand for valuation studies by the main research sponsors (which is small). Of all environmental economics research projects at Dutch universities in the period 1986–1990, only 7 % included some form of valuation. An assessment of future research showed that this percentage may fall to 2 % in the period 1991–1995 (Opschoor et al., 1991).

All four government departments which are directly involved in environmental policy (Environment, Agriculture, Economic Affairs, and Traffic & Public Works) show little interest in monetary valuation that goes beyond an assessment of financial damage. The principal reason is the lack of confidence in welfare-theoretical approaches which are based on the concept of willingness-to-pay.

However, despite this apparent lack of government interest in valuation studies and especially in studies which use "direct" approaches, environmental-economic researchers in the Netherlands have still managed to produce a number of contingent valuation studies, which have been discussed in the previous section. It is to be hoped that the Dutch experience in valuation research will not run to waste, especially since the international attention for this line of research seems to be increasing.

References

Anon. 1985: *IMP Milieubeheer 1986–1990* (Environmental Programme 1986–1990). In Dutch. Ministry of Housing, Physical Planning and Environmental Management, Leidschendam, 184 p.

Bouma, F. 1974: Enkele modellen voor de waardebepaling van rekreatiegebieden (Some models for the valuation of recreation areas). In Dutch. In: P. Nijkamp (ed.): *Milieu en economie* (Environment and Economy). Universitaire Pers Rotterdam, Rotterdam, pp. 153–173.

Hoevenagel, R. 1993: The Contingent Valuation Method: Its Scope and Validity. Ph. D. thesis, Free University, Amsterdam. In prep.

Hoevenagel, R. & H. Verbruggen 1989: De waarde van het milieu (The value of the environment). In Dutch. *Institute for Environmental Studies, R/89–09,* Amsterdam, 46 p.

Jansen, H.M.A. & J.B. Opschoor 1973: Waardering van de invloed van het vliegtuig-lawaai op woongebied rond de potentiele locaties van de tweede nationale luchthaven (Valuation of the effects of aircraft noise on residential areas around the potential locations of a second Dutch national airport). In Dutch. *Institute for Environmental Studies, Series A,* No. 4 and 5, Amsterdam, 95 p.

Jansen, H.M.A., van der Meer, G.J. Opschoor, J.B. & J.H.A. Stapel 1974: Een raming van schade door luchtverontreiniging in Nederland in 1970 (An assessment of damage due to air pollution in The Netherlands in 1970). In Dutch. *Institute for Environmental Studies, Series A,* No. 8, Amsterdam, 222 p.

Klaassen, L.H. & T.H. Botterweg 1974: Projectevaluatie en imponderabele effecten: een schaduwprojectbenadering (Project evaluation and imponderabilia: a shadow project approach). In: P. Nijkamp (ed.): *Milieu en economie* (Environment and Economy). Universitaire Pers Rotterdam, pp. 21–40.

Kuik, O.J., H.M.A. Jansen & J.B. Opschoor 1991: The Netherlands. In: J.-P. Barde & D.W. Pearce: *Valuing the environment: Six case studies.* Earthscan Publications Ltd, London, pp. 106–140.

Linden van der J.W. & F.H. Oosterhuis 1987: *De maatschappelijke waardering voor de vitaliteit van bos en heide.* (The social valuation of the vitality of forests and heath). In Dutch, English summary. Publication by the Ministry of Public Housing, Physical Planning and Environmental Management. VROM 80115/3, Leid-schendam, 46 p.

Opschoor, J.B. 1974: Schade door milieuverontreiniging – het geval van geluidshinder (Damage due to environmental pollution – the case of noise nuisance). In Dutch. In: P. Nijkamp (ed.): *Milieu en economie* (Environment and Economy). Universitaire Pers Rotterdam, Rotterdam, 241–259.

Opschoor, J.B. 1987: Monetary valuation of environmental changes: A review of Dutch case studies and proposals for methodological research. Conference on Environmental Policy in a Market Economy, 8–11 September 1987, Wageningen.

Opschoor, J.B., Folmer, H. Kapteijn, A. Lambooy, J.G. Nentjes, A. Siebrand, J.C. and L.G. Soete 1991: *Environmental Economics in The Netherlands.* A publication of the Netherlands Ministry of Education and Science, Zoetermeer, 54 p,

Chapter 6
Norway

STÅLE NAVRUD & JON STRAND

6.1 Introduction

The development and application of methods for the valuation of environmental goods in Norway has a brief history, as in virtually all other European countries. No studies were done before 1980. Up to the present, however, more than thirty studies have been carried out, and the research field is now very active. It is probably fair to say that Norway is among the countries at the forefront of this research, in a European context. This is due to at least two main factors. First, Norway has been able to maintain strong and stable (although very small) university research environments with competent and interested researchers working on various topics on environmental valuation throughout most of the last decade. Second, there has been considerable support for this type of research and investigation from both research foundations and government ministries and agencies, especially within the environmental sector. The interest in environmental valuation from the point of view of public authorities has clearly been greater in Norway than in most other European countries. However, few of the studies have had any influence on the environmental decision-making process. See also Navrud (1991c) for an analysis of the use of benefit estimation studies in Norway.

In section 2, we will review all the Norwegian valuation studies, according to the environmental commodity addressed. Section 3 will briefly summarize the experiences from the political use of the estimates, and the prospects of benefit estimation in Norway.

6.2 Review of Norwegian environmental valuation studies

Virtually all of the more than thirty Norwegian studies for valuing changes in environmental quality have employed either the Contingent Valuation Method (CVM) or the Travel Cost Method (TCM). Only two studies have used the Hedonic Price Method (HPM). Some other studies to be mentioned here have applied the so-called Multiple Criteria Analysis (MCA), or varieties of this type of method. Also, two studies of implicit values derived from political decisions are reported.

We will go through the studies by types of environmental commodity valued: Air quality, water quality and recreational fishing, noise, forest, recreation and hunting, and preservation of natural resources and biological diversity. Finally, studies with a more direct methodological aim will be reviewed. All the values stated have been converted to 1991 Norwegian kroner (NOK) using the consumer price index.

6.2.1 AIR QUALITY

Several studies have attempted to value changes in air quality, all using the CVM. The earliest is Hylland and Strand (1983), which addressed the issue of maximum willingness to pay (WTP) for particular reductions in air pollution, among a sample of about 1000 persons in the Grenland region of Norway, in the winter of 1982. This has long been (and still is) among the areas most severely affected by industrial air pollution. A CV iterative bidding mechanism was used, and the persons interviewed were asked to value particular air pollution improvements exemplified through pictures depiciting different smog levels in the area. The result indicated a WTP for a "significant" improvement in air quality, of about 1000 NOK per household per year, a rather sizeable figure. A problem with the study was that this figure turned out not to be very sensitive to the degree of pollution reduction indicated by the alternative pictures shown. This might indicate that the quality improvement "paid for" by the persons interviewed was based mainly on the persons' individual perception of what constitutes a "main" improvement, and not on a more objective measure of air quality. A national survey was also conducted, indicating that the Norwegian population as a whole was willing to pay about 0.6 % of their disposable income as a once-and-for-all tax to clean up the environment in the Grenland area. As may be the case with several other studies to be discussed below, this may be subject to so-called "mental account" or "part-whole" bias, whereby respondents tend to focus an overly large fraction of their total willingness to pay for environmental goods in general on the good that is currently being valued.

Strand (1985) conducted a national CV survey of about 2000 persons, attempting to measure WTP for a general 50 % reduction in air pollution in urban areas in Norway. This air quality improvement was claimed to be equivalent to the result of an imposition of a requirement that all Norwegian automobiles be equipped with three-way catalytic converters. Also, in this case, an iterative bidding procedure was utilized. The payment was tied to automobile-related costs and taxes. Annual average WTP was found to be about 1200–2500 NOK per car, or about 600–1200 NOK per person above 15 years of age. This survey was initiated by the State Pollution Control Agency (SPCA) to assess the benefit components in a cost-benefit analysis (cba) of introducing stricter car emission regulations, which the Ministry of Environment (MoE) had asked them to do. However, the cba was completed too late to influence the decision on introducing the measure. In addition, the environmental authorities themselves rejected the benefit estimate, as a result of the critique of the cba (i.e. annual total benefits exceeding annual total costs), the environmental authorities stated that their decisions were based on the best subjective judgement – and that this was the best decision criterion.

An important methodological problem in both studies mentioned above is making the persons interviewed perceive the exact nature of the air quality changes to be valued. The third CV study addressing specific air pollution problems in Norway (Navrud 1988a) suffers less from such a problem. Here the issue was valuation of improved air quality due to reduced emisions of particulates from a ferro-alloy plant in the community of Ålvik in Western Norway. The emision reduction had already taken place when the CV survey of a representative sample of 14 % (i.e. 52 units) of the households in the community was conducted. The nature of the improvement should thus be well known to respondents. A new problem in using the CVM here may then be to make people familiar with the idea of having to pay for an improvement that has already taken place, and where the initial problem perhaps was blamed by many on the polluting company. The result here was, in any case, an average annual WTP of about 1600 NOK per household.

Two other recent studies also try to value aspects of air quality changes. Strand and Taraldset (1991), where the objective is largely methodological, will be described at the end of this section. In Navrud, Pedersen and Strand (1992) the objective was to value social losses from corrosion due to air pollution of a particular historical building. Here, a CV survey of a representative sample of 163 Norwegians and foreigners visiting the old Nidaros cathedral in Trondheim is used to calculate the social losses to "users" (visitors) of the cathedral. To our knowledge, this is the first study valuing the loss of originality of historical monuments due to corrosion, and may thus have significant interest as a model for later studies of similar objects. The results indicate an annual mean WTP to preserve the remaining original parts of the cathedral (through reduced air pollution) of 318 NOK per person visiting the church. The corresponding mean annual WTP for a restored church, where all original parts were lost, was somewhat lower: 278 NOK per person. However, these amounts were not significantly different. Thus, on average, people, at least those visiting the monuments, do not seem to be willing to pay a higher amount to preserve the original rather than having the historical building restored. However, 65 % of the respondents said that the original meant more to them than the restored object, while the remaining 35 % said that they were indifferent. Those who said that the original was more important to them than the restored object had a significantly higher WTP for preserving the original than restoring the cathedral. This, at least, indicates a certain consistency in the responses. To test for amenity misspecification, and part-whole bias in particular, one subsample was asked about the WTP for preserving *all* historical buildings and monuments in Norway before they stated their WTP to preserve the Nidaros cathedral. However, the mean WTP for preserving the cathedral in this two-step procedure was not significantly different from the stated WTP of those respondents that were asked about their WTP for the Nidaros cathedral directly. The WTP for preserving all the Norwegian cultural heritage was also significantly higher than for the Nidaros cathedral alone. This indicates that part-whole bias in this case might be less of a problem than we suspected. Most of the average WTP of the visitors was due to preservation motives, and only 14 % was motivated by the visitors' own "use"/experience of the building. These large non-use values among the visitors indicate that there could also be considerable WTP for this historical building among non-visitors.

6.2.2 WATER QUALITY AND RECREATIONAL FISHING

The largest group of Norwegian environmental valuation studies are those attempting to assess the effects of changes in water quality, especially the effects on fish stocks. The first serious environmental valuation studies in Norway were also done in this area, by Strand (1981a,b). These were spurred by the problem of acid rain affecting Norwegian lakes and rivers, on which significant public attention was focused in Scandinavia in the late 1970s and early 1980s. Most of the early studies on water quality effects concentrate on the issue of reductions in freshwater fish stocks, and the resulting damage to recreational fishing. Some more recent studies, however, also value the effects of improved water quality on all water-related recreational activities, and the non-use value of all effects of improved water quality.

In Strand (1981a), four different national population samples, each of about 1000 persons, were interviewed in-person about their WTP to avoid total extinction of freshwater fish in Norway due to acid rain, over a period of about 10 years. Each sample was faced with one specific additional income tax rate to finance clean-up costs, claimed necessary to maintain fish stocks at present levels (respectively 0.3, 0.6, 1.2 and 1.8 %). The results indicate that the average WTP could be in the neighbourhood of 1700–2750 NOK per year for persons over 15 years of age, a rather sizeable figure. A major problem with the study was that the issue of total extinction of freshwater fish in the whole country was not realistic (although it could be realistic locally, in some parts of southern Norway); and that such extinction could be qualitatively much worse than just a more realistic marginal reduction of the stocks. The study could also be subject to "mental account" biases of the type indicated in connection with the Grenland study above.

Strand (1981b) investigated the recreational value of salmon fishing in Gaula, one of the best salmon rivers in Norway, in 1979 using the TCM. The TC models were constructed from fishing licence information on home addresses for about 1500 of the approximately 6000 recreational anglers visiting the river that year, and from information about the main intention of the trip to Gaula. The estimate of average recreational valuation per angler per day was approximately 335 NOK, for the best-fitting "demand functions". The main weakness of this study was that it was not based on surveys of anglers, and thus all the variables (e.g. frequency of visits, travel costs, income and quality of substitute rivers) had to be constructed from secondary sources.

These two initial studies were later followed up by a large number of studies. Including Strand (1981b), ten studies have used the TCM and/or CVM to estimate the recreational value (use value) of angling. See table 6.1 for a review of the studies. Six of these studies (Navrud 1988b, 1990, 1991a, 1991b, Ulleberg 1988 and Rolfsen 1991) used both the TCM and CVM. Only one of the ten studies estimates the recreational value of saltwater angling (Navrud 1991b); the others concern freshwater angling.

Table 6.1. Review of Norwegian studies on the recreational value of freshwater and saltwater angling

River	Species	Author	Method[1]	Recreational value per angling day[2] (1991-NOK)
Freshwater				
River Gaula	Salmon/ Sea trout	Strand (1981b)	ZTCM	ca. 335
		Rolfsen (1991)	ITCM CVM	440–607 321
		Singsaas (1991)	ITCM	217–339
River Vikedalselv (acidified)	Salmon/ Sea trout	Navrud (1988b)	ITCM CVM	139–190 131–187
River Audna (acidified)	Salmon/ Sea trout	Navrud (1990)	ITCM CVM	214–243 94–274
River Stordalselv	Salmon/ Sea trout	Ulleberg (1988)	ITCM	235–311
River Halling- dalselv	Brown trout	Navrud (1984)	ZTCM	ca. 170
River Tinnelv	Brown trout	Scancke (1984)	ZTCM	ca. 170
Lake Lauvann	Brown trout	Navrud (1991a)	ITCM CVM	119–151 76–103
Gjerstad- skog Lakes	Brown trout	Navrud (1991a)	ITCM CVM	85–95 44–65
* Saltwater				
Sea area near River Audna	Salmon/ Sea trout	Navrud (1991b)	ITCM CVM	27–56 40–65

Remarks: [1] ZTCM = Zonal Travel Cost Method, ITCM = Travel Cost Method based on individual observations, and CVM = Contingent Valuation Method.
[2] An angling day is defined as one angler fishing one day, independent of the number of hours per day.

The TC and CV models used in these studies are quite similar, except for Strand (1981b) and Scancke (1984). While the TC models in the other Norwegian studies are based on the anglers' own statements of the number of visits, travel costs, income, preferred substitute river, etc., these two studies construct the data needed from secondary sources (especially fishing licences) and strict assumptions about the anglers' behaviour. Although multipurpose visits might not be a large problem in the specialized activity of salmon fishing, it could be a serious bias in TC models of trout fishing. Neither of these two studies nor Singsaas (1991) has tried to correct for this potential bias. Strand (1981b), Scancke (1984) and Navrud (1984) base their calculations on zonal observations, while the others use individual observations. By aggregating several individual observations of different variables to zonal averages, the model "conceals" much of the actual variation in the data, and seems to fit the data better than it actually does. Thus, individual observations should be used. Concerning functional forms, all the Norwegian TC studies find a log-linear "demand curve" for recreational fishing to give the best fit. Although all the TC models might be subject to misspecification, all of them have at least tried to include independent variables other than travel costs that might explain the variation in visitation rates (e.g. travel costs and quality of substitute sites, anglers' income, previous angling experience and catch rate)

Although some of the variation in recreational value per angling day between the studies can be accounted for by the differences in the TC models applied, some trends can be identified. There seems to be a clear tendency that the recreational value of freshwater fishing is higher than saltwater fishing. Among the species considered in these studies, atlantic salmon and sea trout are appreciated more than brown trout. Of the salmon and sea trout rivers, those with the largest average size of salmon and the largest stocks of salmon have the highest recreational value per angling day. Correspondingly, the recreational value per angling day in the acidified rivers Vikedalselv and Audna (which have small stocks of relatively small salmon) is about one-half to two-thirds of the corresponding value in two of the top ten rivers in Norway with regard to the amount of salmon caught, the rivers Gaula and Stordalselv. Of these two rivers, River Gaula has the highest catch, which is also reflected in a higher recreational value per day. The three studies of the River Gaula use different TC-models, and one of them (Rolfsen 1991) covers only part of the river. Thus, it is difficult to draw any conclusion on how the recreational value of angling in this river has changed from Strand's first study.

The brown trout lakes surveyed are previously acidified lakes in Southern Norway. They have now been restored through liming and the reintroduction of brown trout. The recreational value per angling day of these is about one-half to two-thirds of that in the rivers Hallingdalselv and Tinnelv, which are two of the best brown trout rivers in eastern Norway. Another interesting result is that when both the TC and CV methods are used in the same study these two independent methods seem to yield results of about the same size. These tests of convergent validity (Mitchell & Carson 1989: 204–206) strengthen the reliability of these estimates. It is also interesting to note that the average size of the recreational value per angling day for freshwater fishing in Norway compares well with similar estimates in the United States (see Walsh et al. 1990, table 1).

Looking at non-use values of fish stocks, Strand (1981b) has been followed up by five other studies using CV surveys to estimate both use and non-use values of fish stocks. Table 6.2 (next page) gives an overview of all these studies.

Four of the studies presented in table 6.2 give the total WTP, i.e. both non-use and use values. It is important to be aware of this to avoid double-counting. In two cases the total WTP has been divided into use and non-use values (Strand 1981a; Navrud 1989). However, all the procedures used for such disaggregation of values are questionable, and there is no single acceptable way of doing this. In Navrud (1991a; 1991b) mostly non-users have been surveyed. Thus, these results represent non-use values.

Unlike the recreational value, it is difficult to see any distinct pattern in how the non-use estimates vary with location-specific factors. The WTP being estimated both per household and per individual also make the comparison difficult. One should here be aware that WTP amounts per individual can often be equal or close to WTP per household, because the individuals often think in terms of household budgets, and act as representatives of households when they are asked to state their individual WTP.

Navrud (1989) conducted a national CV survey of more than 2000 households to estimate the Norwegian population's WTP for increased brown trout and salmon/sea trout stocks in southern Norway due to a 30, 50 and 70 % reduction in European sulphur emissions. Dose-response functions linking reductions in European emissions with Norwegian depositions, water quality and effects on fish populations were used to construct maps and diagrams depicting the changes in the fish populations in Norway's four southernmost counties. These were accompanied by verbal information describing the expected environmental changes to the respondents. The respon-

Table 6.2 Review of Norwegian studies on the non-use values of freshwater fish stocks.

The change in fish stocks valued (national or local population surveyed)	Cause of change	Author	WTP per household (#) or individual (*) per year (1991-NOK)
Detailed description of the increased number of trout lakes and salmon rivers with restored stocks in Southern Norway (national)	Reduced acidification (due to 30–70 % reduction in European SO_2-emissions)	Navrud (1989)	405 # (255–355 is non-use value; the rest is use value)
Avoiding the extinction of the current salmon and sea trout stocks in River Audna (local)	Stop liming, i.e. the neutralization of acid depositions	Navrud (1991b)	120*
Avoiding the extinction of current trout stocks in the Gjerstadskog lakes (local)	Stop liming, i.e. the neutralization of acid depositions	Navrud (1991a)	48*
Avoiding an unspecified "reduction" of the current trout stocks in Oslomarka lakes (local)	Not start liming to neutralize acid depositions	Amundsen (1987)	375 # (both use and non-use values)
Avoiding "some" and "considerable" reductions in the salmon stock in River Numedalslågen (local)	Different operation schemes of the hydropower dams	Carlsen (1985)	43–88 # (only 24–25 % of the households were willing to pay 165–340 per household) (both use and non-use values)
Avoiding extinction of all freshwater fish stocks in Norway (national)	Acidification	Strand (1981a)	1700–2750* (1020–1650 is non-use value; the rest is use value)

dents were, in their valuation, not able to distinguish between the effects on the fish stocks of 30, 50 and 70 % reductions in SO_2 emissions, although the changes were described in detail. However, this may be due to the fact that the respondents were divided into sub-samples, and each respondent got information about and valued only one of these three changes. Thus, the commodity was not misspecified, and people might be able to perceive the differences if they were given information about all three changes. Carlsen (1985), however, is a study where serious commodity misspecification seems to be present. Although methodologically better than Carlsen (1985), commodity misspecification also seems to be a problem in Amundsen (1987).

Navrud (1989) found a mean, annual WTP of about 405 NOK per household for increased fish stocks as a result of 30–70 % reductions in European sulphur emissions. Although bidding games with different start bids were used, this estimate stems from the use of a payment card, which generally gave lower amounts than the bidding game procedures. Four different starting bids were used, and significant starting point bias was observed. The payment vehicle used in this study was a contribution to a national liming fund. Thus, the respondents were asked about their WTP to get the described increment in fish stocks as a result of liming. This was done to limit the number of protest answers, i.e. respondents stating zero WTP not because they have a zero value for the improvement but because they think the polluters (i.e. the other European countries) should pay. A comparison of the resulting annual total WTP estimate of about 630 million NOK to the annual costs of liming of lakes and rivers in southern Norway, indicates that extensive liming to restore local fish stocks is socially beneficial. Only 12–37 % of the total WTP was due to increased use value. Thus, non-use values constitute the major part of the total value of this environmental improvement. The same result was observed in another recent CV survey of improved water quality from reduced nutrient leaching to the North Sea (Magnussen & Navrud 1991; see also chapter 10). Both these studies observed a significantly higher WTP for those living in the affected area compared to those living outside this area.

The positive net benefits from large scale liming found by Navrud (1989) have been used by the Directorate of Nature Management (DNM) to argue in favour of increased funding for liming of acidified water bodies. To document the economic efficiency of liming, DNM has also initiated and funded cbas of local liming projects (Navrud 1990, 1991a, b). Benefit/cost ratios of liming and restocking of acidified water bodies vary from 1.19 and 1.69 in brown trout lakes

(Lake Lauvann and six lakes in the Gjerstad Forests, respectively) to 4.37 in the salmon and sea trout river Audna, using a 7% p.a. discount rate and a time horizon of 20 years. Thus, it seems to be more cost efficient to lime salmon and sea trout rivers rather than small brown trout lakes. However, there might be large variations within these categories of water bodies. The ultimate goal of DNM is to construct a function describing how the cost efficiency of liming varies with different factors. This information will then be used to maximize the net social benefits of limited governmental funds for liming, by liming the water bodies with potentially highest B/C ratios. Thus, DNM seems to have accepted benefit estimation and cba as important tools in freshwater fisheries management. The scepticism towards these techniques seems larger in the sections of DNM responsible for wildlife management, nature and landscape preservation and general recreation, but even in these areas there seems to be a movement towards increasing acceptance.

Among the studies addressing other aspects of water quality are Heiberg and Hem (1987, 1988), Aarskog (1988), Dalgaard (1989) and Navrud and Magnussen (1991: see also chapter 10 of this book). Heiberg and Hem (1987) attempted to value changes in water quality in the Kristiansand Fjord, using two different methods, namely the CVM (in both a local and national study), and a local Simplified Multiple Criteria Analysis (named SMART). The local CV study gave an estimate of about 450 NOK per household per year, and the national study about 680 NOK as a single payment. Aggregated over all individuals locally and nationally, this indicates that the national valuation was in the order of 10 times that of the local valuation, perhaps again indicating mental account biases in the national survey. This was also observed in the local study, where the respondents stated a mean WTP for water quality improvements in two fjords (the Kristiansand Fjord included) which was not significantly higher than the WTP for the Kristiansand Fjord alone. The SMART was carried out using an interactive procedure checking for consistency of preferences, among a set of individuals selected at random locally. This yielded a total local WTP 12–20 times higher than that of the CV study.

Heiberg and Hem (1988) and Aarskog (1988) valued improved water quality in the Inner Oslo Fjord, also using both the CVM, SMART and an ordinary MCA. In contrast with the study described above, the results from CVM and SMART are here in fact quite well in line with each other the. Both give a mean WTP per household per year (for 10 years) in the range of 700–900 NOK, with the CVM yielding the highest figure. The results from this study were used in a cba of measures to reduce water pollution in the Inner Oslo Fjord. The analysis was conducted by the SPCA, and was one of their so-called Locally Adapted Regulatory Impact Analyses (LARIAs). See section 6.3 for a more detailed description of these analyses.

The last fjord study is Dalgard (1989), which used the CVM to value improved water quality in the Drammen Fjord. The results from all three fjord studies are presented in table 6.3 below.

Table 6.3   Mean, annual willingness-to-pay (WTP) per local household for improved water quality in three Norwegian fjords, for users, non-users and on average for both groups. Contingent Valuation (CV) mail surveys. 1991-NOK.

Fjord	Author	Mean WTP per local household per year		
		Users	Non-users	Users and non-users (Weighted average)
Kristiansand	Heiberg & Hem (1987)			447
Inner Oslo	Aarskog (1988) / Heiberg & Hem (1988)	942	522	870
Drammen	Dalgard (1989)	883	433	585

All these studies are based on mail surveys. With a response rate of 40–50 %, one might question how representative the estimated values are for the total local population. However, the estimates were not very sensitive to corrections for the observed small deviations from the actual distribution on age, sex and income in the local populations. The number of respondents varied between 300 and 400. The descriptions of the water quality changes in the CV surveys were quite detailed in all the fjord studies. Colour-coded maps and verbal descriptions of the state of different pollutants before and after the improvement were provided. The physical changes (in oxygen concentrations in the deeper layers, eutrophication, heavy metal and chlorinated hydrocarbons concentrations, and surface pollution of oil and garbage) were "translated" into perceivable measures of water quality. The payment vehicle used was annual sewage treatment fees, which is a "conservative" and realistic payment vehicle. The WTP estimates in table 6.3 refer to a rather large improvement in water quality, from the prevailing situation to a situation with "nearly no pollution". Recreational value per user day before (or after) the change, which will probably vary between different water activities, cannot be calculated from the Kristiansand Fjord and Inner Oslo Fjord surveys, since we have no data on the current number of user days. Neither do we know the increase in the number of user days after the improvement. In the Drammen's Fjord study, however, the respondents were asked explicitly about both current and future number of user days. Using the middle number of the ranges of days that the respondents ticked off, the average number of additional user days was estimated at nine per respondent. This adds up to a total increase of 900 000 user days. Using the respondents' disaggregation of total aggregated WTP into one-third use value and two-thirds non-use value, the total *increase* in use value can be estimated at approximately 6.7 million 1991-NOK. Thus, the recreational value per day *increased* use in the Drammen Fjord will be approximately 7.50 1991-NOK.

In contradiction to these studies of single fjords, Magnussen and Navrud (1991) estimate the WTP for increased water quality in *all* rivers, fjords and coastal areas in the south and southeastern part of Norway (termed the North Sea Plan area). They carried out two CV surveys with in-person interviews, one national survey of 1228 individuals and a local survey in one county of 200 individuals. The samples were divided into different subsamples to test for different biases encountered in CV studies, particularly "part-whole bias"/"mental account bias". (See chapter 10 for a thorough discussion of these methodological tests.) The respondents were asked about their total WTP for the improved water quality in local rivers, fjords and coastal areas (and in the North Sea) due to a 50 % reduction in the Norwegian emissions of nitrogen and phosphorus to the North Sea. The WTP was, as in the fjord studies, measured as the increase in the annual sewage treatment fees. The improvement in water quality was described in great detail by classifying rivers, fjords and coastal areas in four different quality classes. The described changes were closely linked to a physical dose-response model developed by the Norwegian Institute for Water Research. The changes were presented to the respondents as colour-coded maps, colour photos, and verbal descriptions of visible effects and suitability for different uses. Both continuous and discrete choice valuation techniques were used. In the national survey the mean annual, average WTP per household for the described water quality improvement varied between 600 and 5000 1991-NOK in five different subsamples. The most probable estimate of the WTP seems to be in the range of 1000–2000 NOK. The corresponding social cost of this North Sea Plan is in the lower end of this range. The benefit estimate includes both use and non-use value. Only 20 % of the WTP was due to use value. Again the non-use value constitutes the major part of the WTP. The respondents' income, education and whether they lived within the North Sea Plan area or not were the only socioeconomic variables found to have a significant effect on the WTP. Those living in the affected area were willing to pay a significantly higher amount than those living outside, and most (or all) of the respondents' average WTP was motivated by the improved water quality in their *local* rivers, fjords or coastal areas.

We will finally mention one early study on the valuation of oil spill combat in the Norwegian section of the North Sea carried out by Fredrikson et al. (1982), using MCA. Here a number of decision makers and professionals in different fields were asked to state their preferences for different consequences of oil spills, and then a simplified preference map was derived for each person through an interactive computer program. It was thereby possible to derive an overall expert valuation of the different environmental consequences of oil spills, and a consistent decision procedure, given that decisions on clean-up measures would have to be taken by these individuals. A different question is, however, to what degree such preferences represent those of the population at large. On this account we remain somewhat more sceptical, in this study and some other similar studies using MCA.

6.2.3 NOISE

Only two Norwegian studies attempting to value noise reductions have been conducted to date. Incidentally, these are the only two Norwegian studies that apply the HPM. Hoffman (1984) applied data on residential property values to estimate the change in value of this property from increased airport noise in the Bodø area in northern Norway. The results indicate that the market value of housing units decreased by about 1 % per dB increase in the average noise level in areas surrounding the Bodø airport. Larsen (1985) studied the relationship between residential property prices and noise from road traffic in the Oslo area. He found an average reduction in the market value of single-family homes of 0.8 % with an increase of

1000 vehicles per day on the nearest road. While both studies indicate a relationship between residential housing prices and noise nuisance, they are not directly comparable. A particular problem with the latter study is that a higher traffic load can also be associated with a greater risk of accidents and not only with greater noise.

The general hesitation to use the HPM for environmental valuation purposes in Norway is largely due to problems of obtaining relevant data on residential housing prices and the quality of the property, and to the fact that the Norwegian housing market has long been regulated and its prices do not fully reflect the differences in such qualities, and to the general criticism directed against the method from some well-known researchers, notably Mäler (1977). Such criticisms apply as well to the two studies that have been conducted in Norway, and it is unclear what these studies really say about social valuation of reductions in noise levels; no explicit estimates of such valuation have been derived in the studies. Nevertheless, attempts to apply the method in future work should be welcomed. One reason why the situation now seems more ripe for the application of such methods is that the present Norwegian housing market on the whole is functioning more competitively than when the referred studies were done.

6.2.4 FOREST RECREATION AND HUNTING

There are only two studies of the recreational value of forests in Norway. Navrud et al. (1990) used a carefully constructed CV survey to estimate the recreational value of a monutainous forest area that had been subject to three different management practices: clearcutting, selection forestry and no cutting (i.e. preserving the virgin forest.) Representative samples of three groups that visited the forest area Hirkjølen (Eastern Norway) in the summer were interviewed in-person. They included hikers, passing-through car tourists and cottage tourists. The effects of the different forest management practices were carefully described verbally and by a series of colour photos. The hikers and tourists were asked about their maximum willingness-to-pay (WTP) for having selection forestry or no cutting instead of clearcutting in this area. The money was supposed to be used to compensate the forest owners for their losses when they had to give up clear cutting. To make the payment vehicle as realistic as possible, the car tourists and cottage tourists were asked to imagine paying a road toll when entering the area, while the hikers were asked to imagine paying to park their cars at the entrance sites or paying an extra fee for public transportation to the area. There are two main factors that make us believe that the estimated values were minimum estimates of the change in recreational value. First, people's WTP seemed to be restricted by what they were used to paying in road tolls, parking fees etc. and thus did not fully reflect their welfare improvements of the improved "forest quality". Thus, the results seemed to be contingent upon the chosen payment vehicles. Second, only some groups of the summer recreationists and no winter recreationists were surveyed.

Hikers had the highest WTP per visit to the area. Their median WTP per visit (mean values given in parentheses) was 49 (79) NOK for selection forestry, and 65 (104) NOK for preservation of virgin forests, as compared to clearcutting. The corresponding figures for the car tourists were 32 (38) and 43 (50), and 27 (68) and 27 (60) for the cottage tourists. The mean values are severely influenced by the extreme responses of a few respondents.

Hoen and Winther (1991) estimated *both* use (recreation) and non-use values of "multiple use forestry "(i.e. a more cautious forest management) and the preservation of virgin coniferous forests in Norway. This study is described in more detail in the next section.

Sødal (1989) is the only Norwegian study on the recreational value of hunting. He studied moose hunting by hunters in the counties of Østfold and Hedmark. 1467 (73 %) of the 2000 hunters surveyed returned the questionaire in a CV mail survey. Forty-six per cent of the respondents were moose hunters. Both continuous (using a payment card) and discrete CV versions were used. The hunters stated their WTP as the maximum acceptable increase in annual expenses for moose hunting. This is the same kind of CV question that was used in all the previously mentioned CV studies of the recreational value of angling (table 6.1). The mean gross WTP was 3700 NOK per hunter per year. Subtracting the mean costs of hunting of 2300 NOK, the net consumers' surplus is approximately 1400 NOK per hunter per year. The mean gross WTP corresponds well with the results of similar Swedish studies on moose hunting (see chapter 7).

6.2.5 PRESERVATION OF NATURAL RESOURCES AND BIOLOGICAL DIVERSITY

A central topic in the public debate on nature protection in Norway has been that of river preservation. While a significant number of Norwegian rivers have already been developed for hydropower purposes, many exploitable rivers are still left for development or preservation. A general evaluation of these has been made in connection with the so-called Master Plan for water resources (MP). Here, the rivers are ranked on the basis of their financial costs (i.e. construction and operating costs), and on an assessment of the effects of development on different user interests and the local economies. The rivers are then classified in three different categories: one with rivers ready for development, one with rivers to be developed later, and one with rivers to be preserved and not utilized for hydropower development. An extensive research effort has been made, by various types of professionals, to assess potential impacts of developing the different rivers. The impacts on each user group were evaluated on a scale from 4 (very positive impacts) to – 4 (very negative impacts). Taking these "environmental costs" into account, the final ranking of the rivers, which was enacted by the Storting (Norwegian Parliament) in 1986, differs from a ranking that would minimize construction and operating costs per unit of expected energy production. For a further discussion of the MP process, see Navrud (1991c) and Carlsen, Strand and Wenstøp (1991, 1992).

Hervik, Risnes and Strand (1987) and Carlsen, Strand and Wenstøp (1991, 1992) estimate the implicit WTP of the policy makers (representing the citizens in a democratic society) for river preservation embedded in the MP, whereby quite a few projects with low construction costs were in effect protected from development.

Hervik, Risnes and Strand (1987) found that the implicit costs of not choosing this most cost-effective ranking was in the range of 160–760 NOK per household per year. This is the policy makers' implicit WTP for river preservation measures embedded in the MP. To check if Norwegian households were willing to pay this amount as increased annual electricity bills, which is a "conservative" and realistic payment vehicle, a national CV survey with in-person interviews of 2200 individuals was carried out. A bidding game approach was used. Significant starting point bias was observed. The mean, annual WTP per household was estimated to be in the range of 850–1550 NOK, which is well in excess of the implicit costs of the river preservation measures in the MP. A local CV survey of 400 individuals was also conducted to estimate the WTP for preserving one specific river (River Rauma-Ulvåa in Western Norway) from hydropower development. In this local survey, the respondents' information about the effects of hydropower development was much better and less abstract than in the national survey. The mean WTP per household per year was 570–1540 NOK, which is close to the observed WTP in the national survey. As in Magnussen and Navrud (1991), it seems that most of the WTP for a national environmental improvement is motivated by local environmental improvements.

The data from this study of river preservation do not enable us to divide the total WTP into WTP to avoid different impacts of hydroelectric development. Carlsen, Strand and Wenstøp (1992), however, use the ranking procedure in the MP to derive implicit costs associated with each of the different user interests. Using a model that explained 88 % of the variation in ranking procedure, the WTP per energy unit (kWh) of expected electricity production to avoid one unit (on the scale from -4 to 4) worse impacts on nature conservation, outdoor recreation, wildlife, fish, water supply, cultural heritage conservation, agriculture, reindeer husbandry and local economy interests, was estimated at 0.015, 0.027, 0.005, 0.016, 0.017, 0.028, 0.017, 0.015 and 0.109 1982 NOK (multiply numbers by 1.65 to convert to 1991 NOK), respectively. This means, for example, that the politicans are willing to accept an increased electricity price of 0,027 1982 NOK per kWh to increase the index for nature conservation interests by one unit (i.e. from -1 to 0).

The methods employed in these studies are unorthodox, but interesting. We know of no direct precedent for the latter study. Most likely, it cannot easily be repeated in the same form since it relies on a large and very detailed data set, and policy makers who are well informed and aware of the economy/environment tradeoffs involved. This appeared to be the case here, but cannot automatically be assumed to hold for other studies.

Hoen and Winther (1991) conducted a CV survey to estimate the Norwegian population's WTP for multiple use – forestry and preservation of the virgin coniferous forests in Norway. The implicit alternative was continuation of the prevailing rather intensive forest management practice with, e.g. large clear cuttings. The respondents were asked about their annual WTP in the form of environmental taxes on timber and timber-based products. The tax income should compensate forest owners for their income losses due to the restrictions on their forestry operations. A representative national sample of 1204 persons above 15 were interviewed in-person. The CV survey was carefully designed, but commodity Misspecification bias seems to be present, i.e. people had difficulties in perceiving the changes in the environmental good to be valued. The mean annual WTP per household for multiple-use forestry and the preservation of virgin forests was 140–385 and 220–300 NOK, respectively. The corresponding median values were 50–100 and 100–120. The results show that the experimental design in different subsamples has a significant effect on the WTP for multiple use forestry, but not for the preservation of virgin forests. The authors argue that this might be due to the more vague description of the multiple-use forestry option, which also is a relatively new concept to most people. Hoen and Winther (op.cit. table 3) show that people state "preservation of endangered plants and animals" as the most important reason for paying, followed by the related reason "preservation of virgin forests for our descendants". Thus, much of their WTP seems to be motivated by preserving biological diversity in forests.

Another study valuing biological diversity more explicitly is Dahle et al. (1987). They tried to value the existence of the threatened predators, brown bear, wolverine and wolf using a national CV survey. About 2000 persons were interviewed in-person. Since there is an ongoing conflict between farmers and conversationists on the preservation of these species, the respondents were asked for their WTP both for preservation and extinction of these species. Only 5 % had a positive WTP for the elimination of the three species. The mean annual WTP per household for preservation and extinction was 240 and 30 NOK, respectively. This means a net annual WTP for preservation of 210 NOK per household. This shows the importance of asking for both the positive and negative WTP for preservation of goods where there are differing opinions. The positive net WTP for preservation also clarifies the public debate on these issues, where farmer's voices traditionally have been very strong, in favour of controlling and possibly eliminating these animals.

In this survey, the respondents were also asked about their attitude towards how the stocks of these predators shoulde develop, their knowledge of the number of sheep killed by the predators, and how they would change their behaviour if brown bear, wolf and wolverine were present in nearby forest areas. People seem to answer in a consistent way. Those that show a negative attitude towards these species tend to overstate the number of sheep killed by these predators, and also have a negative WTP. The opposite was true for the "conservationists". The survey also confirmed that most people overstated the damage done by these predators to domestic animals. This is probably due to the large media coverage of domestic animal killings. Different subsamples were also given different amounts of information about these three species, but this had no significant effect on their attitude and WTP for the species. Thus, it seems that people have a relatively predetermined opinion about this subject. Neither did the WTP differ significantly between the subsamples where no payment vehicle was stated and those where the respondents were told that they should pay into a preservation/extermination fund. However, the WTP was significantly lower in the subsamples where people were informed about the annual amount paid to the farmers as compensation for their losses due to brown bear, wolf and wolverine (and eagle) attacks: 7 NOK per household. This is an example of how provided information on costs in CV surveys can "anchor" the WTP amounts for environmental improvements.

This survey got large media coverage, and many people, especially farmers' associations, seemed to be sceptical about the validity of the derived WTP amounts. However, many environmentalists and ecologists, although also somewhat sceptical about the valuation methods, used the results from the survey in support of species preservation. DNM, which financed the survey, used its results in arguing for the preservation of bear, wolverine and wolf in their outline of a National Plan (NP) for the management of these species (DNM 1987). Even though DNM, like the environmentalists and ecologists, seems to put most weight on the results from the attitudinal questions, they also use the WTP amounts to support their request for larger governmental funds for monitoring and for researching these species, compensation for damages, to domestic animals and measures for preventing such damages.

6.2.5 METHODOLOGICALLY ORIENTED STUDIES.

Over the last couple of years four studies have been conducted which can be classified as mainly methodological, since their main objective is to attempt to test potential biases of the CVM. Most of the above-mentioned CV surveys also include methodological tests, but their main aim is to come up with monetary estimates that could be used by the environmental authorities, who have sponsored most of them. Two of the four methodological studies have attempted to compare hypothetical and actual willingness to pay for environmental goods through the indicated and actual support of particular environmental organizations. Seip and Strand (1991) conducted a CVM to test the WTP to support the Norwegian Association for the Protection of Nature (NNV). While 62 of the 101 persons interviewed in-person expressed an initial WTP of at least the membership fee of 200 NOK, only 6 (i.e. 10 %) actually joined the organization when subjected to repeated membership drives. This may indicate that the CVM seriously overestimates environmental valuations in some contexts. However, commodity misspecification and uncertainty of provision might explain some of this discrepancy between hypothetical and actual WTP. This poses questions such as: What environmental improvement do people really get by becoming a member of NNV, and what is the probability of getting it? Do people mix up their WTP for collective environmental improvements with WTP for the private good of being a member? Navrud (see chapter 11) tested actual payments to support the World Wide Fund for Nature (WWF) in Norway among a self-selected sample of individuals who voluntarily had expressed interest in the organization by responding to newspaper ads. These results are more encouraging for the validity of WTP estimates from CV studies than Seip and Strand (1991).

Strand and Taraldset (1991) conducted a CV survey with in-person interviews of 104 persons in Oslo. The main objective of the study was to measure the degree of potential "mental account" or "part-whole" bias. One set of individuals is here faced with the issue of valuing particular reductions in air pollution in Norway, first, when this environmental improvement is considered in isolation, and subsequently, when also five other environmental improvements are to be valued. Introducing new environmental goods reduces the average WTP for improved air quality alone to about half of its initial value. In addition, implicit valuations of each of the six environmental improvements are imputed from expressed valuations of all six measures and the individuals' rankings of the measures by importance. Here, the imputed value of the air pollution reductions is less than one third of the initially stated value. This indicates a rather serious mental account bias in the initial answer. This is supported by the results in a second subsample, where people initially were faced with all six environmental improvements and subsequently with the air pollution problem alone. However, this study could be subject to serious amenity misspecification bias, since the descriptions of the environmental improvements are very short.

The fourth study focusing on methodological aspects is Løyland, Navrud and Strand (1991). Ninety persons were interviewed in-person in a CV survey attempting to decompose the value of ecologically cultivated food products in Norway, into private and public aspects of consumption and production. The private aspects include positive individual health effects, better taste and higher suitability for storage, while the public aspects include general health improvement for the whole nation, better environment for domesticated animals, a higher degree of self-sufficiency of food products, reduced pollution from the farms and more diverse agricultural landscape. The two latter public aspects are also environmental aspects, dealing with water quality and aesthetic quality of landscapes. This decomposition procedure was performed in two ways. First, by asking individuals about their WTP (as increased prices) for voluntarily purchasing ecologically produced goods (including only the private aspects), and then the additional WTP for all the public aspects of ecological agricultural production. Second, people were asked to split their total WTP for both private and public aspects, into shares according to their motives for paying. Thirty and seventy per cent of the total WTP appear to be motivated by environmental and other public aspects in the first and second decomposition procedure, respectively. (In the second procedure, the 70 % was distributed with 40 % on environmental aspects and 30 % on other public aspects). Thus, different decomposition procedures give different results. One possible reason for the lower percentage in the first procedure might be mental account/part-whole bias, because the respondents here were asked for their WTP with regard, to private aspects without being informed about the public aspects of ecological agricultural production. The mean, annual total WTP per household for ecologically produced fruit and vegetables, meat products and cereal products was about 300 NOK, in excess of current prices.

None of these four studies can be considered conclusive. They are based on small samples, and have tested only a few selected biases of the method. However, they throw some light on methodological problems of applying CVM, both in Norway, and in more general terms.

6.3 Previous use and prospects of benefit estimates in Norway

So far the benefit estimation studies seem to have been useful for providing support for decisions involving the environmental goods they valued, but they have not played a crucial role in the decision-making process. The main reason for this seems to be the general scepticism towards the methods. This scepticism is partially due to lack of evidence of the validity of valuation methods, and to lack of objective information about the methods' possibilities and limitations among people in public administration, politicians, environmental organizations and the general public. It is particularly unfortunate for the use of benefit estimates that very few people within the ministries and public agencies are trained in environmental and resources economics. Thus, even when the Ministry of Environment (MoE), the State Pollution Control Authority (SPCA) or the Directorate of Nature Management (DNM) initiate and finance benefit estimation studies (which they have often done), they find it difficult to argue in favour of the use of the estimates when faced with critical comments about the methods. This critique from other ministries and public agencies, environmental organisations or the general public is often based on a distorted perception of the valuation methods and their potential biases. Thus, the few benefit estimation practitioners in Norway would benefit from engaging in the implementation of their studies, and in educating the employees of the ministries and agencies in cost-benefit analysis and valuation techniques. So far, this is done only occasionally.

Another obstacle to the use of cba and valuation techniques is the lack of a formal legal basis for doing cbas of projects with environmental impacts and the existing manuals on cbas of public projects. There is a recent general regulation in the Planning and Building Act (and several older regulations in other Acts and their provisions) requiring environmental impact assessments of large projects, but it does not require economic assessment of the impacts. In addition, the existing manuals on cbas of public projects barely mention that there are methods for valuing environmental impact, and recommend not valuing these impacts (Navrud 1991c).

The most sucessful use of the results from benefit estimation in Norway seems to have taken place in connection with the Locally Adapted Regulatory Impact Analysis (LARIA). LARIA is a cost-benefit analysis of potential measures to reduce emissions of pollutants to a specific local recipient. Measures within all sectors of the society are considered. The analysis was developed in 1986 by a project group within the SPCA, which also has carried out the four existing applications on water pollution in the Oslo Fjord and Lake Mjøsa, and noise and air pollution in Oslo and the Sarpsborg/ Fredrikstad area. There was also an advisory group of economists attached to the project group. Benefits of the different measures treated in the LAIRAs were valued according to a set of weights based mainly on previous Norwegian and foreign benefit estimation studies. However, experts' and decision makers' opinions were also used to construct the weights. Stating the benefits as weights, the SPCA deliberately tried to conceal the monetization of benefits from the decision makers, to avoid the analysis being rejected due to the general scepticism towards "placing a value on nature". However, since one of the benefit components with a weight attached to it was "Saved investment and operational costs", the monetary value of the other weights could easily be calculated. Although it is unclear whether the decision makers were aware of the monetization of benefits or not, they seemed to accept the ranking of measures by benefit-cost ratios. Another main weakness of these analyses is that the benefit estimates used to arrive at the set of weights were based on uncritical transfer and use of more or less arbitrarily chosen benefit estimation studies. The dose-response functions used to calculate the physical effects of the different measures are also of varying quality. In spite of these and other methodological weaknesses, the LARIA is a promising approach to more regular and consistent use of environmental benefit estimates. It has led to increased interest in benefit estimation in the environmental sector, and there now seems to be an increasing interest in this field within the transport, energy, agricultural and forestry sectors. The SPCA are now improving the LARIA based on their experiences with the previous ones and the comments from both scientists and economists evaluating their approach. They are also extending the use of LARIA from local to regional and national pollution problems. However, there is a tendency of moving from cost-benefit towards cost-effectiveness analysis. Nevertheless, many of the measures to reduce the emissions of one pollutant by a certain percentage (according to international agreements or national goals) also affect the levels of other pollutants or have other environmental effects. Thus, these effects have to be valued to calculate the cost-effectiveness of the different measures.

The most recent cost-effectiveness analysis conducted by the SPCA, looking at a 50 % reduction in nutrient leaching to the North Sea, was also complemented by a benefit estimation study financed by the Ministry of Environment (see chapter 10). Like many of the previous benefit estimations studies (e.g. Strand 1985, Hervik et al. 1987 and Navrud 1989), this study was done *after* the government had decided to carry out this emission reduction, and thus was only used to support a decision already made.

An important reason for the success of LARIA, is that it is a method developed by the environmental authorities themselves, and thus they find it easier to handle the critics of the results. Another important reason seems to be the involvement of sectoral authorities, decision makers and interest groups at the local level in an early phase of the analysis.

In an attempt to reduce the scepticism about valuation methods, especially the CVM, the empirical valuation studies have become more sophisticated and perform tests for more biases than previously. In particular, the sceptisism about the validity of the non-use values is large. As a reaction to this scepticism, we have started to do experiments on the relationship between hypothetical and actual WTP. Both the research foundations and the Ministry of Environment are now funding projects where the main aim is to increase the validity and applicability of Contingent Valuation estimates; the overall goal being to develop practical tools for evaluation of environmental effects.

To conclude; there is an increasing interest in benefit estimation in Norway, among academics, bureaucrats and decision makers. Most research is now concentrating on the Contingent Valuation Method, and there is a trend in Norwegian benefit estimation of moving from empirical to more methodological research. This can be viewed as a response to the general scepticism about valuing environmental goods, which has limited the actual use of benefit estimates in the decision making process. However, the environmental authorities now want to develop practical and reliable tools for consistent evaluation of environmental impacts in appraisals of projects and regulations in all sectors of society. Partly in response to this, other sector authorities (especially the energy, transport and agricultural sectors) have recently started to look into the possibilities of valuing environmental goods.

References

Aarskog, E.M. 1988: Betalingsvillighet for ytterligere rensing av Indre Oslofjord (Willingness to pay for cleaning up the Inner Oslo Fjord). In Norwegian. M.Sc. thesis, Department of Economics, University of Oslo Centre for Industrial Research, Report no. 871013-2, March 1988, 42 pp.

Amundsen, B.-T. 1987: Rekreasjonsmessig og samfunnsøkonomisk verdsetting av fiskebestanden i Oslomarka (Recreational and non-use value of the fish population in Oslomarka). In Norwegian. M.Sc. thesis, Agricultural University of Norway, 89 pp.

Carlsen, A.J. 1985: Economic valuation of hydroelectric power production and salmon fishing. In Carlsen, A.J. (ed.) 1987): *Proceedings. UNESCO Symposium on Decision Making in Water Resources Planning,* May 5-7 1986, Oslo; 173-82.

Carlsen, A.J., Strand, J & F. Wenstøp 1991: Kvantifisering av miljøulemper ved ulike energiteknologier. Delprosjekt 7: Miljøkostnader og samfunnsøkonomi. Chapter 7: Betalingsvillighet for negative konsekvenser av vassdragsutbygging i tilknytning til Samla Plan for vassdrag. (Willingness-to-pay to avoid negative consequences of hydroelectric development in the "Master Plan for Water Resources".) In Norwegian. Report from the Norwegian Water Resources and Energy Administration (NVE).

Carlsen, A.J., Strand, J. & F. Wenstøp 1992: Implicit environmental costs in hydroelectric development: An analysis of the Norwegian Master Plan for Water Resources. Memo, Department of Economics, University of Oslo. In prep.

Dahle, L., Sødal, D.P & B. Solberg 1987: *Haldningar til og betalingsvillighet for* bjørn, jerv og ulv i Noreg. (Attitudes towards and willingness to pay for preservation of Brown Bear, Wolverine and Wolf in Norway.) Report no. 5/1987, Department of Forest Economics, Agricultural University of Norway, 114 pp.

Dalgard, M. 1989: Drammensvassdraget - en undersøkelse av betalingsvillighet. (Willingness to pay for regulatory actions towards water pollution in the Drammen Fjord). In Norwegian. M.Sc. thesis, Department of Economics, University of Oslo. Centre for Industrial Research, Report no. 881108-2, August 1989, 95 pp.

DNM 1987: Landsplan for forvaltning av bjørn, jerv og ulv. (National plan for management of brown bear, wolverine and wolf). In Norwegian. Report no. 6 - 1987. Directorate for Nature Management (DNM). 37 pp.

Fredrikson, G.W., Ibrekk, H., Johannessen, K.I., Kveseth, K., H.M. Seip, & F. Wenstøp 1982: Oil spill combat: damage assessment using multiattribute utility analysis. Centre for Industrial Research, Report no. 820225-1, 66 pp.

Heiberg, A. & K.-G. Hem 1987: Use of formal methods in evaluating countermeasures to coastal water pollution. In H.M. Seip & A. Heiberg (eds.) 1989: *Risk management of chemicals in the environment,* Plenum Press, London.

Heiberg, A. & K.-G. Hem 1988: Tiltaksanalyse for Indre Oslofjord. En sammenligning av tre forskjellige analysemetoder. Regulatory Impact Analysis of the Inner Oslo Fjord. A comparison of three different methods. In Norwegian. *Centre for Industrial Research, Report no. 880105-1,* September 1988, 67 pp.

Hervik, A., M.Risnes, J.Strand 1987: Implicit costs and willingness-to-pay for development of water resources. In Carlsen, A.J. (ed.) 1987): *Proceedings. UNESCO Symposium on Decision Making in Water Resources Planning,* May 5–7 1986, Oslo: 195–202. (Also published in Norwegian in the journal *"Sosialøkonomen"* no. 3 1985; 3–6 and no. 1 1986; 2–7, and in several special reports).

Hoen, H.F. & G. Winther 1991: Attitudes to and willingness to pay for multiple-use forestry and preservation of coniferous forests in Norway. Report from the Department of Forestry, Agricultural University of Norway.

Hoffman, J.V. 1984: *Flystøy og boligpriser – 1984. Undersøkelse av flystøybelastningens innvirkningen på boligpriser i Bodø.* (Air traffic noise and the value of housing properties.) In Norwegian. Institute of Transport Economics, Working paper, 42 pp.

Hylland A. & J. Strand 1983: *Verdsetting av reduserte luftforurensninger i Grenlandsområdet.* (Valuing reduced air pollution in the Grenland area.) In Norwegian. Department of Economics, University of Oslo, Memo. no, 12–83, 135 pp.

Larsen, O.I. 1985: Veitrafikk og eiendomspriser. (Road traffic and the value of housing properties). In Norwegian, English summary. Institute of Transport Economics, Project report, July 1985, 26 pp.

Løyland, K., Navrud, S. & J. Strand 1991: *Betalingsvillighet for økologiske matvarer i Norge: En betinget verdsettingsstudie.* (Willingness to pay for ecologically produced food in Norway: A Contingent Valuation survey). In Norwegian, Center for Research in Economics and Business Administration, Working paper, 22 pp.

Magnussen, K. & S. Navrud 1992: Verdsetting av redusert forurensning til Nordsjøen (Valuing reduced pollution of the North Sea.) In Norwegian. English Summary. Report B-015-92. Norwegian Agricultural Economics Research Institute.

Mäler, K.-G. 1977: A note on the use of property values in estimating marginal willingness to pay for environmental quality. *Journal of Environmental Economics and Management 4;* 355–369.

Navrud, S. 1984: Økonomisk verdsetting av fritidsfisket i Hallingdalselva i Gol kommune. (Economic evaluation of recreational fishing in the River Hallingdalselv. In Norwegian, English summary. M.Sc. thesis. Agricultural University of Norway. Published in the Norwegian Water Resources and Energy Administration (NVE)'s report series, *"Biotopjusteringsprosjektet – Terskelprosjektet",* Information no. 26 (1987), 121 pp.

Navrud, S. 1988a: *Fordelingsvirkninger i miljøverntiltak i ferrolegeringsindustrien. Case: Bjølvefossen a/s.* (Distributional effects of environmental regulations in the ferro-alloy industries. Case: Bjølvefossen a/s). In Norwegian, English summary. Ministry of Environment, Report T-712, 71 pp.

Navrud, S. 1988b: *Rekreasjonsverdien av lakse- og sjoeaurefisket i Vikedalselva i 1987 – før regelmessig kalking.* (Recreational value of atlantic salmon and sea trout angling in River Vikedalselv- before regular liming). In Norwegian, English summary. Report from the Directorate of Nature Management, 108 pp. Also published in Navrud, S. (1989): *Valuation of environmental goods – methodological and empirical studies of the effects of acid depositions on freshwater fish stocks.* Doctor Scientarium theses 1989:17. Department of Forest Economics, Agricultural University of Norway, Scientific report no. 3/1989.

Navrud, S. 1989: Estimating social benefits of environmental improvements from reduced acid depositions: A Contingent Valuation survey. In H. Folmer & E. van der Ierland (eds.): *Valuation Methods and policy making in environmental economics. Studies in Environmental Science 36;* 69–192, Elsevier Science Publishers, Amsterdam.

Navrud, S. 1990: *Nytte-kostnadsanalyse av vassdragskalking. En studie i Audna.* (Cost benefit analysis of river liming. A case study of River Audna). In Norwegian. Directorate for Nature Management, Report 1990–6.

Navrud, S. 1991a: *Samfunnsøkonomisk lønnsomhet av å kalke utvalgte aurevann i Agderfylkene.* (Social profitability of liming selected trout lakes in the Agder counties.) In Norwegian. Report from the Directorate for Nature Management, 51 pp.

Navrud, S. 1991b: *Samfunnsøkonomisk lønnsomhet av å kalke Audna.* (Social profitability of liming River Audna. An extended analysis). In Norwegian. Report from the Directorate for Nature Management, 35 pp.

Navrud, S. 1991c: The use of benefit estimates in environmental decision-making in Norway. Report to the Environment Directorate, OECD. In J.-P. Barde & D.W. Pearce (eds.) 1991: *Valuing the environment. Six case studies.* Chapter 5: Norway (p. 141–202), Earthscan Publications Ltd., London.

Navrud S., P-E. Pedersen, & J. Strand 1992: Valuing our cultural heritage. A Contingent Valuation survey. Center for Research in Economics and Business Administration (SNF) – Oslo. In Prep.

Navrud, S., Simensen, K. B. Solberg & M.H.A. Wind 1990: Valuing environmental effects of different management practices in mountainous forests in Norway – a survey of recreationsists' preferences and willingness-to-pay. Department of Forestry, Agricultural University of Norway. Paper presented at the XIX World Congress of the International Union of Forestry Research (IUFRO) in Montréal, Canada, August 5–11, 1990.

Rolfsen, J. 1990: Rekreasjonsverdien av lakse- og sjøaurefiske på TOFA's soner i Gaula sesongen 1990. (Recreational value of atlantic salmon and sea trout angling in parts of River Gaula in 1990). In Norwegian. M.Sc. thesis, Agricultural University of Norway.

Scancke, E. 1984: Fisket i Tinnelva. (Recreational fishing in River Tinnelv). In Norwegian. M.Sc. thesis. Department of Economics, University of Oslo.

Seip, K. & J. Strand 1990: Willingness to pay for environmental goods in Norway: A contingent valuation study with real payments. Paper presented at the EAERE conference in Venice, April 17–20 1990. Forthcoming in Environmental and Resource Economics.

Singsaas, T. 1991: Beregning av samfunnsøkonomisk verdi av fritidsfisket etter laks og sjøaure i Gaula-vassdraget i Sør-Trøndelag fylke sesongen 1990. (Estimating the economic value of recreational fishing for atlantic salmon and sea trout in the River Gaula in 1990.) In Norwegian. M.Sc. thesis, Department of Economics, University of Oslo, 70 pp.

Sødal, D.P. 1989: Økonomisk verdsetting av elgjakt. (Economic valuation of moose hunting). In Norwegian, English summary. Doctor scientarum theses 1989:15. Department of Forest Economics, Agricultural University of Norway, Report no. 1/1989, 233 pp.

Strand, J. 1981a: Verdsetting av ferskvannsfisk som kollektivt gode i Norge. Resultater fra en intervjuundersøkelse. (Valuation of freshwater fish populations as a public good in Norway. Results from a survey.) In Norwegian, English summary. Department of Economics, University of Oslo, Working paper, 111 pp.

Strand, J. 1981b: Beregning av samfunnsøkonomisk verdi av fisket i Gaula-vassdraget. (Valuing benefits from recreational fishing in the River Gaula). In Norwegian. Department of Economics, University of Oslo. Memo. November 18, 1981. English short version: "Valuing benefits of recreational fishing in Norway: the Gaula case", in Carlsen, A.J. (ed.) 1987: *Proceedings UNESCO Symposium on Decision Making in Water Resources Planning*, May 5–7, 1986, Oslo; 245–278.

Strand, J. 1985: *Verdsetting av reduserte luftforurensninger fra biler i Norge.* (Valuing reduced air pollution from automobiles in Norway). In Norwegian. Department of Economics, University of Oslo, Memo. no. 1–1985, 89 pp. English short version: "The value of a catalytic converter requirement for Norwegian automobiles: A Contingent Valuation study", Department of Economics, University of Oslo, mimeo, 32 pp.

Strand, J. & A. Taraldset 1991: *The valuation of environmental goods in Norway. A contingent valuation study with multiple bias testing.* Department of Economics, University of Oslo. Memo. no. 2, 1991.

Ulleberg, M. 1988: Rekreasjonsverdien av fisket etter laks (Salmo salar) og sjøaure (Salmo trutta) i Stordalselva i 1987. (The recreational value of fishing for atlantic salmon and sea trout in the River Stordalselv in 1987). In Norwegian. M.Sc. thesis, Agricultural University of Norway.

Walsh, R.G., Johnson, D.M. & J.R. McKean 1990: Non-market values from two decades of research on recreation demand. *Advances in Applied Microeconomics,* Volume 5; 167–193. JAI Press Inc.

Chapter 7
Sweden

PER-OLOV JOHANSSON & BENGT KRISTÖM

7.1 Introduction

Valuation of environmental commodities has both a long and a short history in Sweden. In the 1960s people migrated in large numbers from areas with high environmental quality but also with high unemployment to "overheated" regions with worse environmental quality. In an evaluation of the social benefits and costs of geographic mobility, Dahlberg (1974) asked migrants about their willingness to pay (in terms of annual income reductions) for the opportunity to move back. This was the first Swedish attempt to put a price tag on environmental quality. Bohm (1972) conducted a series of experiments in which public goods were valued. These experiments, like the theoretical inquiries by Mäler (1974), had a large impact on later Swedish attempts to value environmental commodities.

To the best of our knowledge, no valuation studies of environmental commodities were then undertaken until 1985. Since then, 14 studies have been completed. There are also a number of studies under way, but these are not included owing to a shortage of information about the results.

The chapter is structured in the following way: In Section 2, we present a number of studies aiming at the valuation of alternative uses of natural resources. Section 3 summarizes valuation studies of changes in air and water quality. We then turn to a couple of methodological issues raised in some of these studies. In particular, we discuss the use of continuous versus discrete responses in contingent valuation studies, the introduction of uncertainty, willingness to pay (WTP) versus willingness to accept (WTA) compensation, and the overall willingness to pay for an improved environmental quality. The chapter ends with a few concluding remarks.

7.2 Land use conflicts

In Sweden, quite a few studies aiming at the valuation of alternative
and conflicting land uses have been undertaken. Using table 7.1,
these studies can be grouped into four categories: Hunting, virgin
forests, endangered species living in forests, and preservation of the
open landscape. The reason that hunting causes a land use conflict
is that the stock of moose is so large that it causes a lot of damage
to standing timber; hunters prefer a large stock while forest owners
argue for a reduction of the stock.

*Table 7.1 Review of Swedish valuation studies of natural resources.
Mean, annual willingness to pay (WTP) per person.
1991-SEK (Swedish Kroner)*

Publication	Year of study	Commodity	Method[a]	WTP[b]	Payment vehicle[c]	Sample/ resp. rate
1 Mattsson & Kriström (1987)	1986	Moose	CVM	4600	HP	80/0.75
2 Mattsson (1990)	1987	Moose Other game	CVM	4880 3130	HP	2500/0.68
3 Johansson (1990)	1987	Moose	CVM	3560	HP	200/0.67
4 Bojö (1985)	1985	Nature reserve	CVM/ TCM	730/ 760	IT	282/1.0
5 Kriström (1990)	1987	Fragile forests	CVM	95	LS	1100/0.67
6 Johansson (1989)	1987	Endang. species	CVM	85	LS	200/0.61
7 Drake (1991)	1986	Landscape	CVM	750	IT	1089/[d]

Notes: a. Studies no. 4 & 7 are based on interviews. All other studies are based on
   mail surveys.
   b. Annual figures. For studies no. 5 & 6 once-and-for-all payments have been
   converted to annual figures usisng a discount rate of 5 %.
   c. HP = Hunting permit, IT = income tax, LS = lump sum tax.
   d. Not reported.

There are three different hunting studies, all based on the contingent valuation technique. Mattsson has undertaken two surveys in which Swedish hunters are asked about their willingness to pay (WTP) for a hunting permit. In the first study, undertaken in 1986, approximately 80 hunters living in the county of Västerbotten in northern Sweden were asked about their willingness to pay for the opportunity to hunt moose. This sample as well as those referred to below were randomly drawn from a specific register covering all hunters in the contry. The basic valuation question – reported in Table 7.1 – referred to the current year's hunting, but the hunter was also questioned concerning his willingness to pay if the current number of moose was doubled and halved. About 2500 Swedish hunters received a similar questionnaire in 1987, the main difference being that these hunters were asked to value not only moose but also other game species. For the county of Västerbotten, which is represented in both studies, the average WTP for a moose hunting permit turns out to be almost the same in both studies ?? approximately 4600 SEK. This indicates that there is a stability in the answers across (consecutive) years. For the country as a whole, a moose hunting permit is valued slightly higher, up to almost 4900 SEK.

In both these studies, hunters are asked about their willingness to pay for a hunting permit conditional on the outcome of the year's hunting being almost identical to the outcome of the previous year's hunting. Johansson (1990), on the other hand, asked a sample of hunters about their willingness to pay for a hunting permit for the *forthcoming* season. This approach comes closer to the working of a market, since a market forces the consumer to accept or reject an offer conditional on his expectations of the properties of the considered commodity. Economic theory suggests that the resulting ex ante willingness to pay should be lower than the one generated by the "ex post" WTP questions asked by Mattsson (at least for risk-averse hunters). This is also confirmed by the results reported in Table 7.1. The reader interested in a detailed comparison of the two approaches is referred to Johansson (1990).

There are other land use conflicts in which Swedish forestry is involved. In March 1983, it was suggestet that a Nature Reserve, protected from forest harvesting, be created in the Vaalaa Valley in Northern Sweden. In mountainous areas such as the Vaalaa Valley, cutting may cause more or less irreversible damage to the environment. For this reason, the Swedish Environment Protection Agency initiated a social cost-benefit analysis of the two scenarios, i.e. preservation vs. forestry; see Bojö (1985). To estimate the benefits of preserving the area, 282 visitors were interviewed about, among other things, their willingness to contribute to preservation (compensation of economic losses to forest owners), and their travel costs. As is seen from the table, the contingent valuation method and the travel cost method (TCM) both produce an average willingness to pay per visitor of 730–760 SEK (including travel costs of 460 SEK). No attempt was made to estimate a pure existence value by interviewing non-visitors.

Kriström (1990) investigated methods for assessing the value people place on preserving fragile and virgin forests. A random sample of Swedes were shown a map depicting 11 such areas, and were informed that the areas are important for recreation (for present and future generations) as well as for many endangered species. According to an open-ended valuation question, the annual mean WTP for preserving the considered forests is about 100 SEK. We will return to some methodological aspects of this study in a later section.

Johansson (1989) asked a small sample of Swedes (200 people out of which 122 replied) about their willingness to pay for measures taken to save endangered species. The respondents were told that about 300 endangered species – animals, birds and flowers – are living in Swedish forests. If no measures are taken, e.g. a ban on forestry in some areas and the introduction of soft cutting technologies in other areas, all the considered species may become extinct. Therefore, the respondent was asked to make contributions towards programmes that would save some or all of the species. Four different programmes that would save some or all of the species were suggested. First of all, the respondent was asked about his willingness to pay for a programme which would save 50 per cent of the species. The respondent was then asked to contribute to programmes that would save 75 per cent and 100 per cent of the species, respectively. Finally, the respondents was asked to pay (his option price) for a programme designed in such a way that the probability is 0.5 that the programme saves all species and 0.5 that it saves 50 per cent of the species. It turns out that the reported results are in accordance with the predictions of economic theory. For example, the willingness to pay is an increasing function of the number of species preserved. In table 7.1 only the average willingness to pay for the programme saving all 300 endangered species is reported, but in a later section we will come back to this study.

The Swedish landscape is dominated by forests, and agricultural land is continuously converted into forests. With or without intention, farmers produce or maintain a specific landscape which can be considered as a positive external effect of agriculture. There has been much debate in Sweden about the magnitude of this externality. In

1986, more than 1000 Swedes were asked how much they are willing to pay each year in income tax to prevent half of all agricultural land from being cultivated with spruce. The average WTP, as presented in Drake (1991), turned out to be 670 SEK, but more than 80 per cent of the respondents were willing to increase their bids by 20 per cent if the initial bids were insufficient to preserve the agricultural landscape. This raises the average WTP to about 750 SEK.

7.3 Air and water quality

While the air and water quality has improved in several ways in Sweden during the past decades, there are still significant detrimental environmental effects of various activities on air and water quality in Sweden. For example, some parts of the country are badly damaged by acid rain (e.g. the west-coast around Gothenburg) and eutrophication is considered to be one of the main contributors to the water quality problems along the coast-line of the Baltic Sea. Indoor air quality, mainly via the cancer risk that long-term exposure to radon poses, has also been intensively debated during the past years in Sweden. Finally, there has been a debate regarding whether or not gasoline stations should be required to install gasoline vapour recovery systems to reduce gasoline vapour.

These issues have also been the focus of a few studies that have been undertaken to shed some light on Swedes' willingness to pay to improve air and water quality. Table 7.2 gives an overview of these studies.

Johansson and Kriström (1988) made an experiment with the "yes-or-no" (or discrete) valuation question, focusing on the value Swedes may place on improvements in air quality via reduced sulphur emissions. They used a conventional willingness-to-pay question as well as a "willingness-to-offer-jobs" question. The latter question was motivated by the fact that employment/unemployment is of central importance in many countries, and the fact that stringent measures to reduce sulphur emissions in Sweden would mean a (short-run) loss of jobs in Swedish industry. They find a surprisingly high willingness to pay for sulphur reductions; about 6000 SEK/person per year and a willingness to offer (a short run loss) of 150,000 jobs to secure the suggested improvement in air-quality. The latter figure can be converted into money by using figures on value added. The comparison suggests that people are less inclined to sacrifice jobs than income; the jobs-lost question suggests a slightly higher sum – about 4 to 5 per cent of disposable household income. These rather high estimates may be due to a misspecification of the bid-vector. Loosely speaking, "too many" people accepted to pay the suggested cost. We return to this design issue below.

Table 7.2. Review of Swedish valuation studies of air and water quality. Mean, annual willingness to pay (WTP) per person. 1991-SEK (Swedish Kroner)

Publication	Year of study	Commodity	Method[a]	WTP	Payment vehicle[b]	Sample/ resp. rate
1 Katz & Sterner (1987)	1988	Gasoline vapour	CVM	170	GP	800/0.71
2 Johansson & Kriström (1988)	1987	Sulphur	CVM	6000	LS	1700/0.67
3 Aakerman (1988)		Radon	CMS	4300	CP	300
4 Söderqvist (1991)		Radon	HPM	4000-6000	MP	2100
5 Silvander (1991)	1989	Nitrogen loss (angling)	CVM	350	IT	1000/0.65
6 Silvander (1991)	1989	Nitrogen loss (groundw.)	CVM	370	IT	1000/0.69

Notes: a. All studies use mail surveys, except the "hedonic price" approaches used in studies no. 3 and 4. CMS = Constructed market surveys.
b. GP = Maximum increase in gasoline price, IT = income tax, LS = lump-sum tax, CP = constructed price, MP = market price.

Katz and Sterner (1990) investigated consumers' willingness to pay for reduction in gasoline vapours at filling stations. The study was commissioned by the Health and Environmental Department of Gothenburg City Council, the aim being to explore the benefits and costs of reducing vapour from gasoline at filling stations. The sample consisted of 800 people, where 200 were polled at a local gasoline company who already had installed vapour recovery systems, while

600 people were randomly drawn form a register of people in Gothenburg. Katz and Sterner (op. cit) asked the respondents to state how much more they would maximally be willing to pay for gasoline at filling stations already equipped with vapour recovery systems. The average willingness to pay (weighted by gasoline consumption) was found to be about 0.15 SEK per liter of gasoline, while the median was found to be 0.05 SEK per liter of gasoline. These numbers correspond to 170 SEK and 60 SEK per year and car owner, respectively. A regression analysis suggested that, for example, sex, age and annual driving distance have a significant effect on willingness to pay.

Radon radiation is a severe health problem in Sweden. Radon is a radioactive gas which is formed when radium decays, and can cause lung cancer. The problems are due both to the use of alum shale, which has a high content of uranium, as a building material, and soil gas than can enter the home from beneath the foundation. The last decades' energy conservation has increased the radon problem, because the ventilation in homes has been greatly reduced.

Aakerman (1988) collected data on radon concentration, mitigation measures undertaken, if any, the cost of various mitigation measures, household income, age and composition of family, etc. for a part of suburban Stockholm. Using a logit model, she was able to estimate the probability that a household will mitigate, as a function of the mitigation cost, household income, age of house, and so on. In turn, and as is explained in, for example, Johansson (1987), this information can be used to calculate the average willingness to pay for a particular risk reduction. The average radon reduction was 416 bequerels per cubic metre, and the expected annual willingness to pay for a reduction in the subjective risk of getting lung cancer) is 4300 SEK per household. As shown by Aakerman (1988), the probability that a household will mitigate increases with radon concentration and household income, and decreases with the mitigation cost and the age of household head.

Söderqvist (1991) uses information about characteristics and market prices of single-family houses sold in the county of Stockholm during the period 1981–1987 to examine the radon problem. In applying the property value or hedonic price technique, Söderqvist faces the problem that it is only known whether a house is contaminated (>400 Bq/m^3) or not. Still, he is able to arrive at a rough estimate of the average WTP for a non-contaminated house over and above the WTP for a contaminated house. The annual difference turns out to be 4000–6000 SEK. Thus, although Söderqvist and Aakerman use different methods and data sets, their results are surprisingly and encouragingly similar. A study of the radon problem in Stockholm based on the contingent valuation method is under way, and it will be interesting to see what results that method will generate.

Silvander (1991) completed two contingent valuation studies to address the potential benefits of reducing excess nitrogen loss from agriculture. One study concerned the value of improving fishing conditions for anglers, while the other study addressed the value of improving ground water quality by reducing nitrogen loss.

Silvander (1991) sampled 1000 Swedes between 16–74 years of age in the «angling» study. The participants in the survey were presented with different scenarios regarding the effect of eutrophication on the fish population in all Swedish salt and brackish water. One scenario described a possible loss of a specified set of species, while another scenario deseribed situation where all species would become extinct. Using the less servere scenario as a lower bound, we find an average WTP for reducing nitrogen loss of about 350 SEK. (The estimates range from 350 to about 850 SEK depending on the severity of the environmental impact and the payment vehicle).

In his second study of the welfare impacts of nitrogen loss, Silvander (op.cit.) looks into the detrimental effect of excess nitrogen concentrations (above the World Heath Organization limit of 50 ml nitrate/l) in ground water. Again, a representative national sample of 1000 persons was used. In order to test, among other things, the presence of information bias, Silvander (op. cit.) varied the scenario information. Using the "full-information" scenario for those who know that their water contains excess nitrate concentration, he finds an annual, average WTP of 370 SEK per person. His other estimates range from about 260 to 630 SEK depending on the information given and whether or not the respondents knew his water contained excess nitrate.

7.4 Some methodological problems

The difference between willingness to pay and willingness to accept compensation (WTA) for environmental changes is, according to some researchers, a continuing embarrassment for the contingent valuation method. While Hanemann (1991) provides an interesting explanation for the possible disparity between these measures from the viewpoint of economic theory, we may not have reached a consensus yet regarding why many studies show a large difference between willingness to pay and willingness to accept. Mattsson and Kriström (1987) report both WTP and WTA measures in their moose-hunting study, finding that WTA is about 2 to 4 times larger than WTP. Silvander (1991) finds mixed evidence of a large disparity in his studies. The WTA corresponding to the WTP of 350 SEK reported in table 2, is about 15 times higher. In the groundwater study WTA, is, in one case, about 19 times larger than WTP. On the other hand, WTA is about equal to WTP in one scenario in the angling study.

The past decade has seen a shift from the use of the conventional continuous or open ended valuation question to the discrete or closed ended valuation question. These questions differ in how much leeway the respondent is given when he is responding to the scenario presented. In the former case, he is able to state his exact willingness to pay, while he is "only" able to reject or accept a suggested amount in the latter case, an amount that is varied across the sample. The amount of information received by the researcher is therefore very different in these two set-ups and requires very different estimation techniques and study design. In general, the discrete response technique is much more demanding in these two respects, since it requires several assumptions not neeeded in the continuous response case.

There are two reasons why the binary response (at least in the US) is currently the most popular technique, despite the relative drawbacks associated with it. The first is that it resembles more closely our ordinary market decision to reject or accept a given price for a good. The second is that this technique is less vulnerable to strategic responses, since the respondent cannot state a "very large" or a "very small" sum.

The binary response technique needs two sets of assumptions. The first is how to distribute the bids, i.e. the number of different bids, the size of each bid, the number of respondents (ex ante) to each bid and so on. A bad design of the bid-vector can easily lead to badly biased results, as can be seen by imagining a case where everyone accepts the bids used in the survey. In this case we cannot fit a probability distribution, because the sample information suggests that the probability of accepting any bid is equal to one. Several studies may suffer from a bad (unfortunate) design of the bid-vector. Examples include Bishop and Heberlein (1979) and Johansson and Kriström (1988).

When the design rule has been accepted and the survey results collected, it remains to estimate a descriptive statistic on willingness to pay from a set of yes/no-answers to the used bids. Several suggestions have been made in the literature for tackling this problem. However, the estimated mean WTP may be very sensitive to the chosen distributional assumption, which is a substantial drawback of the binary response technique.

This brief discussion suggests that it is probably too early to say which of the two approaches will dominate in the future. Let us now investigate, using the data reported in Kriström (1990), whether or not these two valuation techniques may give different results in a practical application. There is some evidence that the binary response technique tends to give a highes mean willingness to pay than the continuans response technique. It is difficult to explain, disregarding estimation problems, why people may interpret these two types of valuation questions differently. However, psychologists have suggested that people tend to use any type of information as an anchor when providing a valuation under uncertainty.

In the study of preserving "virgin" forests (Kriström 1990) presented in table 7.1, two types of valuation questions were asked; a continuous and a discrete. The sample was split into two subsamples, A and B, consisting of 900 and 200 persons, respectively. Sample A received both types of questions, sample B only the continuous question. The questionnaires were identical in other respects. The response rates were almost exactly the same for both samples. A test of the anchoring hypothesis, i.e. whether the mean WTP differs between sample A and sample B, was rejected. It is useful to have a graphical display of the two distribution functions under scrutiny. Thus, in figure 7.1 we plot the proportion of yes-answers at each given bid, invoking a smoothing procedure to ensure that the probability of obtaining a yes-answer is not increasing in the bid (see Kriström 1990 for details).

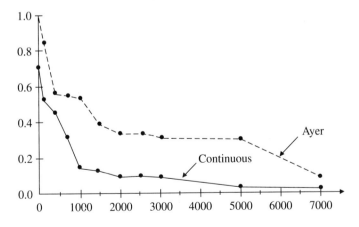

Figure 7.1 Empirical survival functions for the discrete ("Ayer") and the continuous valuation question.
Source: Kriström (1990).

It is interesting to note that the distribution for the binary response data appears to be shifted outwards by a constant. Consequently, both the mean and the median will be higher when calculated from binary data. More generally, one might test the hypothesis that the data are generated by the same distribution. This is, unfortunately, complicated here because the data are grouped. A simple chi-square test suggested, however, that the distributions generating the data are different, i.e. people may think of and respond to these two types of valuation questions differently.

Many public sector programmes involve various elements of *uncertainty*. In particular, the outcome of a proposed change in, say, environmental quality is impossible to predict with certainty. Still, most valuation studies pretend to present respondents with project presentations that suppress any uncertainty or use money measures designed for the certainty case. In a recent study, Johansson (1989) explicitly introduced uncertainty about a programme aiming at the preservation of endangered species living in Swedish forests. In fact, and as mentioned in Section 2, each respondent was asked of his willingness to pay for four different programmes, out of which three had certain outcomes. The basic idea of the study was to check if respondents are able to calculate what is known as the *option price*. In the present context, this is an amount of money such that the expected utility with a programme saving all 300 species with a probability of one half, and every second species with a probability of one half, is the same as the expected utility without the programme (leading to the possible extinction of all 300 species). Economic theory was used to generate a set of hypotheses that were tested on the data. Most of these hypotheses were confirmed, the exception being that male respondents did not show risk aversion. Rather, it seems as if male Swedes have risk aversion when many species are threatened, while they are more inclined to accept risks when only a few species are at stake.

The study confirms that one can meaningfully ask people about their valuation of public sector programmes whose outcome cannot be known in advance with certainty; one cannot reject the hypothesis that the average respondent reported his option price. Since uncertainty is an inevitable aspect of many environmental projects, further attempts to explicity introduce risk into the valuation context seem to be an important challenge for European environmental economists.

Let us finally turn to the sometimes misunderstood fact that one cannot sum the willingness to pay for different environmental "commodities" to obtain the overall valuation of an improved environmental quality. Such an approach would violate the budget constraint. (The basic problem can be illustrated by means of a simple example. Suppose a person in one study is asked of his willingness to pay for a Jaguar, in a second study of his WTP for a Merzedes Benz, and in a third study of his WTP for a Volvo. Apparently, one cannot sum these three unconditional amounts of money and interpret the result as the person's total WTP for cars.) Instead one may ask directly about the total willingness to pay for a specified set of measures taken to reduce environmental damage. This approach was used by Johansson and Zavisic (1989), who report an annual average willingness to pay of 1600 SEK per household. This amount of money is interpreted as being "reserved" for measures such as new or improved pollution treatment plants and purchases of land to preserve species, fragile forests, and the open landscape, etc. Thus, the sum does not include the value of "pure" recreation activities such as hunting or "private" risks such as radon radiation in houses.

The sample (500 randomly chosen grown-up Swedes out of which 250 returned the questionnaire) was also asked to allocate a 100 million SEK increase of government revenues on health care, child care, education, labour market policy, the environment, and other measures. It turns out that the average respondent spends 30 per cent each on health care and the environment. There are, however, considerable regional differences. Those living in depressed but "clean" parts of the country spend more on labour market policy measures and less on the environment than those living in large cities with more severe environmental problems. This result and other similar results presented in Johansson and Zavisic (1989) lend some support to the hypothesis that people can meaningfully state their willingness to pay for various public sector programmes.

7.5 Concluding remarks

Since the 1960s, cost-benefit analysis has now and then been used in the decision-making process in Sweden. For example, several proposed plant closures in depressed parts of the country have been evaluated, the (political) argument being that it would be socially unprofitable to throw people into long-term unemployment. Similarly, electricity generating systems based on domestic renewable resources have been evaluated. The general impression, however, is that these social cost-benefit evaluations have played a minor role in the actual outcome of the decision-making process. Even if a cost-benefit analysis shows that a project is highly profitable to the entire society, the project is not necessarily (or even generally) undertaken, and vice versa.

Very few of the studies summed up in this chapter have had a noticeable impact on decision making. The remarkable exception is the social cost-benefit analysis of the Vaalaa Valley. According to the study, the benefits of preserving the valley unspoiled far exceed the costs (i.e. loss of timber). After the study had been completed in 1985, the Swedish government decided to protect the valley. Therefore, a Nature Reserve was created in the area, implying that the valley will be protected from forest harvesting.

The study by Katz and Sterner (1990) on gasoline vapour may have had an impact on the rate of introduction of vapour recovery systems. The study was initiated by the Health and Environmental Department of Gothenburg City Council, and has been used in the local political debate. At least in part due to the results of the study, one of the largest Swedish gasoline companies is now installing vapour recovery at its gasoline stations across the country. Other gasoline companies are expected to follow suit.

The remaining studies presented in this chapter have not had any direct influence on decision making. In a few cases, there may be an indirect influence. For example, pressure groups may use figures from a study in their attempts to influence policy. It is, however, not possible to even guess what role the environmental studies per se have played in the outcome of decision making in these cases. At the same time, it should be stressed that many of the Swedish valuation studies have been undertaken in order to test methodological issues. We have the impression that this methodological emphasis has been more pronounced in Sweden than in most other European countries. This may, in part, explain the modest influence of Swedish valuation studies on decision making.

References

Aakerman, J. 1988: *Economic valuation of risk reduction: The case of in-door radiation. Stockholm* School of Economics, Stockholm, Sweden, 65 p.

Bishop, R. & Heberlein, T. 1979: Measuring values of extra market goods. Are indirect methods biased? *American Journal of Agricultural Economics 61,* 926–930.

Bohm, P. 1972: Estimating demand for public goods: An experiment. *European Economic Review 3,* 111–130.

Bojö, J. 1985: *Kostnadsnyttoanalys av fjällnära skogar. Fallet Vaalaadalen.* (A cost-benefit analysis of mountainous forests. The case of the Vålå Valley). In Swedish. Stockholm School of Economics, Stockholm, Sweden, 75 p.

Dahlberg, Å. 1974: *Geografisk rörlighet – sociala och ekonomiska effekter.* (Geograp-hic mobility – Social and economic effects). In Swedish. Research report, Dept of Economics, University of Umeå, Umeå, Sweden, 500 p.

Drake, L. 1991: The non-market value of the Swedish agricultural landscape. European Review of Agricultural Economics (forthcoming).

Hanemann, W.M. 1991: Willingness to pay and willingness to accept: How much can they differ? *American Economic Review 81,* 635–647.

Johansson, P-O. 1987: *The economic theory and measurement of environmental benefits.* Cambridge University Press, Cambridge, UK, 223 p.

Johansson, P-O. 1989: Valuing public goods in a risky world: An experiment. In H. Fol-mer, H. & Lerland, E. (eds.): *Valuation methods and policy making in environ-mental economics.* Elsevier Science Publishers, Amsterdam, The Netherlands, 37–48.

Johansson, P-O. 1990: Willingness to pay measures and expectations: An experiment. *Applied Economics 22,* 313–329.

Johansson, P-O. & Kriström, B. 1988: Measuring values for improved air quality from discrete response data: Two experiments. *Journal of Agricultural Economics 39,* 439–445.

Johansson, P-O. & Zavisic, S. 1989: Svenska folkets miljöbudget (The environmental budget of the Swedish people). In Swedish. *Ekonomisk Debatt 17,* 472–474.

Katz, K. & Sterner, T. 1990: The value of clean air: Consumers' willingness to pay for a reduction in gasoline vapours at filling stations. *Energy Studies Review 2,* 1, 39–47.

Kriström, B. 1990: Valuing environmental benefits using the contingent valuation method. *Umeå Economic Studies, 219,* Umeå, Sweden, 168 p.

Mäler, K.-G. 1974: *Environmental economics: A theoretical inquiry.* Johns Hopkins University Press, Baltimore, US, 363 p.

Mattsson, L. 1990: Hunting in Sweden: Extent, economic values and structural pro-blems. *Scandinavian Journal of Forest Research 5,* 565–573.

Mattsson, L. & Kriström, B. 1987: The economic value of moose as a hunting object. *Scandinavian Forest Economics 29,* 27–37.

Silvander, U. 1991: *Betalingsvillighetsstudier för sportfiske och grundvatten i Sverige. (The willingness to pay for fishing and groundwater in Sweden). In Swedish. Dissertation 2, Swedish University of Agricultural Sciences, Dept. of Economics, Uppsala, Sweden, 77 p.*

Söderqvist, T. 1991: *Measuring the value of reduced health risks: The hedonic price technique applied to the case of radiation.* Stockholm School of Economics, Stockholm, Sweden, 85 p.

Chapter 8
United Kingdom

R. KERRY TURNER, IAN BATEMAN & DAVID W. PEARCE

8.1 Introduction

After a decade of neglect, the monetary valuation of environmental benefits and costs is enjoying a revival in the United Kingdom. Much of the cause of the neglect of the subject in the 1970s and early 1980s can be traced to a single major investment – the proposal to build London's third airport (Commission on the Third London Airport, 1970, 1971). The investigating Commission openly embraced cost-benefit analysis as the main guiding principle for selecting the site of the airport. All the sites were controversial. Three inland sites affected open countryside and residential locations. The one coastal site was not opposed by the relevant local governments but did affect the feeding grounds of migratory birds. The Commission chose an inland site on the basis of cost-benefit analysis, with one member signing a minority report which severely criticised cost-benefit technique. The government of the day rejected the majority finding and chose the coastal site. Work commenced on that site only to be halted when it was realised that forecasts of air passenger traffic were not going to be fulfilled. Once demand picked up again, the government chose an inland site for London's third airport. Ironically, the site chosen, Stansted, was not one of the short-listed sites investigated by the Commission, but it had been the priority site prior to the Commission's investigation.

The saga of London's third airport investigation is long and involved (Dasgupta & Pearce 1972). But the implications for the use of monetary valuation were formidable. First, the only environmental effect valued by the Commission was noise nuisance, using a rough-and-ready early version of the hedonic house price approach and contingent valuation. The problem was that the resulting values were swamped by the benefits of reduced travel time. The time-saving noise "trade off" stuck many as unacceptable. Second, the Commission considered, but did not follow through, the idea of valuing a

Norman church at one of the inland sites, using a fire insurance value. The attempt was sufficient for the environmentalists to ridicule the idea of valuing national heritage, even though the Commission did not actually use the value in its final report.

The revival of valuation procedures in the late 1980s might be explained in a number of ways:

First, valuation techniques, notably the contingent valuation approach, had improved substantially during the 1980s. At the time of the airport Commission only travel cost techniques had much currency in the UK. Hedonic property price approaches were still being worked out in the theoretical literature. The intellectual and empirical foundations for valuation were therefore much more powerful in the late 1980s.

Second, a decade of Conservative Party government had brought with it concern for efficiency in government. Politicians sought "value for money" while at the same time facing mounting demands for environmental improvements, not just from domestic lobbies but from the European Commission as well. This led to a search for environmental efficiency. While it remains poorly articulated – there is, for example, no document of any kind in the UK that indicates a procedure for determining environmental priorities – UK government departments have begun to feel their way towards decision-making guidelines. Cost-benefit has inevitably surfaced in this context. Indeed, it is worth recalling that its genesis in the USA in the 1950s was in the context of efficiency in government.

Third, after 1987 all governments were considering their reaction to the "Brundtland Report" (World Commission on Environment and Development, 1987). "Sustainable development" sounded like motherhood and apple pie – something everyone should embrace. Politicans were suspicious, however, since it might also be used to soften the drive for economic growth. Notably, sustainable development as a phrase did not appear more than nominally in UK government statements until 1991, and only then with a change of Prime Minister. But in seeking a response to Brundtland, the UK government commissioned a report on the subject of sustainable development in 1988. It was delivered in 1989. Known as "the Pearce Report" it was published in the same year (Pearce, Markandya & Barbier 1989). The report met with a substantial media interest. While not called for in the terms of reference, the report showed the essential link between sustainable development and monetary valuation.

Valuation therefore entered into the debate through the sustainable development window. And it was valuation that captured the media's attention. Within government a process was established for following through the report's recommendations, one of which was more work on valuation and better dissemination of the research results from other countries.

Fourth, what happened in the UK was happening elsewhere in Europe. Traditionally insulated against "the continent", the UK began to take note of the progress made in other countries, a sign that the UK was truly becoming a part of Europe.

Monetary valuation entered into official government guidelines in 1991. Traditional guidance on economic appraisal has always been given by the UK Treasury. Its technical guide was updated (HM Treasury 1991) and included reference to valuation:

> Some ... costs and benefits can be valued (e.g. travel time, accident deaths avoided, or even option values or existence values). ... Such costs and benefits should always be listed with at least a qualitative assessment of their significance... (HM Treasury, 1991, para.3.18).

A more specific set of guidelines followed also in 1991 (Department of the Environment 1991). This document openly embraced valuation techniques and provided outline guidance on the techniques of valuation.

Monetary valuation remains controversial in the UK. Economists have typically been weak in their popular justifications for its use. Government officials have, with exceptions, limited experience of working with the techniques involved. Some environmentalists remain hostile, though their investment in understanding the philosophy and practice of economic valuation is questionable. Typical anglo-saxon pragmatism prevails. The teqhniques will be used where they seem appropriate and not too controversial. But, as we show in the rest of this chapter, a great deal more activity exists in the UK than many suppose.

8.2 Environmental benefits estimation: the early years

In the UK, the use of valuation teqhniques for securing money measures of environmental benefits/damages began in earnest in the late 1960s and early 1970s, following on from work already well established in North America. Most of these early studies were concerned with the evaluation of recreation benefits. All the studies utilised the Clawson travel cost method (TCM) (zonal variant) to interpret the recreation trip generation equation (Gibson 1974, 1978). The Clawson method was first used in England to estimate the benefits of trout fishing at Grafham Reservoir in what was then Huntingdon-shire (Smith & Kavanagh 1969). Data on visits to Graftham Reservoir by anglers in the 1967 season were used to allocate visitors into distance zones surrounding Grafham. This procedure evaluated what Clawson had termed the demand for the whole recreational experience. A demand curve for the site was estimated by converting the distance variable to a cost equivalent. The total benefits of trout fishing at Grafham Reservoir in 1967 were estimated to be £39,944 (with time costs assumed to be zero) and consumer's surplus was £18,801 (after the payment of £21,143 in charges).

A similar approach was taken in a study of visitors to the coastal resort of Crimdon on the Durham coast (Durham County Council 1971). Benefits at Crimdon for the 1969 season amounted to £182,000 (£114,000 expenditure and £68,000 consumer surplus). The benefits estimate was also adjusted to account for transfer payment effects due to alternative employment opportunities in the local area.

These early recreation benefit studies can be criticised on a number of grounds. The level of aggregation was large, which had the effect of removing variation in visit rates within extensive zones and increasing the R^2 measure of the degree of explanation. The studies also had little predictive capability, the simple Clawson model equation cannot be used as a forecasting equation for visits to other sites.

A number of early studies were concerned with the evaluation of the benefits of new rather than existing recreation facilities. Mansfield (1971) investigated likely recreation benefits derived from a proposal to build a barrage in Morecombe Bay (N.W. England). The basic objective was to estimate the consumer's surplus derived by visitors using Morecombe Bay when the barrage would have become operational in 1981. The method used was to derive a trip attraction model for the Lake District in 1966, to forecast the trips to the Lake District in 1981, and, by means of homogeneity of supply assumption, to predict the levels of trip generation and diversion to Morecombe Bay (Gibson 1974).

According to Gibson (1974) the key assumption in the Morecombe Bay study was that its set of facilities would be viewed by consumers as a homogeneous extension to the Lake District (ie. it was an identical substitute for the Lake District). Two types of benefits could therefore be distinguished – benefits from generated trips and benefits from diverted trips. Visitors were also categorised into day trippers, half-day trippers and holiday makers. The total consumer surplus from recreation for an average week in 1981 was estimated to be £22,880 (for the Bay area).

The identical substitute assumption was used again in a study of a proposed reservoir at Hellifield in Ribblesdale. It was assumed that the reservoir was homogeneous with Morecombe Bay and that the Lake District trip-making function could be utilised. Gibson (1974) commented that the homogeneity assumption and trip diversion formula were open to doubt and that the resulting total benefits estimations of both studies were overestimates.

The benefits derived from recreational fishing on the River Trent in England was investigated as part of a wider study of water supply needs in the East Midlands. Demand curves were derived for various stretches of river and benefits (revenue plus consumer surplus) calculated per stretch (Kavanagh & Gibson 1971; Gibson 1972). The benefits equation included a number of independent variables but only the water quality states coefficients were significant at the 5 % level, R^2 was 0.69. The main limitation of the analysis was the lack of consideration of supply-demand interaction and substitution between stretches. Gibson (1974) warned against the spurious aggregation of individual stretch benefits to get a total fishery quality protection value. This concern over the aggregation of benefits derived from spatially distinct sites is one that has been voiced many times over the years in both the European and North American environmental valuation literature.

The mid 1970s saw a period of consolidation in recreation benefits estimation research. A number of articles appeared which were highly critical of the early UK recreation studies (eg. Common 1973; Flegg 1976). Other researchers sought to improve the application of the basic Clawson method to more complex situations (eg. Gibson & Anderson 1975; Cheshire & Stabler 1976). Both the costs of travel time and the effects of utility derived from travel were much debated issues during this period. A number of writers pointed out that visitor utility may not only be dependent on a particular site but also on the journey itself (Colenutt 1969; Elson 1973; Burton 1966).

Chesire and Stabler (1976) produced an important study of visitors to the Uffington White Horse (landscape attraction) in Berkshire which clarified the visitor behaviour situation and also raised significant question marks against the general applicability of Clawson-type travel cost methods. Cheshire and Stabler identified three distinct categories of visitor: "pure" visitors, who were site orientated; "meanderers", who derive utility from the journey; and "transit" visitors, making their journey for another purpose but calling in at the site in question. Forty-five per cent of their sample was classified as "pure" visitors, but the consumer surplus estimates were only 27 % of that estimated for all visitors.

While they did not recommend any way of dealing with the "non-pure" visitor categories in terms of benefits estimation (within the Clawson methodology) they did suggest that attitude surveys might hold out some promise. Citing a study by Bohm (1972), they made an early call (in the UK context) for what has now become the contingent valuation method (CVM).

Gibson (1978) summed up the early Clawson method dominated research phase by listing four areas of continuing concern:

I) if potential visitors change their residence in order to be near a recreation site, the assumption that all zones have the same distribution of tastes collapses. This type of behaviour would result in a underestimation of benefits by the Clawson method. Essentially what happens is that the price of a trip to a recreation site becomes endogenous. Without correcting for this endogeneity, the estimated slope of a conventional travel cost demand curve will be too flat and the estimated consumer surplus for access value of a site will be too small.

The "endogenous price" problem has, however, been largely ignored in subsequent travel cost demand modelling work. Hundreds of models utilising the basic demand relationship must have been estimated in North America and Europe up to the present day. Most recently (1991) a procedure has been suggested to test for and mitigate this potential bias problem (Parsons 1991).

Parsons argues that the endogeneity may be eliminated using an instrumental variables approach (place of work, job characteristics, etc.). Future surveys should include a question covering the importance of proximity to recreation sites in choosing place of residence. Split data sets could then be used to test for bias;

II) visitors may visit a site as only one of a number visited during one trip. In this case it is not certain how much of an overestimation of benefits there would be;

III) some visitors may derive utility from the journey to a site ("meanderer" category). A complex behaviour pattern may be present, again making it difficult to discern whether benefits are under or overestimated;

IV) journeys may give disutility over and above the reduction in utility due to money and time costs. If this is the case the Clawson method will underestimate benefits.

By the late 1970s therefore the Clawson valuation method was not held in particularly high regard by the small cadre of practising UK resource and environmental economists. The limitations of the technique were reasonably well understood and the restricted range of applications was beginning to be appreciated. There then followed something of a hiatus in environmental valuation research in the UK until the mid 1980s. Only two studies appear to have been undertaken in the late 1970s, both of which used a modified Clawson method. One tried to value the recreational benefits of a nature reserve (Usher 1977) and the other to value wildlife as a recreational resource (Everett 1979).

Everett's Dalby Forest (North Yorkshire) study was based on over 1000 questionnaires completed by day visitors, differentiated by distance zone. Each respondent was also given a score from 0 to 10 indicating his or her interest in wildlife. This data was used to estimate the percentage of the total recreational experience in the survey area that was due to wildlife. Some 93.7 % of the visitors said that they enjoyed the journey to the area and on this basis cost of travel time was assumed to be zero.

Around 48 % of Dalby's visitors said they had never visited the survey area before and 93 % had visited it less than seven times in the 12 months prior to the interview. Everett therefore assumed that the majority of the visitors' house site selections were unlikely to have been affected by the closeness to the Dalby Forest area. The questionnaire also contained a question about alternative competing sites. The answers indicated that a large number of competing sites did exist and that alteration to any of these sites would affect the visitation rate to Dalby.

Evidence was also found that socio-economic groups may alter proportionally with different zones and may have variable behaviour towards visitation, thereby violating a basic Clawson method assumption. In the light of these difficulties Everett concluded that his estimate of total recreational value of £22/ha/pa (£5/ha/pa for the wildlife component) should be viewed as an order of magnitude number only.

8.3 Environmental benefits estimation: recent experience

Since 1985/86 there has been an upsurge of interest in and application of the travel cost method (TCM), both basic forms "zonal" and "individual"; and of the contingent valuation (CVM) method. The application of the hedonic pricing approach (HPM) has been much more limited. Table 8.1. summarises the studies that have been undertaken and presents a short commentary on the methods and techniques adopted, the valuation estimates produced and distinguishing features of the individual valuation studies.

While the UK has lagged behind the expansion of the use of monetary environmental benefits valuation methods (particularly CVM) in the USA and to a lesser extent other countries, the same general trends, with one or two exceptions, have emerged (Bateman, Green, Tunstall & Turner 1991):

I) It has become conventional to at least pay lip service to the need to establish the validity and reliability of the particular valuation method and/or instrument being used in a given empirical study. Validity and reliability together determine the technical acceptability of a valuation method or instrument. But the institutional acceptability of a valuation method or instrument. In a pluralist political and economic system such as the UK, there is a need to assess how a given valuation method might fit (or not fit) into the current "official project appraisal" system, and therefore what the reaction of the "decision-making" system would be to it. It is also necessary to judge how nature conservation agencies, local groups, etc. would react to the use of the monetary valuation methods (Turner & Batemans 1990; Pearce & Turner 1991).

Table 8.1 A review of UK environmental effects valuation studies since 1980. Amounts stated in £s in the year of study

Study	Environmental good	Sample size	Method	Valuation	Remarks
1. Price, Christensen & Humphreys (1986)	Forest recreation	696	ITCM and ZTCM	Reports demand klassticities	An important paper which highlights the difference betwen the elastic price elasticity of demand for a recreation site and the much less elastic general recreation experience demand in the presence of substitutes.
2. Hanley & Common (1987)	Forest recreation	170	ZTCM	Consumer surplus £14.6 to £24.5 per visitor per annum;	Significant difference in the results obtained via CVM (continuous question

Table 8.1 continues

Study	Environ-mental good	Sample size	Method	Valuation	Remarks
			CVM	Average WTP for visitor permit /£1.00 per visitor	format) and ZTCM; latter method results probably represent gross overestimantion of benefits
3. Hanley (1988)	Air polution and amenity loss due to straw burning	100	CVM	Mean WTP £5.18 per household per annum; Mean WTAC £9.6 per household per annum; User values	CVM a face-to-face bidding gane; protest bids excluded; small sample size; divergence between WTP and WTAC results well within expected range (see Hanemann 1991)
4. Turner & Brooke (1988)	Coastal recreation and amenity	200	CVM	Mean WTP £15 per household per annum (locals); £18.8 per household per annum (non-locals); User Values	Payment card format and tax payment vehicle; alternative site analysis included in the full CBA; very limited reliability and validity testing
5. Willis & Benson (1988)	Nature reserve recreation	site 1 = 94 site 2 = 461 site 3 = 463	ZTCM	Consumer surplus £0.6 to £1.7 per visit or £1.02 to £2.3 per visit depending on travel cost estimate; User values	On-site interviews. Test two travel cost assumptions (petrol only vs. petrol + other running costs) producing similar degrees of reliability and explanation. However consumer surplus estimates 33–84 % larger for full cost assumption
6. Hanley (1989a)	Forest recreation	1148	CVM	WTP (visit) wildlife = £0.84 landscape = £0.80 recreation = £0.45 Total = £1.25	CVM used payment card format with an entry fee; low R^2 value was reported. Bid curves estimated. Close-ended wuestioning gave higher bids but less refusals than open-ended.

Table 8.1 continues

Study	Environ-mental good	Sample size	Method	Valuation	Remarks
			ZTCM	Consumer surplus/ capita £0.32; £0.56; £1.7 and £15.13 depending on functional form. User values	ZTCM results were highly dependent on functional form and again a uniformly low R^2 value was reported. Validity of the ZTCM results, in particular, open to question; poor construct validity
7. Hanley (1989b)	Drinking water qua-lity impro-vements (reduced nitrate)	134	CVM	Mean WTP = £12.97 per household	Mail questionnaire sent to residents utilising a payment card and water rates payment card and water rates payment vehicle. A 34% res-ponse rate was achieved and the WTP estimates excluded protest bids. Limited bias and validity testing. Starting point bias tested for and found to be insignificant
8. Harley & Hanley (1989)	Nature reserves/ wildlife sites	site 1 = 145 site 2 = 240 site 3 = 186	CVM ZTCM	WTP £1.13 to £2.53 per adult de-pending on site Consumer surplus/ Capita £1.99 to £2.60; or £7.30 to £9.5 depending on functional form and travel cost components	CVM based on interviews with visi-tors using a payment card and entry fee/ conservation body membership pay-ment vehicle. Re-searchers argue that petrol cost-based travel most estimates are the cost ap-propriate ZTCM re-sults. Only moderate convergent validity
9. Button & Pearce (1989)	Amenity value re-stored ur-ban canal		HPM	Aggregate residen-tial property value increase estimate = £600k	Ball park estimate only for a pre-devel-opment CBA study. Estate agent estimates. *Table 8.1 continues*

Study	Environmental good	Sample size	Method	Valuation	Remarks
10. Penning-Rowsell et al. (1989a)	Beach recreation and quality states	247	CVM	Value/adult visit = £7.7; £6.6; £3.9 & £11.5 depending on quality state; user values	CVM format based on enjoyment per adult visit; no payment vehicle; beach replenishement scenarios
11. Penning-Rowsell et al. (1989b)	Recreation value of beaches	735 at 6 sites	CVM	Value/adult visit = £7.8; user values	CVM format based on enjoyment per adult visit; no payment vehichle
12. Coker et al. (1989)	Recreation value of enviromental improvements to a river corridor	242	CVM	Value/adult visit £0.82; £1.03 WTP per annum per household = £13.9; £16.2; user values	CVM format based on enjoyment per adult visit open question, with a rates payment vehicle (ie. local tax)
13. FHRC (1989)	Recreational value of coastal cliffs	214	CVM	WTP per annum/capita = £1.8, £2.8 depending on starting point in bidding game	CVM incorporating a bidding game with a £0.5 and £1.00 starting point; rates/taxes used as payment vehicle
14. Willis & Benson (1989)	Forest recreation	1843	ZTCM	WTP £1.3 to £3.3 per visit; forest value ⟩ £1/ha to £449/ha	On site interviews with prior cluster analysis to select sites. Allowed statistical tests to select most appropriate definition of travel costs
15. Pennington et al. (1990)	Noise pollution	3472 (house price observations)	HPM	Noise found to be an insigniificant variable in determining house price	House price variation completely explained by neighbourhood and other property characteristics. Retesting with an inferior mode ($R^2 = 0.75$ rather than $R^2 = 0.8$) gave a small negative noise effect

Table 8.1 continues

Study	Environ-mental good	Sample size	Method	Valuation	Remarks
16. Green et al. (1990a)	River water quality im-provement	319 residents at 7 sites	CVM	WTP per anum/ capita = £13.6 (non visitors); = £15.6 (visitors) both with £6.0 S.P.; WTP per month/ capita = £1.5 to £1.8 (non-visitors) and £1.4 to £2.0 (visitors) with £0.5 and £1.0 S.P. Use & non-use values	CVM with bidding game format and water rates payment vehicle; residents liv-ing at least 2km from a river corridor. Questionnaire state-ment attempted to legitimate a refusal to pay. Construct validity testing in-cluded, with only moderate success. Starting point bias found to be signifi-cant. Researchers unable to rigorously differentiate use and non-use motivations.
17. Green et al. (1990b)	Recrea-tional value of beaches	603 at 4 sites	CVM	Value/adult visit £7.5, £7.1, £3.7 and £9.2; WTP per annum/capita = £4.9	CVM with bidding game format and rates/taxes payment vehicle.
			TCM/ CVM	Testing of the relationship be-tween value of enjoyment and distance travelled to site	CVM also used to test the TCM assumption that the value of en-joyment must be high-er for those who tra-vel further (ie. higher travel costs). In a six coastal resort sites analysis only two sites produced the predicted TCM out-come. This is poten-tially a very signifi-cant result and adds to the argument that TCM should only be used in a very con-strained context due, in the analysis, to the lack of construct validity

Table 8.1 continues

Study	Environ-mental good	Sample size	Method	Valuation	Remarks
18. Green & Tunstall (1990)	River water quality improvements	303 residents at 9 sites	CVM	£546, £562 and £582 one-off payments per household	CVM open question format, willingness to pay a lump sum for water quality improvements (three standards); households living adjacent to a river corridor
19. Willis & Garrod (1990)	Open-access recreation on inland waterways	1502	ITCM CVM	Consumer surplus = £3.0 to £0.51 per visit depending on functional form CS = £0.36 per visit	Face to face interviews with canal users; because of the spatial configuration of the waterway ITCM utilised instead instead of ZTCM
20. Benson & Willis (1990)	Forest recreation	1843	ZTCM	National consumer surplus = £53 million per annum: £0.53/capita Average CS/visit = £2.00	On site interviews with prior cluster analysis to select sites. This study presents aggregated national CS estimates based on the work of Willis & Benson (1989)
21. Willis et al. (1990)	Canal and waterway informal recreation	canal 1 = 925 canal 2 = 393	ITCM	Average consumer surplus per visitor canal 1 = £0.29; canal 2 = £0.32	On site interviews. Sensitivity analysis highlighting differences between OLS & ML. techniques
22. Garrod & Willis (1991a)	Amenity value of forests and waterways	1762 to 1826	HPM	Existence of local river/canal or forest amenity increased house price by 4.9% and 7.1% respectively	One of the first rigorous HPM studies in the UK (using house sale prices); subsequently expanded to national scale
23. Garrod & Willis (1991b)	Amenity value of forestry	1031 (properties)	HPM	A 1% increase in proportion of local broadleafs shown to induce a £43 increase in house house price while the same increase in certain confines? shown to reduce house price by £141	National extension of Garrod & Willis (1991a) above. Uses Box-Cox flexible functional form with grid-search to determine statistically optimal parameters

Table 8.1 continues

Study	Environ-mental good	Sample size	Method	Valuation	Remarks
24. Willis & Garrod (1991a)	Forest recreation	126 (21 at each of six sites)	ITCM	Consumer surplus per visitor = £1.4–£2.6; (ZTCM, OLS); £0.06–£0.96 (ITCM, TML); £0.43–£0.72 (CVM)	Important conver-gent validity test study. Zonal travel cost results not con-sistent with ITCM and CVM results. Other CS results reported: £0.4 to £0.8 for ZTCM, (petrol costs only) and £0.4 to £2.3 ITCM (both OLS)
25. Willis & Garrod (1991b)	Dales landscape	1288 (locals) 300 (visitors)	CVM	WTP/capita p.a.	CVM asked individual WTP using a trust fund donation payment vehicle. Question-naire buttressed by pictoral images of possible Dales lands-cape options. Tackles "mental account"/"part-whole" bias problem by asking individuals to work out their recreation budget relative to other components of their household budget eg. other "good causess" etc.
	Landscape abandoned conserved current	visitors £ 24 £ 35 £ 22	locals £ 8 £ 27 £ 26		
26. Hanley (1991)	Preserva-tion bene-fits: flow country (Scotland)	159	CVM	Mean WTP = £16.8 per capita as a once-off payment	Preservation benefits of flow country, landscape and wild-life assets. Mail questionnaire, 40% return rate. Uses a target fund payment vehicle

Table 8.1 continues

Study	Environ-mental good	Sample size	Method	Valuation	Remarks
27. Hanley et al. (1991a)	Heathland conservation in Dorset	237	CVM	WTP = £0.74/visit with entry fee WTP = £9.73/year with annual payment WTP = £25.57/ once-off payment	CVM applied to visitors, with three different payment vehicles and four different informa-tion sets tested. Protest bids excluded
28. Green & Tunstall (1991a)	Coast protection	387 (residents in 5 towns)	CVM	WTP/annum/ capita = £25.16 & £21.9 with 50p and 20p S.P. respectively	CVM using a bid-ding game with a rates and taxes payment vehicle. Starting point bias testing
29. Green & Tunstall (1991b)	River water quality improve-ments	873 (visitors to 12 sites)	CVM	Value/adult/visit = £0.51; £0.6; £0.52 WTP/annum/ capita = £12.08; WTP/month/capita = £1.35 & £1.66 with 50p & £1 S.P. respectively	CVM using a bidding game with water rates payment vehicle. Starting point bias testing
30. Hanley et al. (1991b)	Heathland preserva-tion/wood-land loss	237	CVM	WTP/cap according to different information Categories. No information = £21.54 info on health loss = £20.60 info on species loss = £21.52 info on both losses = £30.59	CVM on heathland loss demonstrates weakly positive informatiion bias. Woodland threat-ened by a road scheme was the context for an ancil-lary mail CVM. Two sets of questi-onnaire distributed with slight wording change ie. "ancient rare woodland threatend"; 40% return rate, no significant information bias found

Resistance to the extended application and use of monetary valuation methods and techniques is likely to be strongest in situations in which there are "soft" environmental values requiring assessment. Environmental values have been variously interpreted and thus perceptions regarding the exact nature and significance of "soft" environmental values are likely to vary widely. In particular, the full ethical significance of environmental degradation is not an issue on which a consensus view is likely to emerge in the short-run (Pearce & Turner, 1990; Turner & Pearce 1992).

If the advances that have been made in environmental valuation procedures continue, there is every likelihood that the official project and programme appraisal system in the UK will encompass an increased if not comprehensive range of monetised environmental impacts (Dept. of the Environment 1991).

Conservation agencies and groups present a more diverse set of responses. All agencies seem to agree that environmental benefits/damages need to be assessed as early as possible in the appraisal process. They also support the general principle of environmental evaluation, within the environmental effects estimation procedures. There are, however, some differences of opinion relating to the acceptability of quantifying and placing monetary values on environmental assets.

Conservationists put forward the following general concerns about any system of environmental evaluation (and monetary valuation in particular):

a) Ecological and landscape/amenity assets should not be viewed on a disaggregated basis (ie. site by site or habitat by habitat) because the total value of the whole stock is substantially greater than the sum of the component parts. This classification and evaluation of say one SSSI against another is not legitimate, they are all equal from a conservation viewpoint. On scientific grounds an holistic view is in any case required because of the danger of "island effects" and resulting loss of biodiversity;

b) if the aim is to quantify more precisely the nature and significance of the UK's remaining stock of environmental assets, then the present planning system does provide a way of establishing preliminary (non-monetary) values for particular sites (ie. what degree of protection or recognition does the planning system currently afford the site – SSSI, NNR, international site designation, etc.) Site designation plus the ownership structure are factors that could be used in any preliminary evaluation "scale" (ranking);

c) there are limits to the monetary valuation approach, both ethical and practical. In the latter context, for example, landscape assets and their appreciation is likely to be a somewhat subjective matter and therefore not easily translatable into a monetary measure.

Decision makers are primarily interested in key issues and the potential for environmental and economic trade-offs. Conservation agencies and groups are resistant to the "trade-off mentality" and seek to retain aggregate stocks of environmental assets and protect them from incremental attrition. These concerns are best accommodated by the introduction of sustainability standards/constraints into the CBA system. Depending on the degree of actual substitution that is both physically possible and practicable, the shadow project approach may offer some flexibility in a given environment/development conflict situation. This approach may also be preferable to changes in the conventional discounting procedure in CBA. Adjustments to the discount rate to accommodate various "environmental concerns" are double-edged. The aggregate effect on the efficiency of resource allocation within the public-sector must not be overlooked (Pearce, Markandya & Barbier, 1989; Pearce & Turner 1990);

II) After a short lived renewed interest in the TCM in the mid 1980s in the UK, there has since been a pronounced loss of confidence in TCM generally and in the zonal variant (ZTCM) in particular;
III) The majority of environmental valuation practioners have been encouraged by the results derived via the CVM, at least as far as use values for a number of environmental assets are concerned;
IV) There has been a growing recognition of the inter-disciplinary nature of CV research. Recent studies are now based at least notionally upon the Fishbein-Ajzen attitude model and articulate willingness to pay as an attitude towards an act (Bateman, Green, Tunstall & Turner 1991);
V) The preferred CV instrument has shifted progressively from bidding games to payment cards to dichotomous choice or referendum;
VI) Going against the general trend, CVM self-completion questionnaires have not been extensively used and telephone interviews have not been used at all in the UK. A high level of non-response to the survey can be a significant problem in postal and self-completion surveys (non-response bias), see Hanley (1989) and Hanley (1991) in which response rates were 34% and 40% respectively.

The choice of field-based or mail/telephone-based surveys provides a potential source of conflict between CV analysts and sponsoring governmental or private agencies. From the analysts' point of view, personal interviews seem to have major advantages over other methods for CV surveys – respondents can be motivated to participate reflectively; information can be communicated and "translated" properly; all CV question formats are feasible options and the presence of the interviewers can sustain respondent interest and commitment through a long interview process. From the research sponsors' viewpoint such a process is expensive because of the difficulty and expense in hiring, training and briefing experienced interviewers. There is also the cost of supervision and monitoring of interview fieldwork, necessary to minimise "interviewer bias". The convenience and relatively low cost of postal surveys is therefore likely to appeal to potential research sponsors.

VII) Again, against the trend, very few HP studies have been undertaken in the UK. While the concept of total economic value (TEV) and its basic subdivision into use and non-use components is generally accepted by UK valuation practioners, empirical estimation of the components as non-overlapping entities is much more contentious an issue. The majority of studies are restricted to use value estimates. A study investigating the value of a range of river water quality improvements in England has sought to shed some empirical light on the different total value components (Green et al. 1990a). In studies of the value of river water quality improvement, samples from a number of different populations asked were interviewed (Green, Tunstall & House 1989). Among the questions asked were, the relative importance of nine different reasons why public money should be spent reducing pollution in rivers and streams – see table 8.2. According to the researchers, the statements include expressions of a generalised user value, option value, bequest value and existence value plus a number of other possible reasons.

The relative weights given to both user and option value are noticeable, as are the weights given to non-use value and the moral aspect in general. However, these reasons did not adequately explain either differences in beliefs as to whether more or less public money should be spent reducing pollution of watercourses, or in individual WTP. Neither did factor analysis reveal a simple structure amongst these beliefs. Green et al. (1990a) concluded that "... no exhaustive and mutually exclusive set of motivations underlying individual preferences for environmental goods has yet been determined. As such, it is unsafe to rely on previous speculations and estimate total WTP as the sum of WTP amounts elicited separately for the different assumed motivations."

Table 8.2 Motivations for increased expenditure on water quality enhancement. 319 observations.

	Mean	Standard deviation
To increase enjoyment of users of rivers	6.5	2.7
To avoid unsightly, smelly rivers	8.8	1.7
To provide for increased demand for leisure and recreation in the future	7.1	2.6
To improve the quality of life	8.7	1.7
To contribute towards the improvement of the environment in general	8.9	1.6
So that clean rivers are there if we want to visit them in the future	8.5	1.9
To conserve wildlife and plants	9.2	1.2
It is a moral issue: we ought not to pollute the environment	9.0	1.7
To ensure a pleasant environment for future generations	9.1	1.4
To ensure public health	9.5	1.1

Scale: 0–10 (0 = not important at all, 10 = most important).
Source: Green et al. (1990a).

The TCM has been the cause of serious concern in the literature in the last few years (Hanley & Common 1987; Hanley 1989a; Green et al. 1990b and Willis & Garrod 1991a). The zonal variant has almost reached the stage of complete rejection in favour of the "individual" version (Garrod & Willis 1991c). However, a number of fundamental TCM problems, first raised in the UK literature in the early to mid 1970s, have not been satisfactorily addressed and continue to lie at the core of the critique of TCM. Most disturbing of all has been the results of a coastal town recreation survey undertaken in the late 1980s (Green et al. 1990b). This study tests a prime assumption of TCM, that the value of enjoyment must be higher for visitors who travel further (incurring higher costs) to visit a particular site. Visitors to six seaside locations in England were asked (via a CVM) to value the enjoyment of their day visit. This data was then compared with the travel costs of the visit. These costs were estimated by using the AUTOROUTE computer program which computes the cheapest, quickest and shortest routes between the origin of the trip and the site in question for day trippers.

Results did not support an unquestioning and extensive use of

TCM in the UK. Only the Dunwich and Spurn Head sites data produced a rising enjoyment value as travel cost and travel time and distance increased. In the case of day trips to Clacton enjoyment value increased as trips were made from increasing distances but only up to a threshold of about one hour's travel time. Beyond the threshold there was no apparent similar relationship. For Filey, no association between the value of enjoyment and distance travelled was found. In the cases of Frinton and Scarborough, the value of the day's enjoyment seemed to be negatively related to distance travelled.

CV studies have become much more sophisticated over time. In terms of reliability, several potential sources of bias remain to be satisfactorily investigated. In the simple CV study case, for example, the minimum sample size is unlikely to be below 400, e.g. a reject rate of 50 %, 100 % response rate, 1 site, 2 payment vehicles and a minimum of 100 respondents WTP by each payment vehicle (Bateman, Green, Tunstall & Turner 1991). Where significant differences are expected between sites, the required sample sizes will be much larger. The studies listed in table 1 indicate that too small a sample size has been a potential problem in a number of cases.

It is also true to say that the issue of temporal bias (for seasonal intervals or longer periods of time) has hardly been addressed at all. Strategic bias does not seem to be a problem in any of the studies reported in table 8.1.

Two studies of heathland and woodland conservation value (Hanley et al. 1991a; and Hanley et al. 1991b) explicitly tested for information bias. No clear significant bias of this type was reported. Starting point bias has been reported as significant in some studies of water quality improvement benefits, especially when a bidding game format was used (Green et al. 1990a; Green & Tunstall 1991b). The higher the initial value used in the bid, the higher the final sum elicited from the respondent. Examination of the distributions of some large data sets (Green & Tunstall 1991b) suggest that it is the extreme bids which are most affected by starting point bias.

The general CVM literature has recently highlighted what has become known as part-whole or mental account bias. Willis and Garrod (1991b) accept the potential for bias and in a study of Yorkshire Dales landscape (mountain scenery) value explicitly set out to minimise it. They set the part-whole problem in the context of the theory of two-stage budgeting (Deaton & Muellbauer part-whole 1981). According to this theory, total income is, in the first stage, allocated to various broad categories of expenditure, e.g. food, recreation, etc. In the second stage a further subdivision within categories, among specific items, e.g. forest recreation, water-based recreation, etc., is made. The individual therefore has several mental accounts, each referring to a category and uses "each account to evaluate some multi-attribute option with regard to the particular multi-attribute reference set that represents the category" (Khaneman & Tversky 1984).

Willis and Garrod recognise that, in responding to questionnaires, individuals may omit to consider all available relevant material. In particular they may not consider their relevant (recreation) mental account. This omission lies at the root of part-whole bias and the authors address this problem explicitly by asking respondents to calculate their "total yearly budget for all environmental issues including those donations and subscriptions that he or she might already have made" (Willis & Garrod 1991b). The mental account question reads as follows: "Bearing in mind how many good causes there are looking for our support today, could you estimate how much money your household spends on a voluntary basis each year on the enjoyment and preservation of the countryside – this might include any donations to countryside causes, membership of conservation or countryside organisations and charges for entry to reserves/parks etc.". This question directly addresses Kahneman and Tversky's fundamental point that decision making is highly context sensitive (while also limiting any incentive towards strategic bias).

In their empirical testing of this approach, Willis and Garrod analyse WTP for different landscape quality states in the Yorkshire Dales. Both visitors and households were interviewed with all the visitors (group V) and half of the households (group A) being asked the mental (recreation) account question directly prior to the WTP question. The mental account question was then omitted from the remaining household (group B) questionnaires, to set up a control. A statistically significant difference was found between the mean WTP and the total recreation budgets of groups V and A (99 % confidence) indicating that, even if part-whole bias were present, it was not a serious problem. (The same test also indicates that strategic bias is not an overriding problem.)

It seems that part-whole bias is a potential problem which will be exacerbated by poor CV instruments. However, with the specification of instruments which encourage considered responses to accurate unbiased information and testing as outlined above, the problem of part-whole bias can probably be reduced to insignificant levels.

Bateman et al. (1991) identify certain variants of mental account type problems. It is noticed that where respondents are asked for evaluations of a category group of goods (e.g. recreation) then WTP may be less than the sum of WTP responses regarding the specific good subdivisions of that category. Willis and Garrod (1991b) tested a similar hypothesis by comparing mean WTP for group A (in the Dales study) with that for group B (who were not given mental account question). They concluded that the inclusion of this extra variable did not significantly affect mean WTP (99% confidence limit).

A variety of payment vehicles have been tested in the UK CV studies – entry permits to nature reserves; entrance fees to forests etc; trust fund donations and taxes. Taxes and rates (a form of local tax) have proved to be the most popular vehicle. A potential problem with payment mechanisms is the degree of trust that the respondent may or may not have that the money raised will in fact be spent on the good in question. Since the UK Treasury does not favour the earmarking of tax revenue, the respondent has presumably to make some judgement about the risk of the possible diversion of funds in the system away from the target good. Equally, the respondents will have to make a judgement about the probability of the good actually being provided and the timescale of this provision. A respondent asked about WTP for, say, the preservation of a woodland via a donation to the National Trust or English Nature should be aware that its acquisition will not necessarily guarantee its long-term preservation (Bateman, Green, Tunstall & Turner 1991). A number of bodies (governmental) will reserve the right to take over the land or change the land use in the future. In this sense, estimating WTP for an SSSI (site of special scientific interest) by asking for a donation to, say, English Nature, which then acquires the land is problematic.

However, there is little evidence reported in the UK studies to indicate significant payment vehicle bias, or to support the concerns reported above. In a pilot study for a large on-going (1991/92) CVM study of the Broadland wetland in Norfolk the tax payment vehicle performed more satisfactorily than other vehicles tested.

The continuous versions of the CV questions format has dominated UK research. The pairwise comparison technique only appears to have been used once (Brown and Green, 1981). An enjoyment per-visit format has, however, been tested by the Flood Hazard Research Unit, Middlesex Polytechnic (see, for example, Penning-Rowsell et al. 1989a, 1989b; Coker et al. 1989). This format was used in order to avoid the problems of introducing a novel entry payment mechanism in the context of currently available environmental goods not subject to charge.

Several tests of convergent validity (by comparing CV and TC results) have been reported by UK researchers. But some of these have been criticised because they have typically been of the total site value, aggregated across the population, rather than of the value per individual (Green et al. 1990b). In any case this form of validity testing is inherently very weak (Mitchell & Carson 1989).

A major study of the Norfolk Broadland wetland area and related flood alleviation schemes is currently (1991–92) underway. The study has brought together three groups of environmental benefits valuation practioners – from the University of East Anglia, Newcastle University and the Flood Hazard Unit of Middlesex Polytechnic. The aim is to estimate (using CVM) the value of water-based recreation and wildlife in Broadland. Personal on-site interviews have been conducted with a sample size of over 2,600 respondents. Both the continuous WTP and discrete WTP formats are under test (continuous format sample = 789; discrete format sample = 1820). A tax payment vehicle was selected after a pilot test (pilot sample exceeded 300). It is planned to augment the use value results with a nationwide postal questionnaire designed to elicit non-use values. The questionnaire design includes checks for pa8.4rt-whole bias and potential respondent confusion between lump sum and annual payment responses and goes to some length to mitigate information bias (via the provision of pictoral and map-based information boards at survey sites).

8.4 Conclusions

Environmental benefits estimation research in the UK has lagged behind that in the USA but most of the same general trends have emerged. Validity and reliability testing has gradually been included in the research, although a formal testing protocol has yet to be established.

Support for the TCM has waxed and waned but now appears to be at quite a low level. The zonal version of the Clawson method now commands little credibility, with researchers restricting their attention to the individual TCM. In the future the use of TCM will be heavily constrained by site and other contextual factors.

Support for the CVM has increased significantly in the last five years or so. Value estimate results relating to a range of environmental goods have shown some "clustering", at least in the case of use values for beach recreation, nature reserve recreation and water-based recreation and amenity. It is also the case that a positive relationship between uniqueness and WTP appears to have emerged in recent studies. Non-use value estimates have been far less numerous and confidence levels in this context are not very high. Personal on-site interviews have been preferred to mail or telephone surveys. The latter may, however, in the future prove a popular option for sponsoring agencies looking for cost-effective research.

Very few HPM studies have been undertaken in the UK but recently two studies (Willis & Garrod 1991a, 1991b) have yielded some promising results.

References

Bateman, I.J., Green, C., Tunstall, S. & R.K Turner 1991: The Contingent Valuation Method. Report to the Transport and Road Research Laboratory, University of East Anglia and Middlesex Polytechnic, Norwich and Enfield.

Benson, J.F. & K.G. Willis 1990: The Aggregate Value of Non-Priced Recreation Benefits of the Forestry Commission Estate. Report to the Forestry Commission, Dept. of Town and Country Planning, University of Newcastle, Newcastle.

Bohm, P. 1972: Estimating Demand for Public Goods: An Experiment, *European Economic Review, 3,* pp. 111–30.

Burton, T.L. 1967: Windsor Great Park: A Recreation Study, *Wye College Studies in Rural Land Use, No. 8,* University of London, London.

Button, K.J. & D. W. Pearce 1989: Infrastructure Restoration as a Tool for Stimulating Urban Renewal – The Glasgow Canal, *Urban Studies, 26,* pp. 559–71.

Chesire, P.C. & M.J. Stabler 1976: Joint Consumption Benefits in Recreational Site Surplus: An Empirical Estimate, *Regional Studies, 10,* pp. 343–51.

Cocker, A. et al. (1989). *An Evaluation of the Recreational and Amenity Benefits of a Flood Alleviation Scheme for Maidenhead,* Flood Hazard Research Centre, Enfield.

Colenutt, R.J. 1969: Modelling Travel Patterns of Day Visitors to the Countryside, *Area, 1,* pp. 43–7.

Commission on the Third London Airport 1970: Papers and Proceeding, Vol. VII. Her Majesty's Stationary Office, London, 440 pp.

Commission on the Third London Airport 1971: Report. Her Majesty's Stationary Office, London, 230 p.

Dasgupta, A.K. & D.W. Pearce 1972: *Cost-benefit Analysis: Theory and Practice.* Macmillan, London, 270p.

Deaton, A. & J. Muellbauer 1980: *Economics and Consumer Behaviour,* Cambridge University Press, Cambridge.

Department of the Environment 1991: Policy Appraisal and the Environment, HMSO, London.

Durham County Council 1971: Crimdon Benefit Study, Durham County Council, Durham.

Elson, M.J. 1973: Some Factors Affecting the Incidence and Distribution of Weekend Recreation on Motoring Trips, *Oxford Agrarian Studies, 2, pp.* 161–79.

Everett, R.D. 1979: The Monetary Value of the Recreational Benefits of Wildlife, *Journal of Environmental Management, 8, pp.* 203–213.

Garrod, G.D. & K.G. Willis 1991a: The Hedonic Price Method and the Valuation of Countryside Characteristics, *Countryside Change Working Paper, 14,* University of Newcastle, Newcastle.

Garrod, G.D. & K.G. Willis 1991b: The Environmental Economic Impact of Woodland: A Two Stage Hedonic Price Model of the Amenity Value of Forestry in

Britain. *Countryside Change Working Paper, 19,* University of Newcastle, Newcastle.

Garrod, G.D. & K.G. Willis 1991c: Some Empirical Estimates of Forest Amenity Value. *Countryside Change Working Paper, 13,* Countryside Change Unit, University of Newcastle, Newcastle.

Gibson, J.G. 1972: The River Trent Recreation Study. In: *Recreation Cost-Benefit Analysis,* Countryside Commission, London.

Gibson, J.G. 1974: Recreation Cost-Benefit Analysis: A Review of English Case Studies, *Planning Outlook: Special Issue,* Newcastle University, Newcastle.

Gibson, J.G. 1978: Recreation Land Use. In: D.W. Pearce (ed.) *The Valuation of Social Cost,* Allen and Unwin, London.

Gibson, J.G. & R.W. Anderson 1975: The Estimation of Consumers' Surplus from a Recreational Facility with Optional Tariffs, *Journal of Applied Economics, 7,* pp. 73-9.

Green, C.H. et al. 1990a: The Economic Evaluation of Environmental Goods, *Project Appraisal 5,* pp. 70-82.

Green, C.H. et al. 1990b: *The Benefits of Coastal Protection: Results from Testing the CVM for Beach Recreation,* Annual Conference of River and Coastal Engineers, Loughborough University, Loughborough.

Green, C.H. & S. Tunstall 1990: The Amenity and Recreational Value of River Corridors. Paper given at the Conservation and Management of Rivers Conference, University of York, York.

Green, C.H. & S. Tunstall 1991a: Is the Economic Evaluation of Environmental Goods Possible? *Journal of Environmental Management* (in press).

Green, C.H. & S. Tunstall 1991b: The Evaluation of River Water Quality Improvements by the Contingent Valuation Method, *Applied Economics, 23,* pp. 1135-1146.

Green, C.H. Tunstall, S. & M.A. House 1989: Investment Appraisal for Sewerage Schemes: Benefit Assessment. In: H. Laikari (ed.) *River Basin Management - V,* Pergamon Press, Oxford.

Hanemann, W.M. 1991: Willingness to Pay and Willingness to Accept: How Much Can They Differ? American Economic Value of Wilderness Areas. In: F., R. van der Ploeg Dietz & J. van der Straaten (eds.) *Economic Policy and the Environment,* Elsevier, North Holland.

Hanley, N.D. 1988: Using Contingent Valuation to Value Environment Improvements, *Applied Economics, 20,* pp. 541-49.

Hanley, N.D. 1989a: Valuing Rural Recreation Benefits: An Empirical Comparison of Two Approaches, *Journal of Agricultural Economics, 40,* pp. 361-74.

Hanley, N.D. 1989b: Problems in Valuing Environmental Improvement Resulting from Agricultural Policy Changes. In: A. Dubgaard & A. Nielson (eds.) *Economic Aspects of Environmental Regulation in Agriculture,* Wissenschaftsverlag, Vauk Kiel, Kiel.

Hanley, N.D. & M.S. Common 1987: Evaluating the Recreation, Wildlife and Landscape Benefits of Forestry: Preliminary Results from a Scottish Study, *Papers in Economics, Finance and Investment, No. 141,* University of Stirling, Scotland.

Hanley, N.D. et al. 1991a: *Heathland Conservation in Dorset. Report to the NCC,* Department of Economics, University of Stirling, Stirling.

Hanley, N.D. et al. 1991b: Design Bias in CV Studies: The Impact of Information Changes, *Working Paper 91/13, Stirling Discussion Papers in Economics,* University of Stirling, Stirling.

Harley, D. & N.D. Hanley 1989: Economic Benefit Estimates for Nature Reserves:

Methods and Results. *Discussion Paper 89/6,* Department of Economics, University of Stirling, Stirling.

HM Treasury 1991: *Economic Appraisal in Central Government: A Technical Guide for Government Departments.* HM Treasury, London, 92p.

Kahneman, D. & A. Tversky 1984: Choices, Values and Frames, *American Psychologist, 39,* pp. 341–50.

Kavanagh, N.J. & J.G. Gibson 1971: *Measurements of Fishing Benefits on the River Trent.* In The Trent Research Programme, The Institute of Water Pollution Control.

Mansfield, N.W. 1971: The Estimation of Benefits from Recreation Sites and the Provision of a New Recreation Facility, *Regional Studies 5,* pp. 55–69.

Mitchell, R. & R. Carson 1989: *Using Surveys to Value Public Goods: The Contingent Valuation Method,* Resources for the Future, Washington D.C.

Parson, G.R. 1991: A Note on Choice of Residential Location in Travel Cost Demand Models, *Land Economics, 67,* pp. 360–64.

Pearce, D.W. & R.K. Turner 1990: *Economics of Nature Resources and the Environment,* Harvester Wheatsheaf, Hemel Hempstead.

Pearce, D.W. & R.K. Turner 1991: *The Use of Benefit Estimates in Environmental Decision-Making: Report to Environment Directorate,* OECD, Paris.

Pearce, D.W., Markandya, A. & E. Barbier 1989: *Blueprint for a Green Economy,* Earthscan, London, 192p.

Penning-Rowsell, E. et al. 1989a: Scheme Worthwhileness. In: *Institution of Civil Engineers, Coastal Management,* Thomas Telford, London.

Penning-Rowsell, E. et al. 1989b: Recreational Aspects of Coast Protection Benefits. Paper presented to the Conference of River and Coastal Engineers, Loughborough University, Loughborough.

Pennington, G. et al. 1990: Aircraft Noise and Residential Property Values Adjacent to Manchester International Airport, *Journal of Transport Economics and Policy,* 24, pp. 49–59.

Price, C., Christensen, J.B. & S.K. Humphreys 1986: Elasticities of Demand for Recreation Site and Recreation Experience. *Environment and Planning A, 18,* pp. 1259–63.

Smith, R.J. & N.J. Kavanagh 1969: The Measurement of Benefits of Trout Fishing: Preliminary Results of a Study at Graftham Water, Great Ouse Water Authority, Huntingdonshire, *Journal of Leisure Research, 1,* pp. 316–32.

Turner, R.K. & I.J. Bateman 1990: *A Critical Review of Monetary Assessment Methods and Techniques.* Environmental Appraisal Group, University of East Anglia, Norwich.

Turner, R.K. & J. Brooke 1988: *A Benefits Assessment for the Aldeburgh Sea Defence Scheme,* Environmental Appraisal Group Report, School of Environmental Sciences, University of East Anglia, Norwich. Also reported on in J-Ph. Barde & D.W. Pearce (eds.) *Valuing the Environment,* Ch. 6, Earthscan, London.

Turner, R.K. & D.W. Pearce 1992: The Ethical Foundations of Sustainable Economic Development. In: L. Freese (ed.) *Advances in Human Ecology,* Vol. 1, JAI Press, Greenwich (pp. 177–195).

Usher, M.B. 1977: Coastline Management: Some General Comments on Management Plans and Visitor Surveys. In: R. Barnes (ed.) *The Coastline,* John Wiley, Chichester.

Willis, K.G. & J.F. Benson 1988a: A Comparison of User Benefits and Costs of Nature Conservation at Three Nature Reserves, *Regional Studies, 22,* pp. 417–28.

Willis, K.G. & J.F. Benson 1988b: *Values of User Benefits of Forest Recreation: Some Further Site Surveys.* Report to the Forestry Commission, Dept. of Town and Country Planning, University of Newcastle, Newcastle.

Willis, K.G. & G.D. Garrod 1990: Valuing Open Access Recreation on Inland Water-ways. *Countryside Change Working Paper, 12,* University of Newcastle, New-castle.

Willis, K.G. & G.D. Garrod 1991a: An Individual Travel Cost Method of Evaluating Forest Recreation, *Journal of Agricultural Economics, 42,* pp. 33–42.

Willis, K.G. & G.D. Garrod 1991b: Landscape Values: A Contingent Valuation Appro-ach and Case Study of the Yorkshire Dales National Park, *Countryside Change Working Paper, 21,* University of Newcastle, Newcastle.

Willis, K.G. et al. 1990: The Value of Canals as a Public Good: The Case of the Mont-gomery and Lancaster Canals. *Countryside Change Working Paper, 5,* Country-side Change Unit, University of Newcastle, Newcastle.

World Commission on Environment and Development 1987: *Our Common Future.* Oxford University Press, Oxford, 383p.

Chapter 9

An assessment of contingent valuation surveys

RUUD HOEVENAGEL

9.1 Introduction

Methods that value environmental change have received much attention from environmental economists. The contingent valuation (CV) method is considered to be one of the most promising (e.g. OECD 1989). The CV method is a survey-based valuation method. It puts a price on environmental change by asking people directly, in mail surveys, in-person surveys, telephone surveys or experimental studies, for their monetary preference for the change in question. The two principal questions of the CV method are:

1. What is the *maximum* sum of money you would be willing to pay (WTP) each month/year to obtain the environmental improvement?
2. What is the *minimum* sum of money you would be willing to accept (WTA) each month/year to accept the environmental deterioration?

Both questions are necessary for establishing a contingent market for environmental change: a constructed market in which respondents, just as in ordinary markets, are able to buy (WTP) and sell (WTA) environmental change.

The above-stated simplicity of the CV method rests on the microeconomic paradigm that people can give "articulated values" for all kinds of environmental change (Fischoff 1991). In other words, it is assumed that people have true hidden preferences for environmental changes and that they are capable of transforming them into monetary units.

The CV method takes its name from the dependency of the stated WTP amounts upon the information presented in the questionnaire. This dependency includes the contents of the information as well as the context in which the information is presented. Such a dependency is essential, as "a policy evaluation tool with results invariant to important changes in these conditions would (...) be misleading and uninformative" (Randall 1986, p. 120).

The first CV survey was carried out in 1961 when Robert Davis interviewed 121 hunters and recreationists to estimate the benefits of outdoor recreation in the Maine woods, USA. (Davis 1963). Since then, the method has been frequently applied in the USA. Particularly after the introduction of Reagan's Executive Order 12291 (February 1981), requiring a Cost-Benefit Analysis for all significant federal actions, there has been a significant increase in CV surveys (for an overview see Mitchell and Carson 1989). It seems that the CV method is regarded as an accepted device to assist the U.S. environmental policy.

In Europe, the CV method has been less frequently applied. Whereas the abscence of a legal obligation to apply a monetary evaluation of environmental policies seems to be the primary reason, it is also true that European policy-makers are sceptical with regard to the validity of the CV method (see also chapter 13).

The aim of this chapter is to assess the CV method. This assessment is based on a review of the literature and our experience through working with the method. Section 2 will start with an examination of the three basic elements of the CV questionnaire; these elements create a highly structured market to confront the respondents with a well-defined situation. Section 3 will deal with the potenntial advantages and disadvantages of the method; the pros and cons will be briefly compared with the ones of other valuation methods. Section 4 will go into the most important potential biases of the method. Section 5 will extend section 4 by summarizing the recommendations that have been formulated in the literature to obtain more valid CV results. Finally, section 6 will present the conclusions.

9.2 The CV questionnaire

9.2.1 A SATISFACTORY TRANSACTION

Compared to valuation methods that are based on observed behaviourial data, fewer assumptions have to be made with regard to the CV method in order to arrive at a correct monetary estimation of environmental change. However, when assumptions are fewer, data requirements are greater (Young & Allen 1986). As the CV questionnaire is the principal device to respond to these requirements, formulating a good questionnaire is crucial.

From a social-psychological viewpoint, CV questionnaires should be formulated in such a way that a "satisfactory transaction" will be established (Fischoff & Furby 1988). A satisfactory contingent transaction will result in valid WTP amounts that can be used in Cost-Benefit Analyses to test for potential Pareto-improvements i.e. the economic goal of the CV method. A satisfactory transaction is defined as a transaction in which individuals are fully informed, uncoerced and able to identify their own best interests. Such a transaction will only take place if the environmental change, the method of payment and the contingent market are well understood by the respondents. As a result, any CV questionnaire should consist of three elements:

1. A description of the environmental change;
2. A description of the method of payment;
3. A description of the contingent market.

In addition, it is recommended that a fourth element be included in the questionnaire: an element consisting of questions related to respondents' attitudes towards the environmental change in question and towards paying for that change, and questions related to respondents' characteristics, such as age, income and education; questions which are useful for providing an internal check of the stated amounts. Sections 9.2.2 through to 9.2.4 will elaborate the above-mentioned three basic elements of the CV questionnaire.

9.2.2 A DESCRIPTION OF THE ENVIRONMENTAL CHANGE

Two steps can be distinguished in defining an environmental change. In the first step all valuable attributes of the change should be identified, a step Fischoff and Furby (1988) called the *substantive definition* of the environmental change. In the second step the location of these attributes should be specified, the so-called *formal definition.*

If researchers have been able to identify all the valuable attributes of the change in question there are three ways to describe them. First, by pointing out each attribute to ensure the respondent's attention. Second, by describing only the "overall" change without referring to its valuable attributes. Third, by describing only the most important or familiar attributes of the change of interest. The first alternative should be followed if unfamiliar environmental change is involved; this option seems most suitable for in-person surveys. The second alternative can only be used if familiar environmental change is involved. However, if this option is followed, researchers have to rely on the identification of the same attributes by all respondents. The third option should be avoided if possible, because mentioning more or other valuable attributes may affect the stated amounts: on the one hand, because simply referring to an attribute increases its importance (Van der Pligt et al. 1987); on the other hand, because people when asked to make some judgement seem to use an heuristic: "what is out of sight is out of mind" (Tversky & Kahneman, 1973). In spite of this, owing to time and money constraints, the third option is generally the option that is followed.

Next to describing the valuable attributes, the context of the environmental change (for example, it matters whether dirty air will be reduced in an industrial landscape or in a park) and the source of the environmental change should also be mentioned if it is likely that they affect the value of the change.

The formal definition of the environmental change involves describing the reference and target level of each valuable attribute. The "overall" reference level of the change of interest corresponds to the state of the world if the contingent transaction is not successful; the "overall" target level to the state of the world if the contingent transaction is successful. Besides describing these levels, the extent of the environmental change, the period in which the environmental change takes place and the certainty that the change takes place should be also mentioned if it is likely that they affect the value of the change.

9.2.3 A DESCRIPTION OF THE METHOD OF PAYMENT

Again two steps can be distinguished in defining the method of payment. First, identifying its valuable attributes, and second, specifying the location of each attribute.

Measuring the value of environmental change means observing all possible transactions involving it, including *money, time, effort* and *discomfort* (Fischoff & Furby 1988). As the CV method asks people for their monetary preferences, the attribute of the method of payment is money. From an economic point of view such a restriction to money is necessary. However, it carries with it the possibility of underestimating the value of an environmental change, if time, effort and discomfort are important substitues. For example, a typical motivation of many respondents stating low WTP amounts is that they already "*do* enough to improve the environment".

Describing the payment vehicle (e.g. taxes) is also part of the substantive definition. In several CV surveys it has been found that the payment vehicle used affects the stated WTP amounts. This effect was not expected and subsequently called payment vehicle *bias*. Nowadays, however, it is argued that the payment vehicle has a value of its own, beyond its ability to obtain the environmental change of interest. Hence, the decision which payment vehicle to use has become a pragmatic one: choose the vehicle that best fits the change in question, and/or the one that will be used if the change is actually implemented.

The first step in the formal definition of the method of payment is related to its reference and target level. The reference level is equivalent to the respondent's current disposable income. Hence, it should be made clear in the questionnaire that respondents are not allowed to include in their reference level taxes they are currently paying for the environmental change in question, or (reallocate) taxes they are paying for other public goods. The target level is the *maximum* WTP amount or the *minimum* WTA amount. Both extremes stem from neoclassical microeconomic theory. The next step is defining the valuation measure that will be used: WTP or WTA amounts. Since many studies have shown large differences between respondents' WTP and WTA amounts, it matters which measure is chosen. this also creates a problem restricting the scope of the CV method to measure of WTP in problems that have a purchase structure reduces its applicability. The certainty of paying is also an element of the formal definition, as the stated amounts will be proportionate to the perception of the obligation to make payment. Hence, the CV questionnaire must convince respondents that they certainly will have to pay for the change. Finally, it should be made clear how often respondents will have to pay, and when they start paying.

9.2.4 A DESCRIPTION OF THE CONTINGENT MARKET

All monetary transactions occur in a social context. The social context in which contingent transactions take place is the contingent market. As this market is unfamiliar to respondents, several aspects should be defined.

First, it should be made clear which organisation will provide for the environmental change if it is likely that this organisation affects the stated WTP amounts. Second, it should be made clear who else will have to pay for the environmental change. Sometimes this commitment is embodied in the change of interest. For example, with regard to national environmental improvements, it is obvious that everyone will have to pay. Defining who else will have to pay is one thing, convincing respondents these others will actually pay is another. Here lies one of the problems in valuing international environmental change. Third, the rule that determines whether the contingent transaction will be completed should be described. Related to this is the question of what respondents will have to pay if the transaction is completed. There are several possibilities, such as paying an (equal) share of the costs, paying the stated amount, etc. By changing these payment obligations, it becomes possible to assess whether strategic bias is a problem (Bohm 1972). This bias stems from strategic (free-riding) behaviour and may result in respondents expressing lower WTP amounts than their true WTP amount, hoping others will pay enough to secure the environmental change.

Finally, the things that are at stake beyond the contingent transaction of interest should be described if it is likely that they affect the stated WTP amounts. For example, if the environmental change in question affects the prices of other goods and services, they should be presented to the respondents. Another aspect is related to the fact that in contingent transactions non-user values, such as existence values, can play a major role. For example, many people donate money to preserve endangered species even though they never expect to see them. As these values are usually not encountered on ordinary markets, it is recommended that they be mentioned in the CV questionnaire. A third aspect that goes beyond the contingent transaction of interest is the fact that using the CV method means that the "market of commodities" will be enlarged. Respondents seem to forget this implicit extension. Therefore, it should be made clear to respondents that, in principle, they could also be asked for their WTP amount for other environmental changes, and to take these other changes into account when stating their WTP for the environmental change in question.

9.3 Advantages and disadvantages of the CV method

9.3.1 INTRODUCTION

Table 9.1 presents the pros and cons of the CV method. The advantages might explain why the interest in the method has increased so rapidly. The disadvantages incorporate the potential biases surrounding the CV method and are directly related to its validity. Section 9.3.2 will elaborate the four advantages of the method; section 9.3.3 will go into the three disadvantages.

Table 9.1 Advantages and disadvantages of the CV method

Advantages	Disadvantages
1. Many environmental changes can be valued.	1. The CV method is based on respondents' intentions to pay.
2. The WTP amount can include non-user values.	2. The CV method depends on the "art of asking questions".
3. The CV method is independent of an existing data-set.	3. The CV method asks respondents to perform an unfamiliar budget decision.
4. The CB method can give a correct monetary estimation of (ex ante) environmental change.	

9.3.2 ADVANTAGES OF THE CV METHOD

The two most important advantages of the CV method are its wider scope and the possibility of measuring non-user values. Many environmental changes can only be valued by means of the CV method, such as the preservation of unique natural areas or the protection of endangered species. This domain includes environmental changes "where markets suitable for] hedonic price or travel cost analyses [do not exist; the policy options under consideration lie outside the range of available amenity data, or past market transaction fail to reflect current information regarding environmental quality" (Hoehn & Randall 1987, p.227).

The CV method is the only method that can measure non-user values directly. These values are important in many fields of environmental regulation. For some environmental changes, such as the preservation of good visibility in the Grand Canyon National Park, they accounted for the major part of the measured benefits (Rahmatian 1987). The CV method is independent of an existing data-set. Contrary to valuation methods that are based on market behavioural data, the CV method creates its own data-set. This carries with it the possibility that specific validity and reliability checks can be built in. Methods based on market behaviourial data, must assume that the microeconomic theory is correct in order to generate results (Pearce & Turner 1991). Finally, under optimal (microeconomic) conditions, the WTP amounts revealed by the CV method will correspond to the correct Hicksian ex ante "compensating" or "equivalent variation". In contrast to this, other methods can only estimate the incorrect Marshallian ex post expected consumer surplus.

9.3.3 DISADVANTAGES OF THE CV METHOD

The stated WTP amounts are intentions to pay. Generally, opponents put forward this hypothetical characteristic of valuation as an argument against the CV method. As the CV method cannot measure what respondents will actually pay, it is hard to refute this argument. However, conditions can be found that predic a close correlation between people's stated amounts and actual payments. Three such conditions, stemming from the attitude-behaviour "theory of reasoned action" of Fishbein and Ajzen (1975), are:

1. The time between stating a WTP amount and the moment of paying should not be too long.
2. Paying for the environmental change should have a voluntary character.
3. The stated WTP amounts and the actual payments should be measured at identical levels of specificity; i.e. the so called "target", "action", "context" and "time" elements of the final valuation question should correspond to the actual payment of interest.

Researchers should take account of these conditions when applying the method. Related to the first disadvantage is the question: "Will respondents state their true value?" In other words, the problem of strategic behaviour. Generally, it seems that this kind of behaviour will only occur if people realize its existence, are willing to use it, and succeed in doing so. Whereas many economists believe that people are willing to behave strategically when valuing public goods, Mitchell and Carson (1989) have argued that the chance of accomplishing this form of behaviour in CV surveys is low. Moreover, the little evidence found in CV surveys (cf. Milon 1989) questions whether respondents realize its existence.

The CV method depends on the "art of asking questions" (cf. Payne 1951), suggesting that the method can be "vulnerable to misuse" (Mitchell & Carson 1987, p. 32). After reviewing the elements that characterize the context of the valuation problem, Brown and Slovic (1988, p.29) stated "the evidence reviewed (...) indicates that seemingly minor contextual factors often significantly affect the assigned values". Moreover, merely changing the frame of a question, while keeping its factual contents, can affect the outcome (cf. Kahneman & Tversky 1984). All these aspects tend to be underestimated by researchers untrained in survey research techniques. On the other hand, there is not much scientific knowledge with regard to how questions should be asked, and information should be presented to ensure that respondents perceive them the way intended (Schuman & Kalton 1985). It is therefore strongly recommended to pretest each CV questionnaire.

The CV method asks respondents to perform an unfamiliar budget decision; most people have never directly stated a WTP amount for environmental change. It is therefore quite unlikely that respondents have some true (hidden) monetary preference for the environmental issues at stake. It seems more likely that people lack well-differentiated values for environmental change and that they derive the specific WTP amount from some basic value (cf. Fischoff, 1991). In other words, respondents' environmental monetary preferences are probably shaped during the course of the CV survey.

Although the microeconomic theory of the CV method is clear with regard to how people should arrive at their WTP amount (i.e. minimizing the expenditure function with the target level of the environmental change as an argument), to date, not much is known with regard to how people actually arrive at their WTP amount. In this respect, it is interesting to look at research findings from cognitive psychology because CV decision-making processes fall within this discipline. In summary, the following processes seem pertinent to the CV method:

– People's behaviour seems to be more consistent with mental processes, such as "suboptimizing" and "satisfying", than with utility maximizing (Schoemaker 1982).
– People seem to have a so-called "bounded rationality" when solving (complex) decision problems, and may resort to simplifications when dealing with them (Simon 1955).
– People, when making decisions under circumstances of uncertainty, seem to use rules of thumb, called heuristics, to reduce difficult mental tasks to simpler ones (Kahneman et al. 1982).
– People seem to make decisiions not with regard to the desirability of outcomes sor end-states as such – as assumed in microeconomic theory – but with regard to how these end-states relate to a reference point that is judged neutral (cf. Kahneman and Tversky, 1979).

(reference: Kahneman, D. and A. Tversky, 1979, Prospect theory: an analysis of decisions under risk. Econometrica, vol. 47, pp. 263–291.).

9.4 Potential CV biases

9.4.1 INTRODUCTION

Whereas the impact of many biases can be reduced by careful design, other biases involve serious threats to the validity of the CV method. It is these biases that will be examined here. (For a complete review of the potential CV biases, see Mitchell and Carson 1989).

Bias can be defined as an *(unexpected) systematic error* from the *true value*. If the stated amounts are unbiased, CV results will be valid. This does not mean there is some everlasting true value left after all CV biases have been eliminated. Contingent values are just as other values, in essence, situational, contextual and relative (Randall, 1988).

Whereas identifying CV biases is a straightforward thing to do, minimizing them is difficult because of the absence of a measurable "true value". Hence, if systematic differences are observed, the right measurement cannot be selected.

Research is necessary to determine whether potential CV biases result in a systematic error. If research shows that systematic questionnaire design changes are characterized by an unsystematic pattern, the bias (and validity) problem changes into a reliability problem. An example of such a transformation seems to be found in the concept of "hypothetical bias". The idea behind this bias is that the hypothetical nature of the CV method will result in respondents stating too high WTP amounts. Until now, however, research evidence related to hypothetical bias does not seem to support such a pattern. In comparison with cash transactions, the hypothetical stated WTP amounts are sometimes lower and sometimes higher.

Three groups of biases will be discussed here: reactive biases (section 9.4.2), anchoring biases (section 9.4.3) and amenity misspecification biases (section 9.4.4). They are the most problematic ones. This section will not pay attention to strategic bias. This bias seems only problematic under "conditions (which) are generally rare in CV studies" (Mitchell & Carson 1989, p.238).

9.4.2 REACTIVE BIASES

When respondents respond to attitude or opinion-related questions, they are aware that their attitudes are being evaluated. This knowledge may affect subjects' responses. For example, respondents may wish to appear socially responsible, ecologically aware, etc. In other words, they may react to the knowledge that their attitudes are being assessed – and consequently colour their responses. These responses have been labelled *reactive responses* by Campbell and Stanley (1963).

Recent developments have put the environment firmly on the public agenda. Media attention has been extensive, and public concern about environmental problems seems to be the norm not the exception. This poses a serious problem for the CV method. Recent research on respondents' attitudes towards environmental issues consistently reports positive attitudes towards these issues with limited behavioural consequences. We are all very concerned, have favourable attitudes towards these issues, but are less prepared to do something about them. Studies, including behavioural measures of energy use, waste-handling and consumer behaviour all show weak attitude-behaviour links. Attitudinal research thus shows a considerable discrepancy between attitudes and behaviour and this is partly caused by the factor of people giving socially desirable answers. It seems likely that such a discrepancy also applies to the CV method.

Whereas the standard solution to avoid reactive responses is to use an indirect attitudinal measure, it is difficult to apply these techniques to the CV method (cf. Hoevenagel & Van der Pligt 1991).

9.4.3 ANCHORING BIASES

There is ample evidence that respondents use the amounts mentioned in the CV questionnaire, such as the starting amount in bidding games or the range of amounts presented on the payment–card, when formulating their maximum WTP amount (see Cummings et al., 1986). The resulting biases are all expressions of the so-called "anchoring heuristic" (Tversky & Kahneman 1974). This (intuitive) rule of thumb is used when people have to make estimates in uncertain or new situations. In these circumstances, people seem to use an(y) initial value to yield the final answer.

Avoiding "anchoring" is difficult as "there is no magic way of preventing respondents from latching onto such weak hints (...) when they have no better way of answering it" (Kahneman 1986, p.193). The only way to avoid anchoring is to present no value clues at all in the questionnaire. This can be done by asking respondents directly for their WTP amount. However, answering such a direct WTP question seems difficult, as it results in an unacceptably large number of non-responses and protest responses (see Desvouges et al., 1983).

Anchoring thus shows one of the basic problems of the CV method. On the one hand, respondents need some assistance when formulating their maximum WTP amount. A bidding game is very useful in this regard because a series of valuation questions will help people to form their attitudes towards paying for the environmental change in question. On the other hand, respondents will use the amounts presented in the CV questionnaire to derive this (biased) WTP amount.

The anchoring heuristic suggests that the more experience respondents have in valuing environmental change, the less anchoring biases will be a problem. Therefore, in order to reduce anchoring, respondents should be allowed to have obtained some experience in valuing environmental change. The second best strategy is to estimate the extent of anchoring. This can be done by using different payment cards or different starting points in bidding games.

9.4.4 Amenity misspecification biases

Mitchell and Carson (1989) distinguish between four amenity misspecification biases: first, symbolic bias; i.e. people (intuitively) react to the more symbolic meaning of an environmental change rather than to the description given in the questionnaire, second, part-whole bias; i.e. people (intuitively) value a more comprehensive environmental change rather than the one described, third, metric bias; i.e. people value (different levels of) the environmental change according to a different metric than the one intended, and fourth, probability of provision bias; i.e. epople perceive a different probability that the environmental good will be provided. Of these biases, the two first-mentioned are the most important.

Both symbolic and part-whole bias are related to the so-called «embedding effect»: the same environmental change is assigned a lower value if the willingness to pay for it is inferred from the willingness to pay for a more inclusive good rather than if the environmental change is valued on its own (cf. Kahneman and Knetsch, 1992). By the same token, these biases are synonymous for respondents stating corresponding amounts for related environmental changes located at different levels of aggregation.

Symbolic and part-whole bias lie at the bottom of a fundamental criticism of the CV method, viz.: "If respondents value many environmental change separately, they end up willing to pay a "total" WTP amount excceding their incomes!" Although this criticism touches upon a tender string of many CV researchers it has not yet been refuted sufficiently.

Two explanations that have been put forward to account for symbolic and part-whole bias are (cf. Hoevenagel, 1991):

in general, people do not have experience in valuing environmental changes directly. As a result, they will lack an "environmentally valuation context" against which they can place the WTP amounts required.

-in general, people tend to ignore information not explicitly mentioned in the questionnaire. Both causal judgment and frequency estimations are clearly affected by the way a problem is presented. "Out of sight, out of mind" offers a reasonable description of respondents' behaviour in these tasks. If we apply this to the CV method, one would expect a tendency to overestimate the value of the change being presented in the questionnaire.

One strategy to reduce these biases is to design the questionnaire in such a way that the respondents' attention is focused on the environmental change of interest within a context that includes the more general class of which that change is an element (see chapter 10 for an empirical application of this approach).

9.5 Recommendations

This section presents an overview of the recommendations that have been developed in the literature to obtain more valid CV results. Some of these recommendations stem from the "State of the Arts" conference held in 1984 (Cummings et al., 1986). However, as these recommendations were based on comparative studies of the CV method and valuation methods based on market behavioural data (i.e. Travel Cost and Hedonic Price methods), they are only effective for the domain of environmental change in which non-user values are excluded. As a result, researchers endeavoured to develop recommendations that could also be used for environmental change where non-user values play an important role. Below, eighteen recommendations are divided into four separate groups.

1. Recommendations related to the environmental change

1.1 Environmental change which is familiar to respondents should be valued (Cummings et al., 1986).

1.2 Environmental change should be valued with which respondents have had prior valuation and choice experience (Cummings et al., 1986).

1.3 Environmental change should be valued where the amounts obtained are related to user values (Kahneman, 1986).

1.4 Environmental change should not be valued that is a highly politically charged policy issue (Freeman, 1986).

1.5 Environmental change should not be valued where the polluter can easily be pointed out.

2. Recommendations related to the survey

2.1 Respondents should be allowed to have obtained some experience in valuing environmental change before they have to value the change of interest.

2.2 In-person surveys are preferred for obtaining contingent valuations. (Mail and telephone surveys should only be used for very familiar environmental change.)

2.3 Each CV questionnaire should be pretested.

2.4 Highly experienced interviewers and a "neutral" survey organization should be used.

3. Recommendations related to the CV scenario

3.1 There should be little uncertainty in the CV scenario (Cummings et al. 1986)

3.2 WTP amounts should be asked (Cummings et al., 1986).

3.3 The CV scenario should be meaningful, realistic and plausible to the respondents (Mitchell & Carson, 1987).

3.4 The "Fishbein and Ajzen" conditions for obtaining a close correspondence between intention to pay and actual payment should be satisfied (cf. Ajzen & Peterson, 1988).

3.5 The CV scenario should be designed in such a way that respondents feel free to abstain from the valuation process and to give zero bids (Mitchell & Carson, 1986).

3.6 The CV scenario should be designed in such a way that respondents focus their attention on the environmental change in question, within a context that includes the more general class of which that change is an element.

3.7 The CV scenario should be designed in such a way that respondents have the opportunity to revise their stated WTP amounts.

4. Recommendations related to the (presentation of the) results

4.1 With regard to the presentation of the results, researchers should justify why certain outliers were deleted, why strategic bias was not a problem in their survey, and present the questionnaire used in the survey (Mitchell & Carson, 1989).

4.2 As CV results are contingent on the contents of the CV questionnaire as well as on the context in which the valuation decision took place, they cannot be interpretatively transferred.

Until now, it has not been possible to give an accurate indication of the divergence between CV surveys meeting all the recommendations presented above and CV surveys that do not. The most one can say is that the first type of survey is more likely to result in valid CV results.

9.6 Conclusions

Contingent transactions are novel monetary transactions. In general, the more novel a transaction, the more details that must be explained, and the more difficult it will be to ensure that those details are understood. Establishing a *satisfactory CV transaction* can therefore be regarded as a major challenge of the CV method. In-person surveys should be used in responding to this challenge, as these surveys make it possible to include more "satisfactory criteria" without making the CV questionnaire too difficult.

Substantial evidence exists that respondents' stated WTP amounts can be biased, indicating that CV transaction are complex phenomena and that CV surveys can yield misleading results. The biases that involve the most serious threats to the validity of the method are reactive biases, anchoring biases and amenity misspecification biases. With regard to reactive biases, the principal problem is the extent to which the stated WTP amounts correspond to socially desirable answers. Both anchoring and amenity misspecification biases ensue from cognitive limitations and an unfamiliarity with valuing environmental change. These biases are difficult to control.

The overview of recommendations shows that an appropriate use of the CV method seems to be restricted to a part of the environmental change the CV method, in principle, can value. It also shows that in order to perform a CV survey correctly much underlying research has to be done, such as pretesting the questionnaire or "training" the respondents in stating contingent valuations. These aspects will have consequences for the popularity of the CV method as more underlying research requires more time and money.

Nevertheless, compared with other valuation methods, the CV method has several important advantages. For example, in most circumstances it is the only method available. This will guarantee further research into the method. Further research is necessary to overcome its major advantages. With regard to these weaknesses it seems that assistance from other social sciences is a prerequisite for placing the method on a higher "validity level".

In a recent paper, Mitchell and Carson used the concept of a learning curve to evaluate the CV method. According to Mitchell and Carson (1987:2–3) the "learning curve for new methodologies" consists of four stages:

> The first stage ... is its invention and initial application. If the method appears plausible and researchers begin to use it, the second or prototype stage is reached. During this stage basic knowledge is acquired about the method's properties, possibilities and limitations. ... Once the method's basic feasibility and validity is established, attention turns to learning how it can be implemented in a routine fashion to obtain information useful to policy makers. Stage three, the early implementation (or production) stage, is characterized by a reduced, but still fairly steep slope to the learning curve as information is acquired about problems in applying the method under different circumstances. ... During this stage learning focuses on how systematically to implement the method in such a way that the quality and cost of its output are acceptable. If the overall results are satisfactory (as judged by peers, journal editors, review panels, and policy analyst consumers), the method may reach stage IV on the learning curve. At this stage the method is regarded as being relatively well understood so attention is directed at making it more cost efficient. During this stage the learning curve gradually flattens until it reaches a plateau.

Mitchell and Carson (1987) concluded their assessment by placing the method near the beginning of Stage III of the learning curve. As we question the presumed establishment of the method's basic feasibility and validity (the end of stage II), we are not as optimistic as Mitchell and Carson. We are more prone to place the CV method in the middle of stage II. We base this position on the many lacunae in our knowledge of people's behaviour when valuing environmental change and on the fact that the three most important biases stem from factors which are difficult to control: (I) human cognitive limitations; (II) an unfamiliarity with stating WTP amounts for environmental change; (III) a tendency to give socially desirable answers.

References

Ajzen, I. & G.L. Peterson 1988: Contingent value measurement: the price of everything and the value of nothing? In G.L. Peterson, B.L. Driver & R. Gregory (eds.) *Amenity resource valuation: integrating economics with other disciplines.* Venture Publishing Inc., State College PA, USA, 260p.

Bohm, P. 1972: Estimating demand for public goods: an experiment. *European Economic Review 3,* 111–130.

Brown, T.C. & P. Slovic 1988: Effects of context on economic measures of value. In G.L. Peterson, B.L. Driver & R. Gregory (eds.) *Amenity resource valuation: integrating economics with other disciplines.* Venture Publishing Inc., State College PA, USA, 260 p.

Campbell, D.T. & J.C. Stanley 1963: Experimental and quasi-experimental designs for research on teaching. In N.L. Gage (ed.) *Handbook of research on teaching.* Chicago, Rand McNally, USA.

Cummings, R.G., Brookshire, D.S. & W.D. Schulze 1986: *Valuing Environmental Goods: A State of the Arts Assessment of the Contingent Valuation Method.* Rowman & Allanheld, Totowa NJ, USA, 270 p.

Davis, R.K. 1963: The value of outdoor recreation: an economic study of the Maine woods. Ph.D. dissertation, Harvard University, USA.

Desvouges, W.H., Smith, V.K. & M.P. McGivney 1983: *A comparison of alternative approaches for estimating recreation and related benefits of water quality improvements.* Office of Policy Analysis, U.S. Environmental Protection Agency, Washington DC, USA.

Fischoff, B. 1991: Value elicitation: is there anything in there? Mimeograph. Department of Social and Decision Sciences, Carnegie Mellon University, Pittsburgh, USA 41 p.

Fischoff, B. & L. Furby 1988: Measuring values: a conceptual framework for interpreting transactions with special reference to contingent valuation of visibility. *Journal of Risk and Uncertainty 1,* 147–184.

Fishbein, M. & I. Ajzen 1975: *Belief, Attitude, Intention and Behaviour: An Introduction to Theory and Research,* Addison-Wesley, Reading Mass, USA, 571 p.

Freeman, A.M. 1986: On assessing the state of the arts of the contingent valuation method of valuing environmental goods. In R.G. Cummings, D.S. Brookshire & W.D. Schulze (eds.) *Valuing Environmental Goods.* Rowman & Allanheld, Totowa NJ, USA, 270 p.

Hoehn, J.P. & A. Randall 1987: A satisfactory benefit cost indicator from contingent valuation. *Journal of Environmental Economics and Management 14,* 226–247.

Hoevenagel, R. 1991: A contingent valuation (CV) experiment to test "part-whole bias". Paper presented at the annual meeting of the European Association of Environmental and Resource Economists, Stockholm.

Hoevenagel, R. & J. van der Pligt 1991: Contingent valuation applications: Willingness, intentions but what about behaviour? Paper presented at EAERE annual meeting, June 10–14 Stockholm, Sweden, 21 p.

Kahneman, D. and J.L. Knetsch. 1992: Valuing public goods: the purchase of moral satisfaction. Journal of Environmental Economics and Management, vol. 22, pp. 57–70.

Kahneman, D. 1986: Comments. In R. G. Cummings, D.S. Brookshire & W.D. Schulze (eds.) *Valuing Environmental Goods.* Rowman & Allanheld, Totowa NJ, USA, 270 p.

Kahneman, D. & A. Tversky 1984: Choices, values, and frames. *American Psychologist 39,* 341–350.

Kahneman, D., Slovic, P. & A. Tversky 1982: *Judgement under uncertainty: heuristics and biases,* Cambridge University Press, New York, USA, 555 p.

Milon, J.W. 1989: Contingent valuation experiments for strategic behaviour. *Journal of Environmental Economics and Management 16,* 293–308.

Mitchell, R.C. & R.T. Carson 1986: Some comments on the State of the Arts report. In R.G. Cummings, D.S. Brookshire & W.D. Schulze (eds.) *Valuing Environmental Goods.* Rowman & Allanheld, Totowa NJ, USA, 270 p.

Mitchell, R.C. & R.T. Carson, 1987: *Evaluating the validity of contingent valuation studies.* Discussion paper QE-87-06, Resources for the Future, Washington, D.C.

Mitchell, R.C. & R.T. Carson, 1989: *Using Surveys to Value Public Goods: The Contingent Valuation Method.* Resources for the Future, Washington DC, USA, 463 p.

OECD, 1989: *Environmental policy benefits: monetary valuation.* Paris, 83 p.

Payne, S.L. 1951: *The art of asking questions.* Princeton Univ. Press, Princeton, USA, 249 p.

Pearce, D.W. & K. Turner, 1991: The use of benefit estimates in environmental decision-making. Draft final report, OECD, Paris, 61 p.

Pligt van der J., Eiser, J.R. & R. Spears 1987: Comparative judgements and preferences: The influence of the number of response alternatives. *British Journal of Social Psychology, 26,* 269–280.

Rahmatian, M. 1987: Component Value Analysis: Air Quality in the Grand Canyon National Park. *Journal of Environmental Management 24,* 217–223.

Randall, A. 1986: The possibility of satisfactory benefit estimation with contingent markets. In R.G. Cummings, D.S. Brookshire & W.D. Schulze (eds.). *Valuing Environmental Goods.* Rowman & Allanheld, Totowa, NJ, USA, 270 p.

Randall, A. 1988: Total and Nonuse Values. In J.B. Braden & C.D.Kolstad (eds.) *Measuring the Demand for Environmental Quality.* Elsevier Science Publishers, Amsterdam, The Netherlands, 370 p.

Schoemaker, P.J.H. 1982: The expected utility model: its variants, purpose, evidence and limitations. *Journal of Economic Literature, 20,* 529–563.

Schuman, H. & G. Kalton, 1985: Survey Methods. In G. Lindzey & E. Aronson (eds.) *Handbook of Social Psychology, Volume I.* Random House, New York, USA.

Simon, H.A. 1955: A behavioral model of rational choice. *Quarterly Journal of Economics, 69,* 174–183.

Thaler, R. 1986: Mental accounting and consumer choice. Marketing Science 4, 199–214.

Tversky, A. & D. Kahneman 1973: Availability: A heuristic for judging frequency and probability. *Cognitive Psychology 5,* 207–232.

Tversky, A. & D. Kahneman 1974: Judgement under uncertainty: heuristics and biases. Science, 185. 1124–1131.

Young, T. & P.G. Allen 1986: Methods for valuing countryside amenity: An overview. *Journal of Agricultural Economics 37,* 349–364.

Chapter 10

Valuation of reduced water pollution using the Contingent Valuation Method – testing for mental accounts and amenity misspecification

KRISTIN MAGNUSSEN

10.1 Introduction

Public goods and services, environmental goods included, are not traded in competitive markets, and hence they command no market price. Yet, we need benefit estimates for these goods in order to be able to do benefit cost assessments related to environmental issues. To measure the economic value of such commodities, non-market valuation techniques must be used. One of these techniques is the Contingent Valuation Method, CVM. The CVM attempts to induce survey respondents into revealing their valuation of a hypothetical change in the provision of some non-market good via a contingent market. The respondent is given a description of the commodity to be valued, the current level of provision and the proposed change in that level. The payment mechanism by which the posited change is to be funded is also presented. The respondent is then asked to carefully consider the proposed change and state his or her maximum willingness to pay (WTP) for, or minimum willingness to accept (WTA) compensation to forgo, the change. From the elicited values, consumer's surplus associated with the change can be derived. For an overview of the method, see Mitchell and Carson (1989).

The traditional approach in CVM is to focus on a single commodity in each survey. If aggregate values are desired, one simply adds up the values obtained for each commodity or commodity piece. An issue of recent concern is the valuation of commodity package components. As noted by Hoevenagel (1990):

> one of the main criticisms with regard to the CVM, [is], viz.: When respondents value X different Contingent Valuation (CV) goods separately, they end up with giving a "total" WTP exceeding their income. This criticism touches upon a tender string of many CV practitioners, and to this day, has not been sufficiently refuted by them.

Strand and Taraldset (1991) when describing earlier and present emphasis on biases in CVM, also emphasize mental accounts (or part-whole bias) whereby individuals tend to focus too much of their total valuation of a large set of environmental goods on the particular object to be valued. Psychological studies suggest that the outcomes of human cognitive decision-making processes are sensitive to the context in which the problem is presented (Tversky & Kahneman 1981). To the degree that people tend to focus on the single commodity discussed in the survey, this may give biased results ("focusing effects").

Suppose that in response to a Contingent Valuation (CV) question we find the average WTP to be Norwegian kroner (NOK) 200 per year per household for an improvement in water quality in a specific river. The theory of mental accounts suggests that the CV instrument has revealed WTP for a greater entity than this, possibly WTP for a general improvement in environmental quality in a larger geographic area.

The aim of this chapter is:
1) to evaluate use of the CVM for assessing the value people place on reduced water pollution. Special emphasis will be on the existence of "mental accounts" and "amenity misspecification";
2) by empirical data estimate the value of reducing Norwegian nutrient leaching to the North Sea by 50 per cent (called the North Sea Plan, NSP).

We will first examine what is in the literature on the concepts "mental accounts" and "amenity misspecification" ("part-whole bias"), where both concepts seem to give explanations of why one can have "focusing effects" in CV studies. We will then derive testable hypotheses, and test them on data from a study of WTP for reducing by 50% Norwegian Nitrogen(N) and Phosphorus(P) leaching to the North Sea.

10.2 The theory of mental accounts and amenity misspecification

10.2.1 Mental accounts

Kahneman and Tversky (1984) and Thaler (1985) suggest that people tend to partition expenditures into "mental accounts". As an example, Tversky and Kahneman (1982) talk about an "entertainment account", wherein an expenditure level of X dollars is allocated to, for example, a dinner and a show. They have observed that pre-purchased tickets to a theatre are often not replaced when lost (in experimental markets) whereas loss of the cash earmarked for the purchase of the tickets is replaced. To explain this, they assert that separate mental accounts must exist for "cash" and for "entertainment". Kahneman and Tversky (1984:346) propose:

in order to evaluate a multi-attribute option, a person sets up a *mental account* that specifies the advantages and disadvantages associated with the option, relative to a multiattribute reference state (emphasis added).

They further suggest that people balance advantages and disadvantages associated with the option and compare this to the reference state. They divide between *minimal, topical* and *comprehensive* accounts. The minimal accounts include only the differences between the two options, whereas for the topical account the reference level is determined by the context within which the decision arises. A comprehensive account includes a context broader than the special situation where the option arises. Kahneman and Tversky suggest that people typically will use topical accounts in framing decisions. They find support for this in their experiments (Kahneman & Tversky 1984).

In earlier articles, Tversky and Kahneman (1981; 1982), use the concept "psychological account" for the concept of mental accounts. This notion describes what goes on when people have to decide about actions which will give rise to a compound output, which implies a series of changes in a single attribute. A psychological account is defined as "an outcome frame which specifies 1) the set of elementary outcomes that are evaluated jointly and the manner in which they are combined, and 2) a reference outcome that is considered neutral or normal" (Tversky & Kahneman 1981:456).

They propose that people tend generally to evaluate acts in terms of minimal accounts which include only the direct consequences of the act, because this simplifies evaluation. There are situations, however, where the choice situation may be evaluated in terms of a more inclusive account.

They further induce that the topical organization of mental accounts leads people to evaluate losses and gains in relative rather than absolute terms, resulting in large variations in the rate at which money is exchanged for other things.

Thaler (1985) argues that the budget constraint that has the largest effect on behaviour is the current income flow rather than the present value of life time wealth. The budgeting process, either implicit or explicit, tends to occur on a month-to-month basis. Second, expenditures tend to be grouped in categories. Potential expenditures are considered within their category. The tendency to group purchases by category can violate the economic principle of global optimization. Given the existence of time and category specific budget constraints, the consumer evaluates purchases as situations arise. Formally, the decision process can be modelled by saying the consumer will buy a (market) good, x, at price p if

$$\frac{u\,(x,\,p,\,p^*)}{p} > K_{it} \qquad\qquad (10.1.)$$

where p^* is the reference price for a commodity, x. $u(x,\,p,\,p^*)$ is the total utility connected with a transaction, and K_{it} is a constant for category i in time period t.

Global optimization would lead all the K_{it} 's to be equal and the budget process described here would be irrelevant. According to Thaler, there is evidence that individuals do not act as if all the K's are equal. This brings up the issue of rational and irrational behaviour. This general topic will not be pursued further here. See Elster (1989) for a more general discussion on this topic.

Some authors have considered what Kahneman and Tversky's theory could mean for CV results. Walbert (1984) says that the existence of mental accounts could conceivably create an "aggregation bias". In searching for a payment by which to determine WTP for a specific public good, it is possible that a respondent may tap a "mental account" and use the same figure for several public goods. That is, if people use such environmental accounts to determine their WTP for a specific good, how can we obtain the value of a specific public good, such as reduced water pollution in a specific river or greater safety from a regulation controlling hazardous wastes? If this is not possible, then how do we interpret the bids obtained for an isolated commodity? This poses a problem for the interpretation of average bids obtained from CV studies, and for the aggregate valuation of public goods.

Walbert (op. cit.) cites Schulze et al. (1983), who raise some further questions in regard to this problem:

> ... What determines the composition of any one account – are accounts hedonic in nature – or perhaps functional?

... Are account lines more or less rigid, i.e. with but $ 10 in the entertainment account and faced with the desirable opportunity to attend a concert costing $ 20, may not the individual reallocate income *across* account lines, and, if so, what is the *meaning* of an account?" (Schulze et al. 1983, as cited in Walbert 1984).

These questions still remain to be answered.

Also Cummings, Brookshire and Schulze (1986) in their assessment of CVM note that if people think in terms of "mental accounts", this may have serious implications for the CV exercise. In deriving a value for a specific environmental good, the obtained value may in fact apply to some more aggregate commodity. That is, the CV measure may relate to something akin to an "environmental account", as opposed to the specific environmental good in the CV study.

Several studies report comparisons of values obtained by CVM when an environmental amenity was valued in isolation and within a broader policy package. Kahneman (1986) refers to a study where the "key observation" is that there is a class of problems in which people's answers to preference questions seem quite insensitive to the numbers that are mentioned in the survey. These results stem from a telephone study where different groups of respondents were asked to state their willingness to pay for maintaining fishing in some different regions of Ontario, Canada, and in all Ontario, respectively. Kahneman reports that the three groups gave "strikingly similar" demand functions. He interprets the results as indicating that people seem to be willing to pay about as much to clean up one region as another, and almost as much for any one region as for all Ontario. He also argues that people seem to answer such questions as if they had been asked "What do yo want to do about keeping fish in the lakes" and "How important is the issue to you?" The dollar number merely expresses the strength of the feeling that is aroused by these questions (Kahneman 1986:191). Kahneman calls this "symbolic demand" because the question elicits expressions about how high they value the actual amenity, and for symbolism, quantity is sometimes irrelevant.

Experiments demonstrate that when a commodity was valued in isolation the measures differed from the values for the same commodity valued within a context of other commodities. But to a certain extent they "should" differ, due to ordinary substitution and income effects.

10.2.2 AMENITY MISSPECIFICATION

The term "amenity misspecification" is first used in Mitchell and Carson (1989), and is a class of what they call "scenario misspecification". According to them, misspecification occurs when "the respondent incorrectly (from the standpoint of theory or policy) perceives one or more aspects of the contingent market and the good to be valued" (p. 246). Amenity misspecification is considered to be a problem because individuals tend not to have previously well-defined values for many of the goods valued in CV studies. Therefore, there is considerable potential for them to ignore some or all of the details in a scenario, or to distort them by unconscious use of judgemental heuristics ("rules of thumb"). The effect of these distortions may be to completely invalidate a contingent valuation study (Mitchell & Carson 1989:249). Referring to the classification of Mitchell and Carson, we can divide amenity misspecification into symbolic, part-whole, metric and probability of provision bias (table 10.1).

Table 10.1 Categories of amenity misspecification (Mitchell & Carson 1989).

1. Symbolic

2. Part-whole
   2.1 Geographical
   2.2 Benefit
   2.3 Policy Package

3. Metric
4. Probability of provision

Symbolic bias means that the respondent in his WTP/WTA statement does not value the particular amenity in question, but rather a symbol connected with that amenity. Part-whole biases may be classified as geographical part-whole, benefit part-whole or policy package part-whole. Geographical part-whole bias means that the respondent when asked, for example, to value water quality improvements in one river, is unable to separate that river's value from he value of the county's or country's rivers, and thus values a larger amenity than the one asked about. Benefit part-whole bias occurs when respondents are unable to differentiate between benefit subcomponents or between the subcomponents and the value for all types of benefits. When the respondent is asked to value an amenity which is only a part of a policy package, it is possible that the respondent may have difficulties in separating the amenity per se from the rest of the policy package and therefore again values a bigger amenity than the researcher is interested in.

Bergstrom and Stoll (1987) argue that the reliability of piecewise evaluation is sensitive to the manner by which component values are elicited. Because of limitations of the human cognitive decision-making process, the context of the bidding question itself may affect stated values for commodity package components.

They suggest that there are at least two procedures for eliciting total WTP for a change in an environmental policy component, q_1, by using CVM. One can use a 2-step bidding process, that is, the respondents state their WTP for the overall policy, q, in a first step and partition out their WTP for the change in q_1 in a second step. Alternatively, a 1-step process can be carried out, in which the respondents state their WTP for a change in q_1 directly.

Bergstrom and Stoll suggest that the 2-step approach makes it easier for the respondents to isolate their value for the package component, q_1. With the 1-step approach, respondents may have a difficult time isolating WTP for the one component because of the lack of reference to WTP for the overall change in the commodity package. The 2-step process on the other hand, requires respondents to calculate WTP for the overall change in q first. Thus they expect that the 2-step approach gives more accurate valuations of commodity package components. This was tested in a setting where the "package" (q) was a farmland protection program, which had four major components, one of which was protection of environmental amenities. A separate value was obtained for this component (q_1). They found that WTP for an overall change in the commodity package, q, was not significantly different from the stated WTP for the element q_1 when this was obtained in a 1-step approach. Bergstrom and Stoll (1987) argue that WTP for q_1 must be less than WTP for q unless the value associated with all other farmland protection components taken together is zero or negative.

They also suggest that a respondent's ability to value components may be sensitive to the exact manner by which component values are elicited. For example, the test described indicates that CV respondents provide component valuations more consistent with theoretical expectations when a 2-step bidding approach, rather than a 1-step approach, is used.

10.2.3 ARE MENTAL ACCOUNTS AND AMENITY MISSPECIFICATION SYNONYMOUS?

The "traditional" consumer theory and theory of value, require that subjects in CV experiments do consider income and other goods trade-offs in formulating their WTP. The economic theory of value assumes that individuals have perfect knowledge over all states of the world, alternative actions and post action states of the world, that is, the individual is aware of all possible goods/services (and their prices) that he might buy, as well as savings alternatives, his income, and his preferences regarding all combinations of purchased goods/services and savings. Based on such perfect knowledge, the individual selects purchases such that the ratios of marginal utilities to prices for all purchased commodities are equated (Deaton & Muellbauer 1980).

As described in sections 10.2.1 and 10.2.2, mental accounts bias and amenity misspecification bias both violate some microeconomic principles because money is not supposed to have labels attached to it (Thaler 1985), and people are supposed to be able to place values on each specific commodity. They thereby cause problems in interpreting CV results.

Mental accounts/amenity misspecification is treated in two recent European studies. In these two studies, the "mental account" notion is used as an explanation for "part-whole bias". According to Hoevenagel (1990):

> Part-whole bias is part of the so-called amenity misspecification biases ... A possible explanation for part-whole bias is found in the notion that people may think in terms of "mental accounts" when making budgetary decisions. When making allocative decisions, individuals seem to focus on groups of commodities instead of individual commodities.

Strand and Taraldset (1991) have also conducted a survey testing for these biases and ascribe some of the results to mental account bias.

I would argue that there is a difference between the concepts "mental accounts" and "amenity misspecification" ("part-whole bias"), at least theoretically. Mental accounts assume that people *do not have* values for particular goods and that money may have different labels for different groups of goods, and thereby question the usefulness of CVM at all. As explained by Hoevenagel (1990), mental accounts imply that rather than allocate NOK 200 to an environmental improvement for a local river basin, NOK 250 to an improvement in air quality and NOK 150 to obtain some lower noise level, an individual may allocate NOK 600 to something akin to an "environmental account". Decisions about allocation are then made as the need or opportunity for environmental improvements arise (i.e. when respondents *really* have to pay to the environmental improvement in question, which is never the case in CVM questionnaires).

On the other hand, amenity misspecification, as defined in Mitchell and Carson (1989), includes misspecification by the surveyor, misconception of the survey's meaning by the respondent and shortcomings in the respondents' decision making process, i.e. this is a communication problem.

This means that "amenity misspecification" is a broader concept than mental accounts. To a greater extent it assumes that people *do have* values for different commodities, but they may "confuse" these with a greater package and need "help" to get the value right. The surveyor's aim is to avoid confusion and misconceptions in a CV survey, but he cannot prevent respondents' lack of values for the good in question. Therefore, I think it will be wise to keep these two notions separate. But they are not mutually exclusive.

It can also be difficult to distinguish between some of the categories of "amenity misspecification" (see table 10.1), for example "part-whole bias" and "symbolic bias". I will, therefore, mainly use the concept "amenity misspecification". But one should note that some authors (for example Hoevenagel 1990 and Strand Taraldset 1991) have used "part-whole bias" as a synonym for "mental accounts". Since we do not make any attempt to say if the effects are due, for example, to geographic part-whole bias or symbolic bias, the concept "amenity misspecification" will be used.

10.3 Formal derivation of the concepts mental accounts and amenity misspecification

The theory of mental accounts is reminiscent of the theory of two-stage budgeting. We will take this theory as the point of departure to derive how the theory of mental accounts or amenity misspecification differ from "ordinary" consumer theory. But first, we will give a brief review of some aspects of the theories of separability of preferences and two-stage budgeting. The two following sections draw heavily on Deaton and Muellbauer (1980) who give a more detailed description of these theories.

Separability of preferences.

According to this theory, commodities can be partitioned into groups so that preferences within groups can be described independently of the quantities in other groups. This implies that we can have a subutility function for each group and that the values of each of these subutilities can be combined to give total utility. Suppose there are six (market) goods, x_1 and x_2 = food, x_3 and x_4 = housing and fuel, x_5 and x_6 = TV and watching sports. Then, if the separable groups, foods, shelter and entertainment are formed, the utility function, u, can be written:

$$u = v(x_1, x_2, x_3, x_4, x_5, x_6)$$
$$= f[v_f(x_1, x_2), v_s(x_3, x_4), v_e(x_5, x_6)],$$

(10.2.)

where $f()$ is some increasing function and v_f, v_s and v_e are the subutility functions associated with food, shelter and entertainment, respectively. There is no reason why each subutility function could not have one or more deeper subgroupings within it, nor should we rule out the possibility that some groups may contain only one good. If we put all this together, we get the utility tree: the individual commodities are the utmost twigs that join together to form branches that, in turn, join up to form the tree.

Two-stage budgeting.

This theory implies that the consumer can allocate total expenditure in two stages: at the first or higher stage, expenditure is allocated to broad groups of goods (food, shelter, entertainment), while at the second, or lower stage, group expenditures are allocated to the individual commodities. At each of these stages, information appropriate to that stage only is required.

At the first stage, allocation must be possible given knowledge of total expenditure and appropriately defined group prices. At the second stage, individual expenditures must be functions of groups expenditures and prices within the group only. Both of these allocations have to be perfect in the sense that the results of two-stage budgeting must be identical to what would occur if the allocation were made in one step with complete information.

One possibility of extension/modification of the basic theory of two-stage budgeting, is the requirement that the decision at each stage can be thought of as corresponding to a utility maximization problem of its own. For example, different foods would be chosen so as to maximize a food subutility function subject to a food budget constraint, while the fuel utility function would determine the allocation to fuel and so on. For this latter to work, we must be able to define appropriate price and quantity indices for the group so that the utility maximization procedure can be defined.

Two-stage budgeting involves both aggregation (to construct the broad groups) and separable decision making (for each of the group subproblems). The two ideas, separability of preferences and two-stage budgeting are intimately related to one another, but are not equivalent. Neither one implies the other. However, separability is both a necessary and sufficient condition for the second stage of two-stage budgeting.

If any subset of commodities appears only in a separable subutility function, the quantities purchased within the group can always be written as a function of group expenditure and prices within the group alone.

Maximization of utility in stage 2, must imply that v_f, v_s and v_e are each maximized subject to whatever is spent on food, shelter and entertainment. If this were not so, v_f, v_s and v_e could be increased without violating the budget constraint, so that, since f is increasing in its arguments, utility cannot be maximal. Hence, the expenditure on x_1 and x_2 with prices p_1 and p_2, is the outcome of maximizing $v_f (x_1, x_2)$ s.t. $p_1 x_1 + p_2 x_2 = y_f$, the total expenditure on food, so that:

$$x_i = g_{fi} (y_f, p_1, p_2); \quad i = 1,2 \qquad (10.3.)$$

for the Marshallian subgroup demands.

We are concerned with changes in an environmental commodity. The change consists of a change in a policy package, $q = (q_1, q_2, q_3)$ from an initial situation q^0 to an after policy level, q^1. Initial utility level is u and initial income is y. P_f, P_s, and P_q are pricevectors for the group of goods food, shelter and environment, respectively, and x_f and x_s are as defined above.

As the point of departure, we take the theory of two-stage budgeting. We have

$$u = v(x_1, x_2, x_3, x_4, q) = f[v_f (x_f), v_s (x_s), v_e (q)], \qquad (10.4.)$$

where $x_f = (x_1, x_2)$

$x_s = (x_3, x_4)$

$q = (q_1, q_2, q_3)$.

If the policy package is to be changed, the consumer's problem is:

Max $v(x_f, x_s, q)$ (10.5.)

s.t. $x_f P_f + x_s P_s + P_q q = y$

If only a policy component is to be changed, the consumer's problem is:

Max $v_e (q_1, q_2, q_3)$ (10.6.)

s.t. $\sum_{i=1}^3 P_i q_i = y_e$

where y_e is the total expenditure on "environmental goods" (found by solving the maximization problem in 10.5.) and P_1 denotes the price of good q_i (where i $= 1, 2, 3$).

This leads to the following Hicksian Compensating (HC) measures for the total policy package, q, and one element, q_i, respectively:

$\text{HC}_q (p, q^1, q^0, u) = y - e(p, q^1, u)$ (10.7.)

$\text{HC}_{qi}(p, q_i^1, q_i^0, u) = y_e - e(p, q_i^0, u_e)$ (10.8.)

If the theory of mental accounts is correct, it implies that the respondent confronted with the change that leads to the maximization problem 10.6. perceives this as the same problem as in 10.5. It follows that the two HC measures elicited in this case will be equal, whether the respondent is asked to value all q or only one element, q_i.

If we assume amenity misspecification, the respondents are believed to have some values/preference ordering for $q_1, q_2, \ldots q_K$, but confuse it with the larger entity, q. With some "help" they will be able to reveal their "correct" value for the element. It means that if we ask directly for (10.8.) we might get (10.7.), but with "help" (for instance by the 2-step valuation approach of Bergstrom and Stoll (1987)), the respondents will reveal their value for q_i.

The concepts of "mental accounts" and "amenity misspecification" are difficult to keep separate in practice. It will be difficult to separate biases due to people's shortcomings in decision making and the surveyor's mistakes in conducting the survey. We could distinguish between them by knowing that if mental accounts are present we would always get the same value whatever the commodity being valued, and irrespective of the number of steps. However, we would probably experience that people in a second stage will lower their WTP, and would not be able to tell whether this was due to their "true" value or was stated to "please" the surveyor. ("Since they ask me to give a separate value for q_i, I ought to have a particular value attached to it".) This implies that in practice we will hardly be able to tell what is "mental account bias" and what is "amenity misspecification" or "part-whole bias". However, to keep it straight, we will reserve the concept "mental accounts" only for situations where this is "true" in a strict theoretical way, i.e. people perceive the maximization problem in 10.6. as the same as that in 10.5. Otherwise, we will name it amenity misspecification.

10.4 Hypotheses to be tested

We want to look at the following questions:

1) Do people act in accordance with the theory of "mental accounts" or "amenity misspecification" in CV studies?
2) From what we have said above, the problem of interpreting CV results would probably be greater, the more inclusive potential mental accounts are. Therefore, we will test for mental accounts on several "levels".
3) Are the estimated values of policy elements influenced by what we consider to be the "total resource" or the "total policy package"?

By standard value theory, one can obtain a unique value measure for different policy elements, q_1, ...q_K, and for $q = (q_1, q_2, ... q_K)$. If the mental accounts hypothesis is correct, one would expect receiving the same WTP for q_1 as for q_2 as for q_K as for $q = (q_1, q_2, ..., q_K)$. For example, if a CV study reports an average WTP for reduced air pollution in a particular city to be NOK 200, this could actually represent the respondents' WTP for air pollution abatement in the whole country, or may be for general pollution abatement in the country. This obviously would make interpreting CV results difficult and would also cause problems for aggregating stated values. It should also be clear that the more "inclusive" the environmental accounts are, the larger the problems they could cause for interpreting CV results. The theory does not tell how inclusive they should be, although Kahneman and Tversky's (1984) suggestion that people tend to calculate in "minimal/topical accounts" to lessen the burden of desicion making is encouraging for CV studies.

  An often suggested solution to focusing effects is to design the CV scenario in such a way that attention is focused on the environmental commodity of interest within a context which includes the more general commodity class within which the commodity is a component. Two possible ways of doing this are decribed by Mitchell and Carson (1989:251–252):

> Among general strategies to minimize part-whole biases are inclusion of a description of the larger entity in the scenario, with a warning not to confuse the larger entity with the amenity changes being valued; and making the description of the good more salient by the use of such descriptive devices as maps. Another strategy which appears to be compatible with respondents' cognitive process, is to have them first value the total resource, even if this is not the subject of the study, and then have them allocate their total WTP amounts for the component of interest.

Two questions remain, however: what is the proper "total resource" and, does it matter what we consider to be the "total resource"? We would suppose that it is often not obvious what should be considered the proper "larger entity", and that this choice could influence the values obtained for the amenity in question.

In this survey we set out to estimate a value of a 50 % reduction in N and P leaching in a region, S. We would obtain the Hicksian Compensating measure using what Bergstrom and Stoll (1987) called a 1-step approach:

$$HC_S\,(q_S^0, q_S^1, u^0) = y - e(p, q_S^1, u^0). \tag{10.9.}$$

Since there are programs for improvement in several kinds of pollution, we might consider the program for pollution reduction as the proper "total resource" or policy package. In this case we would have to partition the holistic valuation (HC_P) into valuations of water pollution, air pollution, etc. This might be called a 2-step-approach. First, we would obtain:

$$HC_P\,(q_P^1, q_P^0, u^0) = y - e(p, q_P^1, u^0) \tag{10.10.}$$

Thereafter we would ask for WTP for the reduced leaching in region S, HC_S^P. Here subscript S denotes the commodity of interest and superscript P denotes the bigger commodity valued first, pollution reduction. Throughout, subscripts in HC connections denote the commodity valued, and superscripts denote the commodities valued in the first step. S = 50 % reduction in water pollution in region S, P = package of 4 pollution measures, E = package of 4 ennvironmental improvement measures. E is more inclusive than P, which is more inclusive than S.

If we think that the relevant policy package is environmental improvement, E, the Hicksian Compensating measure for the package is:

$$HC_E \ (q_E{}^1, q_E{}^0, u^0) \ = \ y - e(p, q_E{}^1, u^0) \qquad (10.11.)$$

In a second step we would obtain WTP for the pollution package, $HC_P{}^E$ (described above), and in a third step we would obtain $HC_S{}^E$.

If the theory of mental accounts is correct, we would expect receiving the same average WTP for water quality improvement in a region S as for the pollution abatement program, P, as for the environmental improvement program, E, when these are all revealed in a 1-step approach. At the most extreme, we would expect the following hypothesis, H_{01}, to be true:

$$H_{01} : HC_S \ = \ HC_P \ = \ HC_E$$

However, as discussed above, it could still cause problems if we have less inclusive mental accounts. Therefore we want to test if the stated WTP (using a 1-step approach) for any of the amenities listed above are equal. Formally, this can be expressed as:

$$H_{02} : HC_i \ = \ HC_j \text{ for } i \neq j, \text{ where } i \text{ and } j \ = \ S, P, E, LW.$$

If we find that $HC_i = HC_j$, but that HC_i obtained in a 2 – or 3-step approach is smaller than HC_i obtained in one step, it tells us that mental accounts in the "purest" form are not present, but that we may have some focusing effect.

$$H_{03a} : HC_S{}^P \ < \ HC_S$$

$$H_{03b} : HC_S{}^E \ < \ HC_S$$

$$H_{04} : HC_P{}^E \ < \ HC_P$$

Finally, we want to test whether the "size" of the policy package valued in the first step, influences the stated bids.

$$H_{05} : HC_S \ = \ HC_S{}^P \ = \ HC_S{}^E$$

If we find that these hypotheses do not hold, it means that the results in a CV study will depend on what we define as the "policy package". A listing of the hypotheses to be tested is given in table 10.2.

Table 10.2 A summary of the hypotheses to be tested. For definition of symbols, see table 10.3.

$H_{01} : HC_S = HC_P = HC_E$
$H_{02} : HC_i = HC_j$ for $i \neq j$, where i and j = S, P, E, LW.
$H_{03a} : HC_S^P < HC_S$ $H_{03b} : HC_S^E < HC_S$
$H_{04} : HC_P^E < HC_P$
$H_{05} : HC_S = HC_S^P = HC_S^E$
Alternative hypotheses: Not H_{0i}, where i = 1, 2, 3, 4, 5

10.5 Design of the survey

Norway and the other countries around the North Sea have agreed to reduce substantially nutrient leaching (Nitrogen and Phosphorus) to the North Sea. This survey was conducted to measure the social benefits of a 50% reduction in Norwegian nutrient leaching to the North Sea. The program to achieve this is called the North Sea Plan (NSP).

The survey was conducted in February 1991, by an opinion poll institute. 1228 persons randomly selected from all of Norway were interviewed in their homes. The selected sample appears to be representative with respect to age, sex and income. Five different questionnaires, each representing different subsamples, were used in the survey.

In the first subsample we used iterated discrete choice to reveal WTP, in addition to an open WTP question. This subsample was again divided into six subsamples, each consisting of 120–130 respondents. These subsamples differed only with respect to the bids in the discrete choice question. These answers will not be treated in this paper, but will be analyzed elsewhere.

The remaining respondents were divided into 4 subsamples, each consisting of about 120 respondents. In all of these subsamples we used a payment card to elicit WTP. The amounts on the card ranged from NOK 0-12 000 per year and also showed the corresponding monthly expenses for some of the annual amounts. A main question was the WTP for the North Sea Plan. The respondents were asked to state the maximum amount in NOK/year they would be willing to pay in *increased* sewage taxes to achieve the given improvements in water quality in the NSP area.

Table 10.3 Overview of WTP questions in different subsamples and definition of abbreviations used

SUB-SAMPLE	WTP QUESTIONS
1	1. Max WTP for NSP?; NSP-1-STEP; corresponds to HC_S 2. Max WTP for local water quality improvement (current pollution level class 3/4 or 2)?; LOCAL CL 3/4 and LOCAL CL 2
2	1. Max WTP for 4 pollution measures? (50 % reduction in air and water pollution, noise and littering in Norway); PACK-POLL-1-STEP; corresponds to HC_P 2. Max WTP for NSP?; NSP-2-STEP; corresponds to HC_S^P 3. Max WTP for LOCAL CL 3/4 and LOCAL CL 2
3	1. Max WTP for 4 environmental measures? – Reduction in global pollution causing climate changes and depleting the ozone layer, – Save threatened plant and animals in Norway, – Reduce Norwegian air-, water-, noise- and littering pollution by 50 % – Conservation of Norwegian nature and nature resources; PACK-ENV; corresponds to HC_E 2. Max WTP for PACK-POLL?; PACK-POLL-2-STEP; corresponds to HC_P^E 3. Max WTP for NSP?; NSP-3-STEP; corresponds to HC_S^E 4 Max WTP for LOCAL CL 3/4 and LOCAL CL 2?
4.	1. Max WTP for LOCAL CL 3/4 and LOCAL CL 2?; LOCAL CL 3/4-1-STEP and LOCAL CL 2-1-STEP; corresponds to $HC_{LW-3/4}$ and HC_{LW-2} 2. Max WTP for NSP?

The differences between the subsamples were that, in two of them, the respondents were asked to reveal their WTP for different packages of environmental goods prior to revealing their WTP for NSP. For an overview of the differences with respect to WTP questions in the subsamples, see table 10.3. Appendix 1 includes a translation of the WTP questions in subsample 3 and a short description of the other questions.

In subsample 1 (questionnaire Q_1), after some introductory questions about the problem, the first WTP question was for the North Sea Plan. Thereafter the respondents were asked to state which local water body they found most important to clean up, and their WTP for cleaning it up. In subsample 2, before the WTP question for the NSP, the respondents were asked to state their WTP for a package of 4 pollution abatement measures (PACK-POLL), which would reduce water pollution by 50%, reduce noise problems in cities and towns by 50%, reduce air pollution by 50% and reduce littering by 50%. After having stated their WTP for this package, they were asked to divide this sum into amounts for each part of the package. Thereafter, the questionnaire was similar to Q_1. In subsample 3, some more questions were added before Q_2. First, respondents were asked to rank 5 areas of society, of which environmental protection was one. Thereafter, they were asked to give WTP for a package of 4 environmental improvement measures (PACK-ENV), of which one was the reduction of air, water, noise and littering pollution by 50% (similar to PACK-POLL). After this, the questionnaire was similar to Q_2. Questionnaire 4 was similar to the one used in subsample 1 except that the WTP question for the "local" water water *body* was was given before WTP for the NSP. This change made it necessary to modify slightly the sequence of information and other questions asked, and this subsample is therefore not fully a part of the test, but will be used only to supplement the other results.

In addition to the WTP questions and the ordinary background questions, we included several questions related to the respondents' use of fresh and salt water in Norway. This section included questions about their priorities for water quality improvement in different rivers and sea-areas, which water quality factors they found most important, which activities, how many days, they spent by fresh water and the sea, and whether or not they would use fresh and salt water more if it was less polluted, etc.

This survey was conducted in order to find WTP for reduction of nutrient leaching (Nitrogen and Phosphorus) to the North Sea, not for "all kinds" of water pollution reduction. We pointed this out in the introduction to the questionnaire, where we described different water pollution problems and asked the respondents to give weights to what they thought should be given priority among nutrient leaching, acid rain and heavy metals.

It was also important that the NSP would reduce water pollution not only in the coastal area of the North Sea, but also in the watercourses in the area. This is quite a complex amenity to value, and it was a challenge to explain the benefits from the NSP in a proper manner. We chose to use coloured maps and cards. The respondents were shown a card (appendix 2) where water quality was divided into four classes (extremely polluted, markedly polluted, modestly polluted, not polluted), as is commonly done by the Norwegian Water Research Institute (NIVA). For each water quality class, which was symbolized by different colours, the card had illustrative colour-pictures, symbols for possible water usage (boatable, fishable, swimmable, drinkable) and short verbal descriptions of water quality. Then the respondents were shown one card with two maps of the North Sea Plan area (appendix 3). (They were still allowed to look at the card for water quality.) One map showed the current situation with respect to water quality in this area, where the four different water quality-classes again were symbolized by different colours. The other map showed expected water quality in the same area with 50 % reduction in nutrient leaching. We had good cooperation from researchers at the Norwegian Institute for Water Research, who from their current knowledge, predicted expected changes in water quality in the different water sources, due to a 50 % reduction in nutrient leaching.

Our experience was that this way of giving information worked well. It rather quickly gave an optic impression of the current water quality status and the expected improvements. The respondents could easily locate "their" water body of main interest and investigate the situation there. Still, it probably was difficult for the respondents to separate out values for nutrient leaching only.

10.6 Main results from the survey

The main summary results from the survey are shown in table 10.4.

The WTP amount stated in the first WTP question in the different subsamples, which we would expect to be equal given the presence of mental accounts, is seen as the upper values in each column in table 10.4.

Table 10.4 Mean WTP (in NOK/year) for different goods in diffe-
rent subsamples. For definition of these goods, see table
10.3. Numbers in upper parentheses are sample size and
numbers in lower parentheses are standard deviation.

GOODS	SUB-SAMPLE			
	1	2	3	4
PACK-ENV			3054 (116) (3987)	
PACK-POLL		3366 (123) (4562)	1985 (115) (2922)	
NSP	1943 (114) (2937)	1107 (119) (1623)	592 (117) (878)	
LOCAL CL 3/4				1125 (28) (1324)
LOCAL CL 2				1301 (32) (1301)

As can be seen from table 10.4, WTP for a package of 4 environmental goods (PACK-ENV) and WTP for a package of 4 pollution measures (PACK-POLL) are both quite high and quite similar amounts,
while WTP for NSP is quite a bit lower, and WTP for "quality
improvement in most important local water" is even lower. In these
numbers all reported values are included. Outliers have not been
taken out, because we did not find unreasonably high stated WTP.
Results of the t-tests conducted on the differences between the first
reported WTPs are reported in table 10.5.

As shown in table 10.5, WTP for the 2 packages of environmental
improvement, where PACK-POLL in fact is included in PACK-ENV,
is quite similar. The data support that they are not significantly different, although WTP for the "smallest" package is in fact larger than
WTP for the more inclusive one. However, there is a significant
difference (at the 5 % level) between the WTP for these two packages
on one hand and WTP for NSP and the local recipient on the other
hand. The difference between WTP for NSP and the local recipient
is considerable, but significantly different at the 10 % level only
where current pollution level is assumed to be class 2. There are not

Table 10.5 T-tests on differences between mean WTP for the first valued (package of) good. (Variances are assumed to be unequal.)

	|T-VALUE|	SIGNIFICANCE LEVEL (2-TAILED) P-VALUE
PACK-ENV-1-STEP – PACK-POLL-1-STEP	0.57	0.573
PACK-ENV-1-STEP – NSP-1-STEP	2.41	0.017
PACK-POLL-1-STEP – NSP-1-STEP	2.88	0.004
NSP-1-STEP – LOCAL CL 3/4-1-STEP	1.62	0.108
NSP-1-STEP – LOCAL CL 2-1-STEP	2.20	0.030
LOCAL CL 3/4-1-STEP – LOCAL CL 2-1-STEP	0.47	0.643

any significant differences between mean WTP for local recipients whether they are lifted from pollution class 3 or 4 to class 1 or from class 2 to class 1.

Referring to the hypotheses, we have to reject H_{01}. All the values given in the first valuation step are not equal. However H_{02} is rejected for $HC_E = HC_S$ and $HC_P = HC_S$ and $HC_E = HC_{LW}$ and $HC_P = HC_{LW}$. But we fail to reject the hypothesis for $HC_E = HC_P$ and $HC_S = HC_{LW-3/4}$. In hypotheses 3 and 4, we wanted to test whether respondents will lower the value for the package element, when this is elicited in two or three steps. We find that (see table 10.4):

HC_S^P (NOK 1107) $<$ HC_S (NOK 1943) and

HC_S^E (NOK 592) $<$ HC_S (NOK 1943) and

HC_P^E (NOK 1985) $<$ HC_P (NOK 3366).

These differences are significant at the 0.5 % level (table 10.6).

The last hypothesis concerned whether WTP for the good in question differs if it is obtained in a 1-step, 2-step or 3-step approach. We compare the WTP for NSP when the most inclusive good was respectively, PACK-ENV and PACK-POLL, with WTP for the NSP directly elicited. Using Bergstrom and Stoll's concepts, we compare the value of q_1 obtained in a 1-step, 2-step and 3-step valuation approach. The WTP-values are given in table 10.4. on the NSP-row, and the t-values for the differences of the means are given in table 10.6 below.

Table 10.6 T-values for differences between mean WTP in 1-step, 2-step and 3-step valuation of the NSP and 1-step and 2-step valuation of PACK-POLL. (Variances are assumed to be unequal.)

	|T-VALUE|	SIGNIFICANCE LEVEL (2-TAILED) P-VALUE	SIGNIFICANCE LEVEL (1-TAILED)
NSP-1-STEP – NSP-2-STEP	2.67	0.008	< 0.005
NSP-1-STEP – NSP-3-STEP	4.71	0.000	< 0.005
NSP-2-STEP – NSP-3-STEP	3.04	0.003	< 0.005
PACK-POLL-1-STEP – PACK-POLL-2-STEP	2.80	0.006	< 0.005

We find that H_{05} has to be rejected.

$$HC_S \neq HC_S^P \neq HC_S^E$$

This implies that what is chosen as the "total package" definitely influences what is obtained as the WTP for the good of interest. We see that a 2-step approach considerably lowers WTP for the NSP, as compared to a 1-step approach (from NOK 1943 to NOK 1107), as was found in Bergstrom and Stoll's (1987) study. But there is also a big difference between WTP for the NSP obtained in a 2-step and 3-step approach (from NOK 1107 to NOK 592).

10.7 Discussion and conclusion

Two recent European studies deal with the existence of mental accounts. Hoevenagel (1990) concluded that Dutch households did not state their total value for environmental improvements when valuing the prevention of a further deterioration of the Dutch forests and heaths. However, he suspects that some kind of focusing effects (Hoevenagel names this "mental accounting") may have been present. In a recent study of WTP for reduction in air pollution in Norway, Strand and Taraldset (1991) also found support for focusing effects.

In the present study, the tests on the existence of mental accounts (hypotheses H_{01} and H_{02}), give some quite interesting results. On a "high" level of aggregation and a rather "fuzzy" description of the goods to be valued, mental accounts seem to be present. When asked about WTP for a more familiar and less inclusive good, people seem to be able to state a smaller value for a smaller good. This indicates that valuation of well known and well defined goods give more valid results. This supports the advice given in CV literature, to describe the good and payment vehicle as accurately and realistically as possible. It also tells us that in testing for these biases, the way of doing it and the goods valued, may influence the results of the test. These results also indicate that the CVM may not give valid results for all kinds of public goods, i.e. there are limits to the use of the CVM.

The results concerning hypotheses H_{03} and H_{04} seem to suggest that by a 2-step valuation approach the respondents will lower the stated values for the component goods in CV surveys. But it was not generally the case, as in Bergstrom and Stoll (1987), that the value for the package and the component valued in one step were similar. Therefore, we cannot without further investigation conclude as Bergstrom and Stoll that a 2-step approach will give more valid valuation of policy package components due to shortcomings in respondents' cognitive decision-making processes.

Due to ordinary substitution and income effects, one would expect rather lower values for NSP in subsample 2 and subsample 3 than in subsample 1. This is so because, in the former cases, NSP may be considered a part of the greater entity. Although some differences therefore may be expected for purely theoretical reasons, the result of the tests concerning the influence of choice of "total entity" and the choice of 1-, 2- or 3-step approach, is problematic in the practical use of the CVM. Some may argue that it is obvious what is in the "total package", and that having respondents value "packages" of goods before the good of interest is irrelevant due to theory. I would argue that in practice it is often not obvious what should be chosen as the bigger entity since the environmental authorities have programs on most environmental areas. It is just "by accident" that some improvements are valued and some are not. These results then imply that the often suggested solution to "focusing effects" (to have respondents value "the bigger entity" first) is ambiguous.

We found no significant difference between WTP for local water improvement to class 1 for those respondents who considered current pollution level to be class 3/4 and those who considered it to be class 2. This indicates that it is not easy for people to distinguish between marginal changes in environmental quality, suggesting that the CVM can not give precise and accurate values for marginal environmental changes. Rather it may give an interval for an "environmental change". The same conclusion is reached in earlier studies, e.g. in Hylland and Strand (1983) and Navrud (1989). Hylland and Strand valued marginal changes in visibility in the Grenland area in Norway. Navrud valued increased fish stocks due to 30%, 50% and 70% reductions in acid rain in Southern Norway and found very small differences in WTP for these different improvements. In these studies, the respondents were not told that they were to value different marginal changes of the environmental good in question. If the respondents had been informed about this at the start, it would probably have been easier for them to perceive the differences between the marginal changes.

To conclude, the study did not support that people state the same value in CV surveys whatever amenity is valued. But for very inclusive packages of environmental improvements and "loose" descriptions of the payment vehicle, this seemed to be the case. This result underlines the importance of well-defined goods and payment vehicles for obtaining valid results in CV studies. The small differences in WTP for different marginal water quality improvements question whether people are able to value different marginal changes. We found that WTP for the good in question, differs according to what is chosen as the "total entity" and to whether or not the value is obtained in a 1-step, 2-step or 3-step approach. This leaves us with the unanswered question: What is the appropriate total entity and how many "steps" should we use in obtaining WTP for a specific good?

In the end this is an empirical question, and has to be decided contingent upon which programs for environmental improvements, payments etc. the authorities have at the time the survey is undertaken. We will have to choose how inclusive the actual package ought to be, and most important, the results obtained must be interpreted with these assumptions strongly borne in mind. We also note that it is impossible to conclude definitely about the existence or non-existence of mental accounts/amenity misspecification because some effects may be due either to these phenomena or to ordinary substitution and income effects. It would therefore be useful to consider all these concepts in the same study.

References

Bergstrom, J.C. & J.R. Stoll, 1987: A test of Contingent Market Bid Elicitation Procedures for Piecewise Valuation. *Western Journal of Agricultural Economics. Vol. 12* Number 2.

Cummings, R.G., D.S. Brookshire & W.D. Schulze, (eds), 1986: *Valuing Environmental Goods. An Assessment of the Contingent Valuation Method.* Totowa, N.J. Rowman and Allanheld.

Deaton, A. and J. Muellbauer, 1980: *Economics and Consumer Behavior.* Cambridge University Press.

Elster, Jon, 1989: *Nuts and Bolts for the Social Sciences.* Cambridge University Press.

Hoevenagel, R. 1990: The Validity of the Contingent Valuation Method: Some Aspects on the Basis of three Dutch Studies. Paper presented at the Congress "Environmental Cooperation and Policy in the Single European Market", Venice, Italy, April 17-20.

Hylland, A. & J. Strand, 1983: *Verdsetting av redusert luftforurensning i Grenlandsområdet.* (Valuation of reduced air pollution in the Grenland Area) Report no 12, August 1983. Departement of Economics, University of Oslo. (In Norwegian)

Kahneman, D. 1986: Comments. In: R.G., Cummings, D.S. Brookshire and W. D. Schulze, (eds). *Valuing Environmental Goods. An Assessment of the Contingent Valuation Method.* Totowa, N.J. Rowman and Allanheld.

Kahneman, D. § A. Tversky 1984: Choices, Values and Frames. *American Psychologist Vol.39.* No. 4:341-350.

Mitchell, R.C. & R.T. Carson 1989: *Using Surveys to Value Public Goods: The Contingent Valuation Method. Resources for the Future,* Washington, D.C.

Navrud, S., 1989: Estimating social benefits of environmental improvements from reduced acid depositions: A Contingent Valuation Survey. In: H. Folmer & E. van Ierland: Valuation methods and policy making in environmental economics. *Studies in Environmental Sciences 36.* Elsevier Science Publishers, Amsterdam, pp 69-102.

Schulze, W.D. et al, 1983: Methods Development in Measuring Benefits of Environmental Improvements: Experimental Approaches for Valuing Environmental Commodities. Vol.2. Draft manuscript of a report to USEPA. As referred to in Cummings et al. (eds) 1986.

Strand, J. & A. Taraldset 1991: The valuation of environmental goods in Norway: A contingent valuation study with multiple bias testing. Memorandum from Department of Economics, University of Oslo. No 2, March 1991.

Thaler, R. 1985: Mental Accounting and Consumer Choice. *Marketing Science. Vol. 4* No.3. Summer 1985: 199-214.

Thaler, R. & H.M. Shefrin 1981: An Economic Theory of Self Control. *Journal of Political Economy. 39,* April: 392-406.

Tversky, A. & D. Kahneman 1981: The Framing of Decisions and the Psychology of Choice. *Science. Vol. 211,* 30. January: 453–458.

Tversky, A. & D. Kahneman 1982: The Framing of Decisions and the Psychology of Choice. In: R. Hogarth (ed): *New Directions for Methodology of Social and Behavioral Science: Question Framing and Response Consistency. No. 11.* San Francisco: Jossey-Bass, March 1982:3–20.

Walbert, M.C. 1984: Valuing Policies which Reduce Environmental Risk: An Assessment of the Contingent Valuation Method. Ph.D. Dissertation, University of New Mexico, Albuquerque.

Appendix 1

Questionnaire, subsample no. 3

Instructions to interviewers are shown in parentheses.

Question 1
(Show card A) On this card we have mentioned some areas of society. Which of these areas do you think should be given highest priority in the time coming, which should be given next to highest priority etc?

(education and research, health and social care, sports and culture, environmental protection, foreign aid)

Question 2
(Show card B) On this card we have mentioned different tasks within the environmental protection area. Which of these tasks would you give highest priority, next to highest, etc?
(Conservation of all threatened plant and animal species in Norway, 50% reduction in Norwegian pollution to air and water, noise and garbage, Conservation of nature areas and resources, 50% reduction in global pollution which might cause global warming and depletion of the ozone layer.)

When you answer the following questions, remember that there might be other causes that you would also want to spend money on and that you have a limited amount to spend. Also remember that this amount comes in addition to whatever you already pay in taxes and fees.

Question 3
(Show payment card) What is the maximum amount your household is willing to pay per year in higher prices and taxes to implement *all* the measures mentioned on the card above (show card B again)?

Question 4
How concerned are you about environmental issues?

(active, very concerned, moderately concerned, not very concerned, environmental protection is exaggerated)

Question 5
(Show card j) Now, we will ask you some questions about pollution in Norway. To improve environmental quality, it is possible to implement measures in addition to those already decided on. We will mention 4 possible measures which will all imply approximately the same costs to society and therefore to yourself. We will also mention some possible consequences of no measures.

i)   50 % reduction of emissions to water. Consequences of no measures: reduced drinking water quality, reduction of fish stocks in fresh water, reduced possibilities for swimming and recreation by fresh and salt water.
ii) 50 % reduction of noise problems in towns. Consequences of no measures: reduced welfare and reduced working capacity in towns.
iii) 50 % reduction in emissions to air. Consequences of no measures: health problems, reduced sights, smell and damage to plant growth.
iv) 50 % reduction of garbage problems in Norway. Consequences of no measures: reduced welfare in towns, pollution of ground water, health problems, less effective use of nature resources.

(Show payment card) What is the maximum amount your household is willing to pay per year for implementing the 4 measures as mentioned on this card, by increased prices and taxes on commodities and services? Note that these measures are only a part of the measures in the above questions (Repeat, if necessary, the measures in question 2). Therefore, you are not meant to pay this sum in addition to what you have already said you are willing to pay, but as a part of this.

Question 6
How would you divide this amount (in question 5) between the possible measures?
   Norwegian fresh and salt water areas receive polluting discharges from several sources. Different discharges result in different effects. The pollution authorities consider the following 3 problems to be the most important: acid rain, discharges of heavy metals and nutrient

leaching. (Show card 1) This card illustrates damage from different water pollution sources. Take your time and study this card before answering the next question.

Question 7
How would you assign priorities to Norwegian efforts in the 3 areas on a scale of 100 points? Give most points to the area you think should be given the highest priority, fewest points to the area of least priority.

(-measures against acid rain, -measures against heavy metals, -measures against nutrient leaching)

It is important to note that in the rest of the questionnaire we will be concerned with nutrient leaching only. By nutrient leaching we mean that nutrients are being discharged to water from agriculture, sewage, aquaculture and industry. Agriculture and sewage are the main sources of nutrient leaching. (Show card 2) This map shows fresh and salt water areas in Norway. With freshwater areas we think of lakes, waters and rivers. With salt water areas we think of the coast area, fjords and the sea. We have named only a few of the water sources on this map. Different colours signify different levels of nutrient leaching. (Show card 3). This card explains more about which pollution level the different colours on the map imply.

Question 8/9
(Show card 2 and 3) To which 3 of the main watercourses/fjords and coast areas mentioned on this map do you find it most important to reduce nutrient leaching?

(Read) Norway and the other countries around the North Sea have committed themselves to reduce nutrient leaching to the North Sea. The area from the Swedish border to Lindesnes is included in the treaty, that is, the area shown on these maps. We will call this the North Sea Plan area. (Show card 4)
   This card shows 2 cards of the North Sea Plan area. We have named only a few of the water sources. The first map (A) shows the current situation. Map (B) shows improvements in water quality if the leaching to the North Sea is reduced by 50%. The different pollution levels implied by, the different colours on the map, can be seen on card 3. Note that the North Sea Plan will not only reduce emissions to the North Sea, but will also imply improved water quality in all rivers and lakes in the area. Take your time to study the maps so that you can see how the water quality improvements will influence the watercourses

and sea areas you are most interested in. Remember, however, that we cannot include all details and local variations on a map like this.

(Show card 4 and 3 still) If emissions of nutrients to the North Sea are reduced by 50%, this will mean improvements in water quality as shown on map B. This will imply that households, industry, agriculture and the public sector must spend more money on pollution control. The sewage tax you pay to the municipality today provides for water quality as shown on map A. To achieve improved water quality as shown on map B, the sewage tax has to increase. The sewage taxes for a household varied in 1990 from NOK 670–6400. Average sewage tax was about NOK 2500.

When you answer the following questions, remember that there might be other causes you would like to spend money on and that you have a limited amount to spend. Also remember that this amount comes in addition to whatever you pay in sewage taxes today.

Question 10
(Show payment card) Earlier you said that you would pay... NOK to reduce discharges to water by 50%. To reduce nutrient leaching in the North Sea Area so that water quality in this area becomes as shown on map B, what is the maximum amount your household is willing to pay per year in increased sewage taxes? Note that reduction of nutrient leaching by 50% in the North Sea Plan Area is included in the measures you were willing to pay for earlier. This is not payment in addition to, but as a part of whatever you have said you are willing to pay earlier.

Other questions

Related to WTP questions:
- Why pay 0 NOK?
- WTP for local water source?

Related to fresh and salt water usage:
- Most important local water source where nutrient leaching should be reduced?
- Pollution level in local water source?
- Use of fresh and salt water respectively in 1990:
  (-which activities, how many days, most used area)
- most important water quality factors to be improved
- increased use of fresh/salt water if water quality improved?
  (-yes/no, how many days)

Socio-economic variables:
- Age
- Sex
- Income (personal and household)
- Education level
- Marital status, county, type of residence, number of persons in household, types of persons in household, number of incomes in household, income source, occupation, political party.

Appendix 2. Card 3:

Nutrient leaching – water quality classes

Water quality class	Suitable for:	Water quality description
1. NOT POLLUTED		

	Drinking	Clear water
	Swimming	Enough oxygen
	Fishing	Little algae growth
	Boating	Stones are not overgrown

2.   MODERATELY POLLUTED

		Weakly muddy water
	Swimming	Little oxygen in deep water
	Fishing	Some algae growth
	Boating	Slippery stones, partly overgrown with algae

3.   MARKEDLY
      POLLUTED

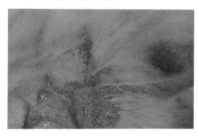

	Markedly muddy water
	Partly lack of oxygen in deep water
Fishing	Marked algae growth
Boating	Stones are markedly overgrown
	Bad living conditions for species of salmon

4.   EXTREMELY
      POLLUTED

	Extremely muddy water
	Extreme lack of oxygen
	Extreme algae growth
Boating	Species of salmon cannot live there
	Fungi and bacteria are common

Appendix 3. Card 4:

Nutrient leaching in the North Sea Plan area

| MAP A: CURRENT POLLUTION LEVEL | MAP B: EXPECTED POLLUTION LEVEL WITH 50% REDUCTION IN NUTRIENT LEACHING |

COLOUR Codes:

        Group 1: Not polluted

        Group 2: Moderately polluted

Group 3: Markedly polluted

Group 4: Extremely polluted

—— Limit for the North Sea Plan area.
In this area water quality both in fresh and salt water will be improved as a consequence of the North Sea Plan.

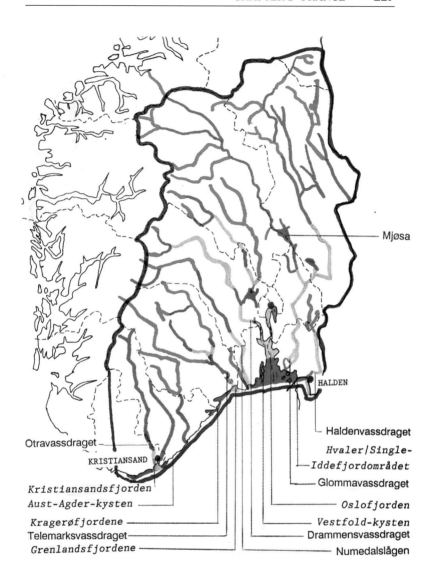

Map A

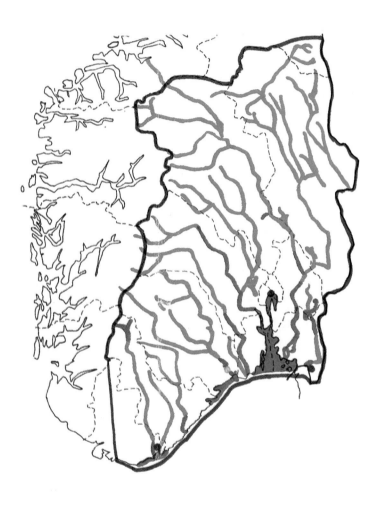

Map B

Chapter 11

Willingness to pay for preservation of species – An experiment with actual payments

STÅLE NAVRUD

11.1 Introduction

The contingent valuation (CV) method is one of the most used techniques for valuation of environmental goods. Mitchell and Carson's (1989, p. 2–3) definition of the method is:

> The CV method uses survey questions to elicit people's preferences for public goods by finding out what they are willing to pay (WTP) for specified improvements in them. The method is thus aimed at eliciting their WTP in dollar amounts. It circumvents the absence of markets for public goods by presenting consumers with hypothetical markets in which they have the opportunity to buy the good in question. The hypothetical market may be modelled after either a private goods' market or a political market. Because the elicited WTP values are contingent upon the particular hypothetical market described to the respondents, this approach came to be called the contingent valuation method.

A question which has been raised since the birth of the method with the Davis (1963) study is whether the CV method can provide valid data on people's willingness-to-pay (WTP) for public goods. Will people actually pay the amount they say they are willing to pay? How well can the CV method, as a measure of intended behaviour, predict people's actual behaviour? Real-payment or "simulated" markets serve as a particularly useful criterion against which to judge the accuracy of hypothetical scenarios. However, no single test is definitive. Even if there are large differences between the result of a CV study and a real-payment experiment, the reason may lie in its poor design rather than in the method itself.

This study is an attempt to test the validity of the CV method by comparing behavioural intentions and later actual behaviour with respect to WTP for a specific environmental good, namely the preservation of global biological diversity. The WTP for this public good was tied to the private good of becoming a member of the World Wide Fund for Nature (WWF).

This chapter first examines the different types of validity. Special emphasis is put on criterion validity and the Ajzen-Fishbein conditions for behavioural intentions to be reasonably good predictors of later behaviour. In section 3, the experiment and the questions asked are described, and in section 4, the results are presented and discussed. Section 5 summarizes and concludes the experiment.

11.2 Validity

In their examination of validity, Mitchell and Carson (1989, chapter 9) distinguish between three types of validity – content, construct and criterion validity. Content validity involves the issue of whether the measure adequately covers the construct's domain, i.e. an assessment of the CV questionnaires to see if they ask the right questions in an appropriate manner. This criterion differs from the others in the manner that it is based on subjective judgement.

In the second type of validity, construct validity, a measure is validated by comparing it with other measures that theory suggests it should be related to. There are two forms of construct validity, convergent and theoretical validity. Convergent validity involves measuring whether the measure is correlated with other measures of the same theoretical construct. This includes comparing CV results with corresponding estimates elicited from alternative valuation techniques like the Travel Cost (TC) and the Hedonic Price (HP) methods. A positive correspondence is interpreted as validating both measures, since neither is a superior measure of the underlying construct. The large number of these studies shows a suprisingly high level of convergent validity. See, for example, Cummings, Brookshire and Schultze (1986) for a review of eight such convergent validation studies. The theoretical validity asks whether the measure is related to other constructs in a manner predicted by theory. This is assessed in CV studies primarily by regressing the WTP amount on a group of independent variables believed to be theoretical determinants of the WTP amount. This type of validity has been demonstrated in many CV studies.

Criterion validity (or predictive validity) is measured through comparing the CV results with the value of semi-private goods as measured in simulated markets. Bohm (1972) and Bishop and Heberlein (1979, 1986) have shown that the correspondence between hypothetical and simulated markets is quite strong for goods which are well understood and familiar to the respondents, television programme and hunting permits, respectively. However, we do not know whether the CV method can accurately value public goods such as water and air quality improvements or endangered species preservation.

In general, there is a need for testing the validity of the large non-use values that have been observed for most environmental goods. There have been very few studies using real-payment markets to test the criterion validity of non-use values observed in CV studies. The obvious reason for this is the lack of actual markets for public goods, and the difficulties in constructing such markets.

In a CV survey, Seip and Strand (1990) asked a sample of 101 persons about their WTP for membership in the Norwegian Association for the Protection of Nature (NNV). Then, the 62 persons that stated a higher WTP than NNV's annual membership fee (200 NOK) were made subject to two mail membership drives by NNV, receiving membership application forms with a letter urging them to join the association. In the drive no reference was made to the previous CV survey. Only 10 % (i.e. 6 persons) joined the association and paid the membership fee. One of the reasons for this large discrepancy between intended and actual behaviour seems to be that people are mixing the valuation of the private membership good with a much more comprehensive and poorly defined set of environmental goods associated with NNV. Another reason is the lack of foreknowledge of an obligation to pay in accordance with one's verbal statements. Providing this knowledge in CV surveys has been shown to have a positive impact on the correspondence between contingent values and actual payment for both a private and a public good (Kealy, Montgomery & Dovido 1990). They asked two different samples of undergraduate students about their WTP and collected actual payments for a choclate bar and a donation to reduce acid rain. They also found the predictive validity of the CV study to be the same for the private and the public good. For both commodities the change from hypothetical to simulated markets did lead to a change in observed "preferences". 75, 72 and 95 % of the students paid their hypothetically stated amount for the private good, the public good and the public good with an explicitly stated payment obligation, respectively.

The reported study is different from the two studies above in several ways. First, the CV study was conducted in the untraditional way of looking at people's voluntary response to a newspaper ad asking for their support to combat the extinction of species by becoming members of the World Wide Fund for Nature (WWF). No specific amount was mentioned, and the respondents would have had to devote time and money by filling in their names and mailing the ad to WWF. Second, in contradiction to the Seip and Strand study, the focus in the CV study is not on the private good of becoming a member of an environmental association, but more specifically on the public good of preserving endangered species. This will hopefully reduce the risk of mixing up the private membership good with the public good of global biological diversity. Third, in contradiction to both studies above, the public good to be valued is described in great detail, and the respondents could take all the time they needed before responding. This is in sharp contrast to in-person interviews where the respondents have to come up with their WTP in a very short time.

Several CV studies have focused on endangered species, e.g. Brookshire, Eubanks and Randall (1983) valued the Grizzly bear; Stoll and Johnson (1984) the Whooping crane; Hageman (1985) the Blue whale; Boyle and Bishop (1986) valued the habitat for several endangered species (a nature preserve); Boyle and Bishop (1987) the Bald Eagle and the Striped shiner; and Dahle, Solberg and Sodal (1987) valued Wolf, Brown Bear and Wolverine. In contrast to these studies, the reported study will not try to come up with a benefit estimate of preserving specific species, but attempt to test the criterion validity of CV studies. The assumed lack of criterion validity seems to be one of the largest obstacles to wider use of CV estimates in environmental decision making in Norway (Navrud 1991), and probably also in other developed countries.

The results from this study will be analysed within the criterion validity framework of Ajzen-Fishbein (1977). According to Ajzen and Peterson (1988), the Ajzen-Fishbein model gives three conditions for behavavioral intentions to be reasonably good predictors of later behaviour:

1) The behaviour under consideration must be completely under a person's volitional control, i.e. the person can decide at will to perform it or not perform it.

    The more the performance of the behaviour is contingent on the presence of appropiate opportunities or on possession of adequate resources (e.g. time, money, skills, cooperation of other people etc.), the less the behaviour is under purely volitional control.

2) The intention must not have changed in the interval between the time it was assessed and the time the behaviour is observed. The longer the time interval, the more likely is the occurrence of unforeseen events that may change the intention.

3) The measurement of intention must correspond in its level of generality to the behavioural criterion.

Any intention and any behaviour can be defined in terms of four elements:
i)   the action involved,
ii) the target at which the action is directed,
iii) the context in which it occurs, and
iv) the time of its occurrence.

The more similar (i.e. identical levels of generality and specificity) the action, target, context and time elements of the intention are to the elements of the behaviour, the stronger should be the statistical relation between them.

According to Azjen and Peterson (1988), the first condition may not be a serious problem in the context of CV studies, because people are usually spending the amount they are willing to spend. However, it is recommended that the respondents are instructed explicitly to take into account alternative uses for their money. The second condition can easily be met by keeping the time interval between intended and actual behaviour to a minimum. However, since changes in the intentions of different individuals are often likely to balance out, aggregate intentions, as measured in CV studies, can be relatively stable over time. Thus, the correspondence between intended and actual behaviour at the aggregate level can also be quite high over time. The third condition, which is closely related to the previous "hypothetical bias" of CVM, seems to be the most difficult condition to meet in CV surveys.

The experiment will be analysed to see to what degree the different conditions are met, and how this has influenced the observed relation between intended and actual behaviour.

11.3 Method

The experiment was a three step procedure:

1) An untraditional CV survey where WWF asked people to express their support for combatting the extinction of species by responding to newspaper ads.
2) An offer to become a member of WWF and further information about WWF's work to preserve global biological diversity were sent to those that responded to the ad.

3) A telephone survey of a sample of the respondents that actually paid the membership fee and a sample of those that did not pay was conducted to identify the reasons for the observed divergence between behavioural intentions stated in step 1 and the actual behaviour in step 2.

In March 1990, WWF Norway had four one-page, colour ads in one of Norway's largest newspapers, informing people and asking for their support to preserve the world's endangered species by becoming a member of WWF. The ads described in detail the species extinction threat and the benefits of species preservation. At the end they said:

"In WWF we are working for the preservation of biological diversity. For this work we, of course, need money. However, most of all we need people: people to take on responsibility and personally care about the environment, people to put pressure on the politicans, authorities, and other decision makers, And people in international aid organizations (like NORAD) to ensure that new development projects respect nature. We need industrial leaders, opinion creators, church leaders and environmentalists who are willing and pushing for reduced pressure on natural resources. For every 'vote' we get, we become a bit stronger in the struggle for this planet. It is the only one we have."

Then there was a reply coupon that said: "Yes, I will contribute with my vote as WWF friend." In this first step of the experiment, persons responded to the ad by filling in their name and address and returning the reply coupon to WWF. They had to pay the postage themselves.

It should be noted here that the newspaper ads were not constructed with the purpose of being a CV study. The author was not involved in the construction of the ads, but was brought in after step 1 and 2 had been completed. Therefore, some part of the observed divergence between intended and actual behaviour might be due to the poor design of the CV instrument, especially the lack of an explicit payment obligation and specific amount. In contrast to ordinary CV studies, the respondents are a self selected group of people, not a random sample of the general population or some specific interest group. This is expected to increase the correspondence between intended and actual behaviour. The results of this study might therefore overstate the criterion validity of ordinary CV studies ceteris paribus.

Less than one week after they responded to the ad, the respondents received an offer to become a member of WWF together with general information about WWF's campaign "Preserve nature's diversity". Enclosed was also a post money order saying, "Yes, I will support WWF with an annual contribution", with the possibility of ticking off amounts ranging from NOK 75 for "Youth friend" and NOK 125 for "Support friend" to NOK 1000 for "Elite friend". Membership fees and their size were not mentioned in the newspaper ad. In this second step, the persons that responded to the ad were supposed to pay the annual membership fee and become members of WWF.

In the third step, a telephone survey of two random, and presumably representative, samples of the respondents was conducted to identify the reasons for the observed discrepancy between intended and actual behaviour. One sample of those that actually paid the membership fee (hereafter named members) and one of those that did not pay (hereafter named non-members) were interviewed in January and February 1991. 45 non-members and 21 members were interviewed. This is 3.4 and 5.0% of the two populations, respectively.

The non-members were first told that the telephone survey was a scientific study that had nothing to do with WWF, and that there was no payment obligation connected to the survey questions. The fact that the majority of the people that responded to the ad had not become members was mentioned before they were asked an open question about their reasons for not becoming a member of WWF.

Then the following list of possible reasons was given, and the respondents asked to state which of the reasons had influenced their decisions not to pay the WWF membership fee;

1) ENV.ORG = You already pay annual membership fees to other environmental organisations
2) FINANCE = Your financial situation became worse after you had responded to the ad
3) LATER = You could not afford to become a member last year, but you would like to do it later
4) SUPPORT = You responded to the ad to show your general support for preservation of species – not to pay an annual membership fee
5) LABOUR = You responded to the ad because you were willing to contribute with voluntary labour for WWF – not to pay an annual membership fee
6) HIGH FEE = The annual fee, which is NOK 75 for children and NOK 125 for adults, was too high. You would be willing to pay a lower membership fee.

If the answer was "yes" to HIGH FEE:
What is the highest annual membership fee you would be willing to pay to WWF in their work to preserve the global species diversity?

7) GOODS = You were not willing to pay an annual fee, but bought goods from WWF's gift catalogue, and supported the organisation in that way.
   If the answer was "yes" to GOODS:
   Approximately how much did you spend on this last year?
8) DONATE = You would rather donate money to specific preservation projects than pay an annual membership fee to WWF
9) OTHER = Did you have other reasons for not becoming a member of WWF, than the ones mentioned above? State them.

The respondents were allowed to state more than one reason.
   The members were asked the following questions:

1) REASON = Did you respond to this ad because you were willing to support WWF with monetary donations, e.g. through membership, or did you do it to show your general support to this work without supporting it with money?
   Four alternatives were given:

   - PAY   = Were willing to pay something (e.g. through membership in WWF)
   - SUPPORT   = Would show general support; pay nothing
   - PAY/SUPPORT   = Both monetary and general support
   - DON'T KNOW

2) WHY PAY = Your answer to REASON was SUPPORT.
   If you would show your general support without paying anything, why did you then become a member of WWF?

For both non-members and members, data on the following socio-economic background variables were collected;

   - AGE   = the respondent's age in years
   - INCOME   = the respondent's personal monthly income, when income tax is deducted
   - SEX   = the respondent's sex; 0 = women, 1 = man
   - RESIDENCE   = the respondent's residence; 0 = the counties of Oslo and Akershus, 1 = other counties in Norway

For members, the annual membership fee paid was also recorded. There are several different annual membership fees to choose among from NOK 75 as a "Youth friend" to NOK 1000 as an "Elite friend".

11.4 Results and discussion

A total of 1349 persons responded to the newspaper ads, and received the offer to become a WWF member, and in that way support the fund's work to preserve biological diversity. 423 persons became WWF members. This is 31.4%, or less than one third, of those that said they were willing to support WWF in their species preservation work. This is a much lower share than Kealy, Montgomery and Dovido (1990) found in their experiments. However, this share is three times higher than what Strand and Seip (1990) found. The mean annual WTP per person in a random sample of those that became members was found to be NOK 194. The WTP varied from NOK 75 to 500. The median value was NOK 125 (1 NOK = 0.12 ECU = 0.15 $).

According to Johnson (1991), the conventional wisdom is that donations always will understate WTP because of free riding. Willingness to donate might also be influenced by, e.g. the perceived cost-effectiveness of the donation vehicle or the recipient organisation, the degree to which contributing is regarded as a social responsibility or direct source of satisfaction, the likelihood that a donation will be matched by sufficient similar donations to change noticeably the amount of public goods available, and the availability of convenient donation vehicles and information about donation options. In this WWF study, the overall effect of these factors seems to be an under-statement of WTP. Johnson (1991) also points out that aggregating estimated real or hypothetical donations could overstate the value of resources for which there are close substitues. This last point can hardly be the case for biological diversity. Therefore, the aggregate donations of the persons that became members, should be viewed as a lower estimate of the value put on this resource by the Norwegian people. However, the main aim of this study is to test the criterion validity of CV surveys, not to put a value on biological diversity.

Table 11.1 shows that 67% of those who became members of WWF stated that they responded to the newspaper ad because they, at least partly, were willing to pay something to support WWF's work for preservation of species. Nineteen per cent stated they responded to the ad only to show their general support, not because they were willing to make any monetary contribution to this work.

The reason given for still paying the WWF membership fee was that they were convinced by the material sent to them by WWF.

Table 11.1 Distribution of the different reasons of WWF members to respond to the newspaper ad. 21 observations. Percentage.

Reason[1]	Percentage
PAY	38
SUPPORT	19
PAY/SUPPORT	29
DON'T KNOW	14
	100

Remark: 1 Definition of the different reasons are given in chapter 11.3 under the variable named REASON.

Table 11.2 Review of the distribution of the different reasons given by non-members for not paying the membership fee to WWF. Each person was allowed to state more than one reason.

Reason[1]	No. of respondents	No. of obs.	Percentage
ENV.ORG	10	43	23
FINANCE	12	43	28
LATER	19	43	44
SUPPORT	28	42	67
LABOUR	2	42	5
HIGH FEE	10	42	24
GOODS	2	42	5
DONATE	11	43	26
OTHER	16	45	35

Remark: 1 For a definition of the different reasons, see chapter 11.3.

In contrast to this, the percentage showing general support of those that did not become WWF members was 67 %, see table 11.2 (reason: SUPPORT). This is the reason stated by non-members for not paying the membership fee. This indicates that maybe as many as two-thirds of those that did not pay did not consider the ad as a WTP question. Thus, these individuals' intended behaviour was different from the assumed one that was to be tested by measuring their actual WTP.

In addition, 24 % of non-members said that the WWF membership fee, whose size was unknown when they responded to the ad, exceeded their WTP (table 11.2, reason: HIGH FEE). On average these persons were willing to pay NOK 83 annually, while the minimum annual membership fee was NOK 125 and 75 for adults and children, respectively. Respondents stating this reason, or that they responded to support WWF with free labour, or to pay towards a specific preservation project (table 11.2, reasons LABOUR and DONATE, respectively) also indicate that the intended behaviour was not stated as WTP for preservation of species. Thus, it makes no sense to test it against actual WTP. Of the non-members, at least 26 % can be said to express a payment obligation by responding to the ad. These respondents gave, as their *only* reason for not becoming a member, either that they lacked money (reasons: FINANCE and LATER), 21 %, or were members of another environmental organisation (reason: ENV.ORG), 5 %. However, this number might be larger, since these reasons are also stated by others, but together with other reasons.

The reasons for not paying given in table 11.2 were read to the respondents, and this pre-selection of reasons might have influenced their answers. Therefore, an *open* question about the reason for not paying was asked before the question with pre-selected reasons. Then, 31 % said they had forgotten it or hadn't had the time to pay, 22 % couldn't afford it, 18 % had thought of their response as a general support and not as a payment obligations, 9 % supported other non-governmental organisations (not including environmental organisations), 2 % were members of other environmental organisations, 2 % gave other reasons and 16 % gave no reason. The relatively large percentage that gave no reason indicates that people had forgotten the reasons why they didn't pay. Remember that the telephone survey was carried out 9–10 months after they received the offer to pay the membership fee. For these respondents, pre-selected reasons could have had a particularly strong influence on their response.

Compared with table 11.2, it seems as if the "general support" reason was given by fewer persons. However, the fact that many had forgotten about it or hadn't had the time to pay, can also indicate that their response to the ad was not perceived as a payment obligation. Thus, as many as 51 % (i.e. 22 + 9 + 2 + 2 + 16 %) of non-members can be interpreted as perceiving the intended behaviour as a payment obligation.

If we assume our sample to be representative, and that all members and 26–51 % of the non-members viewed their action as a payment obligation, it means that 664–895 persons responded to the ad, perceiving it as a WTP question. Considering that 423 persons became members, this means that as many as 47–64 % of those that said they were willing to pay actually paid. The WTP question in the ad could be misunderstood, and we do not know for sure whether the respondents actually viewed their response to the ad as a supportive action with no payment obligation attached, or gave this reason as an easy way out when interviewed about the reasons for not paying.

The reasons for not paying, given by pre-selected options or as an open question, clearly show that there was a large percentage of non-members that perceived their response to the newspaper ad as a general support rather than a payment obligation. Can this be seen as a result of violating any of the three conditions in the Azjen-Fishbein model for criterion validity?

The first two of these conditions for behavioural intentions to be reasonably good predictors for later behaviour seem to be met. It was completely voluntary to respond to the WWF membership anouncement (Condition no. 1), and it took a maximum of one week for the persons mailing the coupon stating that they wanted to become a WWF member until they received an offer to become a member, together with information about WWF and a money order showing the different membership fees to choose from (Condition no. 2).

Regarding the third "Correspondence condition", there seems to be some discrepancies between the elements in the description of the behavioural intentions and the elements of the actual behaviour. Azjen and Peterson (1988) distinguishes between the action target, context and time elements of this condition.

The action involved when measuring intended behaviour was focused more on the willingness to support (i.e. giving one's vote more in general than donating money) preservation of species (i.e. a public good) than the measurement of actual behaviour, which focused solely on the willingness to pay for the private good of becoming a member of WWF. Membership fees and the size of these were not mentioned explicitly in the newspaper ads. The measurement of intended behaviour, therefore, seems to be more general than the measurement of actual behaviour. The target at which the action is directed is the same in both measurements. The ad and the information sent to the respondents both clearly state that WWF's main task is to work for the preservation of species.

Concerning the context and time elements, it can be argued that there are differences between the intended and actual behaviour. The context when expressing intended behaviour is more general than when the behaviour take place; supporting the preservation of species (public good) as compared to paying a membership fee to an environmental organization (private good). The time dimension is also more general in the case of intended behaviour. Actual behaviour is measured as paying an annual membership fee while the intended behaviour is just a general support, with no description of the time dimension.

These differences in action, context and time elements of the intended and actual behaviour seem to have been perceived by many of the respondents, and mainly those that did not become members. This can, however, only partly explain why less than one third of the respondents actually became members.

The discrepancy can also be due to the relatively poor design of the WTP question, apart from the issue of being too general. Remember that initially this question was not designed as part of a CV survey. Thus, if the experiment had been constructed in a way that all three conditions of Azjen and Fishbein were met, and the WTP question had been designed according to, for example, Mitchell and Carson (1989), it might have shown a larger degree of correspondence between intended and actual behaviour. However, the special design of this CV study might also have led to a more "dedicated" sample of respondents than "ordinary" CV surveys (by mail, telephone or in-person interviews). Thus, the result from this experiment might understate the share of the respondents that overestimate their WTP in "ordinary" CV surveys. This can be one of the reasons why this study yielded a better correspondence between hypothetical and actual payment than the Seip and Strand (1990) study. However, I think the main reason, which was also stated by almost all the respondents that didn't pay, was a diffuse and general description of the environmental good in that CV survey. Therefore, the WTP given in that CV survey was for a much broader set of environmental goods than the more private good of a membership in an environmental organization.

Table 11.3 shows the differences in the background variables between members and non-members. The age and sex composition is approximately the same in the two groups. Income is larger for non-members than for members of WWF, but not significantly larger at the 10 % level. Due to the small sample sizes, the differences between the two means must be 50 % or more to be significantly different in a one-tailed t-test at the 10 % level (Mitchell & Carson 1989, appendix C). The percentage of people residing in the urban Oslo and Akershus counties is higher among those that became WWF members. However, in general these background variables are not able to explain the different actions taken by members and non-members.

Table 11.3 Comparison of WWF members' and non-members' income (NOK per person per month, when income tax is deducted), age, sex, and place of residence.

Variable[1]	Members			Non-members		
	Mean	St.dev.	Obs.	Mean	St.dev.	Obs.
Income	7213	6956	20	9182	8661	40
Age (years)	34.81	19.73	21	33.06	13.41	34
Sex	0.476	0.512	21	0.489	0.506	45
Residence	0.286	0.463	21	0.444	0.503	45

Remark: Sex and residence are dummy variables.
- Sex: 0 = female, 1 = male
- Residence: 0 = Oslo and Akershus counties,
   1 = Other counties in Norway

11.5 Conclusion

The aim of this simple experiment was to test the criterion validity of the Contingent Valuation (CV) method for valuation of environmental goods, i.e. "Will people actually pay what they say they are willing to pay ?" This is one of the few studies to test the criterion validity of the large non-use values observed in CV surveys. The results are analysed within the framework of the Ajzen-Fishbein conditions for behaviourable intentions to be reasonably good predictors of later behaviour.

The good to be valued is preservation of the world's endangered species, and the payment vehicle is annual membership in the World Wide Fund for Nature (WWF) in Norway. The CV survey is done in the untraditional way of measuring the response to a series of four one-page colour ads in one of Norway's largest newspapers. This yields a self-selected, and probably more enthusiastic, sample of respondents than a survey of a random sample of the general public. Thus, the results from this exercise might overestimate the validity of ordinary CV surveys. On the other hand, the ads were initialy not

constructed as a CV survey, and lacked an explicit payment obligation. Therefore, a more carefully designed CV scenario could have
improved the validity.

1349 persons responded to the ads, stating that they were willing
to support WWF in their work for the preservation of endangered
species. No specific amounts were mentioned in the ads. There is a
possibility that the respondents had perceived their response as a
general, not monetary, support for WWF's work. Actual behaviour
was measured as the number of respondents actually paying an
annual membership fee to WWF. The correspondence between behavioural intentions and actual behaviour seemed poor. Only 423
persons, i.e. 31 % of the respondents, actually paid.

A telephone survey of random samples of those that didn't pay
(named non-members) and those that paid (named members) was
carried out. It revealed that 26–51 % and 67 % of the non-members
and members, respectively, had responded to the ad expressing
monetary, not general, support to WWF. This difference in the generality of the context where intended and actual behaviour is measured means that part of the "Correspondence condition" in the
Azjen-Fishbeinn model is not met. The other two conditions for
behavioural intentions to predict actual behaviour, "Volitional control" and "Unchanged intentions" seem to be met. Assuming that all
members and 26–51 % of the non-members perceived the ads as a
WTP question, the correspondence between intended and actual
behaviour improves from 31 to 47–64 %.

To conclude, the results from this experiment, which utilize the
information from one of the few existing markets for non-use values
of environmental goods, are quite encouraging for the CV method's
ability to predict actual behaviour. It also shows the paramount
importance of a carefully constructed CV survey that in all aspects
corresponds to the actual behaviour. This means that the CV scenarios should be policy oriented if the results are going to be used to
justify decisions, and they should contain an explicit payment obligation.

This is a small scale experiment of one particular public good
using a very untraditional CV design. Therefore, one should be very
careful in drawing a general conclusion about the predictability of
CV surveys from these results. More experiments involving actual
payments for non-use values of public goods are needed to verify the
results gained from CV surveys.

References

Ajzen, I. & M. Fishbein 1977: Attitude-behaviour relations: A theoretical analysis and review of empirical research. *Psychological Bulletin 84,* 888–918.

Ajzen, I. & G. L. Peterson 1988: Contingent value measurement: The price of everything and the value of nothing? In G.L. Peterson, B.L. Driver & R. Gregory (eds.): *Amenity Resource Valuation. Integrating economics with other disciplines.* Venture Publishing Inc., P. 65–76.

Bishop, R.C. & T.A. Heberlein 1979: Measuring values of extramarket goods: Are indirect measures biased? *American Journal of Agricultural Economics 61,* 926–930.

Bishop, R.C. & T.A. Heberlein 1986: Does Contingent Valuation work ? Chapter 9 in Cummings et al (1986).

Bohm, P. 1972: Estimating demand for public goods: An experiment. *European Economic Review 3,* 111–130.

Boyle, K.J. & R.C. Bishop 1986: *The economic valuation of endangered species in wildlife. Transactions of the Fifty-First North American Wildlife and Natural Resources Council.*

Boyle, K.J. & R.C. Bishop 1987: Toward total valuation of Great Lakes fishery resources. *Water Resources Research 5,* 943–950.

Brookshire, D.S., Brookshire, L.S. & W. Schultze (eds.) 1986: *Valuing environmental goods: An assessment of the Contingent Valuation Method,* Rowman & Allanheld, New Jersey.

Dahle, L., Sødal, D.P. & B. Solberg 1987: Haldningar til og betalingsvillighet for bjørn, jerv og ulv i Noreg. (Attitudes towards and willingness to pay for preservation of Brown Bear, Wolverine and Wolf in Norway). Report no. 5/1987, Department of Forest Economics, Agricultural University of Norway, 114 pp.

Davis, R.K. 1963: The value of outdoor recreation: An economic study of the Maine Woods, Ph.D. dissertation, Harvard University.

Hageman, R. 1985: Valuing marine poulations: Benefit valuations in a multi-species ecosystem. *Adm. Report No. LJ-85 22.* La Jola: National Marine Fisheries Service, South-West Fisheries Center.

Johnson, F.R. 1991: Measuring existence values: Environmental altruism and the missing behavioural link. Paper presented at the EAERE conference in Stockholm, June 11–14 1991. 12p.

Kealy, M.J., Montgomery, M. & J.F. Dovido 1990: Reliability and predictive validity of contingent values: Does the nature of the good matter? *Journal of Environmental Economics and Management 19,* 244–263.

Mitchell, R.C. & R. Carson 1989: *Using surveys to value public goods: The Contingent Valuation Method.* John Hopkins University Press, Baltimore

Navrud, S. 1991: Norway. In J.P. Barde & D.W. Pearce (eds.): *Valuing the environment. Six case studies.* Chapter 5 (p. 141–202). Earthscan Publications Ltd., London.

Seip, K. & J. Strand 1990: Willingness to pay for environmental goods in Norway: A contingent valuation study with real payments: Paper presented at the first annual conference of the European Association of Environmental and Resource Economists, Venice, April 17–20 1990. Forthcoming in Environmental and Resource Economics.

Chapter 12

Starting to value the environment: The Australian experience

JEFF BENNETT

12.1 The policy context

Environmental policy making has been the source of much controversy in Australia over the last two decades. Governments at both State and Federal levels have been lobbied vigorously by pro-development and pro-conservation groups. Often, conflicts of interest have flowed over into public protests and demonstrations. Because of the strength of feelings involved in many of the environmental decisions faced by politicians, it has been difficult for them to determine accurately the political consequences of the alternatives. The choices faced have therefore been invidious for politicians as well as creating social tension and the wastage of scarce resources within the decision making process itself. Politicians have sought, in the facet of these difficulties, a more "arm's length" choice calculus.

At the same time, groups of policy analysts and policy advisors have pressed for more objective assessments to be made of the tradeoffs involved in environmental decision making.

The result of these pressures has been the increased use of more structured review processes. The most common of these is the Environmental Impact Assessment (EIA) process which is based on Federal Government legislation. The earliest forms of EIA involved the documentation of the physical impacts on the environment of development projects. As the process became more sophisticated, with heavier demands being placed on it, a shift toward the inclusion of social and economic affects has occurred. Most recently, the EIA process has begun to require, in an albeit tentative way, the quantification of impacts to enable projects to be assessed within the framework of a benefit-cost analysis.

Other venues for policy review and recommendation – such as Commissions of Inquiry and departmental investigations – have embraced similar movements toward the quantification of the effects of environmental change.

The movement toward environmental valuation has not been without some deal of resistance. Some members of environmental lobby groups have rejected completely the principle of valuing the environment using dollars as a numeraire. Criticism has also been levelled at some of the measurement techniques used by economists to value the environment. It has been claimed that the measurements so derived are inaccurate. Some bureaucrats tasked with the development and implementation of the EIA process have also been reluctant to change from the established physical science approach to one which incorporates economic valuation.

12.2 The role of economists

There has been a small but active group of economists working in Australia to establish environmental valuation as a useful tool for policy makers. The earliest studies were undertaken almost three decades ago. The early studies centred on the concept of a threshold value: if an environment is conserved, development benefits of $x m would be foregone. Whilst essentially not a valuation exercise, this type of analysis has provided decision makers with bench marks to guide their policy making. This was the case for one of Australia's pivotal environmental conservation cases – the proposal to dam the Franklin River for hydro electricity generation. Saddler, Bennett, Reynolds and Smith (1980) estimated the additional costs of alternative power generation capacity, suggesting that the value of the conservation of the river needed to be in excess of approximately 700,000 Australian dollars (A $) in the current year for conservation to be optimal. Policy makers decided not to construct the dam. The influence that the Saddler et al. study had on that decision is difficult to establish, but its results were part of the information matrix on which the decision was made.

The travel cost method has been used to value the recreational benefits of natural environments for nearly two decades in Australia. Its use has often been at the behest of governmental agencies. For instance, Ulph and Reynolds (1980) were commissioned by the Australian National Parks and Wildlife Service to value the recreational benefits supplied by the Warrumbungles National Park in New South Wales as a demonstration of the technique's effectiveness.

The hedonic price technique has seen less exposure in Australian applications. However, Abelson (1979) used the method to value the costs of aircraft noise around Sydney's international airport.

The limitations of these methods – notably their ex post rather than ex ante focus and their restriction to a narrow range of environmental benefits – has led to a growing interest in the Contingent Valuation Method (CVM). The CVM can be tailored to measure the values of projected changes and is adaptable to a wide variety of applications. The growth in interest has been manifested by an increasing number of empirical studies employing the CVM but also by a growing level of controversy surrounding the method's suitability.

12.3 Australian contingent valuation studies

Australia has witnessed over a decade of active applications and development of CVM. The applications have been scattered over a wide variety of issues, with the chief developmental influences coming from the writings of United States researchers such as Randall, Bishop, Mitchell and Carson.

The impetus for the studies undertaken has been mixed. Early studies were largely undertaken within University research programmes but as the credentials of the method have become more established, more studies have been conducted under the auspices of government agencies or commissions of inquiry. In general, the studies have not gained strong acceptance in the policy context. Whilst the valuations estimated by a number of the studies have been used indirectly by policy makers in formulating resource use decisions, others have been actively rejected largely because of their controversial nature. A selection of Australian CV studies will now be reviewed. All amounts are stated in Australian dollars (A $) in the year of the study.

12.3.1 FLY CONTROL

Johnston (1982) investigated the value of improved fly control brought about by the biological control of animal dung. The study formed part of Johnston's doctoral research but was funded by the Commonwealth Scientific and Industrial Research Organization (CSIRO) as part of an ex post evaluation of its Entomology Division's research programme into the introduction of the dung beetle.

The questionnaire designed by Johnston asked respondents for their willingness to pay (WTP) for the CSIRO research programme. The payment mode used was an increase in local taxes, the revenue from which would be paid into a research fund earmarked for fly control. The overall sample of 537 households was split into two subsamples: respondents in the first sub-sample were given an open ended WTP question whilst the remaining respondents were presented the same question in the context of an iterative bidding game.

Perhaps the most interesting feature of this study was Johnston's attempt to validate the mean willingness to pay an estimated A $13.40 per annum using information on the value of fly protection derived from the estimated demand curve for the marketed substitute good, personal insect repellant.

The Johnston study therefore featured a number of key characteristics. It was designed in accord with what were state-of-the-art features; it was essentially policy driven; and it was embellished with an attempt at validation. The use of a parallel validation study was indicative of the degree of scepticism displayed toward the CVM by main stream economists and non economists.

12.3.2 EXISTENCE BENEFITS

An adjunct validation exercise was also a feature of the Bennett (1984) analysis of the existence benefits supplied by the continued preservation of the Nadgee Nature Reserve in New South Wales. The main part of the study used a questionnaire designed to ask respondents their once-off willingness to pay to protect the Reserve from development, given that no direct use benefits would be available from its preservation. The adjunct study was an exercise in experimental economics where a sub-sample of respondents were asked willingness to pay questions of various types to establish the degree, if any, of biases induced. Included amongst the questioning styles was an incentive compatible, anti free riding, question which was used as a validation bench mark.

Whilst the study was not directed at a specific policy initiative it was assisted by the Australian and New South Wales National Parks Services. Its results were used by Service personell to argue for the preservation of wilderness areas irrespective of their visitor profiles.

12.3.3 THE CROWN OF THORNS STARFISH

The Great Barrier Reef Marine Park Authority (GBRMPA), the government funded management agency for the Great Barrier Reef, commissioned Carter, Vanclay and Hundloe (1987) to estimate the value of reef management and control of the Crown of Thorns Starfish. At the time of the study it was feared that the starfish would pose a significant risk to the coral living on the Reef. The purpose of the valuation exercise was to gain an appreciation of the benefits of starfish control, relative to the costs, and to establish the viability of a user-pays funding mechanism.

Vicarious users of the reef were presented with the CV vehicle designed for the task via a mail survey whilst reef visitors were approached by direct interview. The payment mode used was a once only donation to a trust fund set up to manage the reef or an increase in entrance fees to be paid to a trust to manage the reef. The mail survey used an open ended WTP question whilst the iterative bidding technique was employed in the direct interview.

No direct policy initiative arose from the Carter et al. study. One reason for this was that subsequent ecological research suggested that the rapid growth in starfish numbers was a phenomenon that was subject to a process of natural control. However, the results of the research have encouraged GBRMPA to investigate further the prospect of levying a 1 % surcharge on all reef tours to fund their operation.

12.3.4 FRASER ISLAND

In 1990, a Commission of Inquiry was established by the Queensland Government to investigate the future use of Fraser Island, the world's largest sand island. As a component of its submission to the Inquiry, the Queensland Department of Environment and Heritage commissioned Hundloe, McDonald, Blamey, Wilson and Carter (1990) to estimate the conservation value of the hardwood forests on the island.

The study was the first in Australia to use the dichotomous choice referendum model form of the CVM. The questionnaire was administered by a mail survey and asked for respondents' willingness to pay an annual increase in taxes. Both visitors and vicarious users were surveyed.

The format of the dichotomous choice presented to respondents was the source of some criticism. Respondents were presented with opposing views of the future of the forests – one prepared on behalf of the timber industry and the other on behalf of conservationists. It was argued in the Commission of Inquiry that such a presentation forces a polarization of views and hence causes the formation of a biased, bimodal distribution of willingness to pay. Furthermore, information on willingness to accept compensation was not gathered from the respondents who preferred the pro-logging option.

The results of the study indicated that the aggregate WTP for the preservation of the Fraser Island forests was in the order of $600m per annum. The magnitude of this estimate was cause for a rekindling of CVM scepticism. In particular, it was suspected by the Commission that the questionnaire had resulted in significant overstatement of willingness to pay bids by respondents. One potential cause for this was identified as a failure to separate forest values from the preservation values of the entire Island.

As a result of this scepticism, the CV results were not given prominence in the Commission of Inquiry's final report. However, on the basis of other information, the Commission did recommend to the Queensland Government that the forests be preserved and the Government has subsequently accepted that advice. The CV results were used to support the payment of compensation to timber workers whose jobs would be lost as a result of the new Government policy.

12.3.5 CORONATION HILL

The most widely publicized and contentious CV study undertaken in Australia to date has been the Australian Government's Resource Assessment Commission (RAC) analysis of the environmental costs likely to arise from a proposed mining operation of Coronation Hill. Coronation Hill is an ore body located in the Kakadu Conservation Zone, an area of approximately 50 square kilometres, which altough not part of the Kakadu National Park, is part of the Park's ecosystem.

The questionnaire designed by the RAC research team Imber, Stevenson and Wilks (1991) involved a two stage dichotomous choice model. Respondents were asked if they would be willing to pay for the preservation of the Conservation Zone through replacing lost government revenue from mining and an increase in park management expenditure. Two sub-samples of respondents were formed: the questionnaires presented to each group differing in respect of the extent of the described impacts on the environment caused by the projected mining operations.

For even the minor impact scenario, the result of the RAC study indicated a substantial cost if mining were permitted at Coronation Hill. The value of these costs was estimated at A $647m per annum for at least ten years. This figure can be compared with the A $82m estimate for total net present value of mining. The extent of the RAC estimate created a considerable debate in the national media. Much criticism was levelled at the study because of a perception that the estimates of costs were simply "too high". Specifically, Brunton (1991) suggested that respondents were enjoying a "moral free lunch" by voting with "play money". He suggested that to compare such "play money" bids with the "real money" earned by the mining operation was fundamentally flawed. Moran (1991) criticised the study as being biased for a number of reasons – an inadequate framing of the environmental effects of mining in the context of other complementary and substitute goods; a lack of familiarity with the good involved; and inadequate understanding of the price item being valued. In particular, Moran used the approach of dividing the value of the Conservation Zones environment as derived by the CVM by the area of the Zone and comparing the per hectare value so determined with other real estate. It was shown that the Zone was more valuable than downtown Tokyo on a per hectare basis.

The criticism did not go unchallenged. Carson (1991), who had been appointed as a consultant to the RAC for the Coronation Hill project, responded. He criticises the critics' "glib characterizations", asserting that they demonstrate "a complete lack of understanding of welfare economics". The comparison between the value of the Conservation Zone and downtown real estate is dismissed on the grounds of the distinction between the values of public and private goods. Carson asserts that the evidence provided by US studies suggests that CVM can be used across a wide range of goods, some of which are relatively unfamiliar to respondents. He also argues that the differences detected between the major impact and minor impact scenario values show that the respondents were well aware of the good involved.

Because the Australian community, and more specifically, its policy makers are largely unfamiliar with the CVM and its potential for assisting decision making, it was particularly easy for the critics to castigate the study. Such was the level of the controversy which arose from the CV study that the RAC's final report on mining at Coronation Hill incorporated its findings only in a descriptive manner; the values derived were not used in any explicit benefit-cost analysis of the proposed mine. The campaign the critics launched to discredit the RAC findings must therefore be regarded as a success. It did not, however, succeed in its overall objective of ensuing to go-ahead of mining as the Australian Government subsequently decided to declare the Zone part of Kakadu National Park, thus preventing the operation of a mine. The rationale for the decision finally rested on matters relating to aboriginal heritage rather than environmental consequences.

12.4 The policy significance of Australian CVM's

The track record of Australian CVMs as key impacts on policy making can only be described as weak. Whilst most studies have produced results which may have had some influence on decisions taken, no study has been instrumental in swaying a choice one way or the other. Nor is the strength of the record improving. It is true that a number of recent major policy making processes have involved CV studies, but the results of these studies have proved so contentious that their usefulness as decision making aids has been significantly limited. Many policy makers now view the technique as suspect and even in circles where confidence in CVM is high, a reluctance to use it has now developed because of the fear that its results will increase rather than decrease the extent of friction in the community. It is apparent that the reception given to the Coronation Hill CV results has provided a firm brake on the rate of growth in the use of the technique.

12.5 The future of CVM in Australia

There is little doubt that improvements can be made in future CV studies in Australia. Weaknesses have been exposed by the criticisms levelled at previous studies, and these will cause practitioners to reconsider and refine their approaches. There is more doubt currently that practioners will be called upon to undertake these refinements given the level of scepticism held for the method by policy makers.

One factor which has fuelled this scepticism, limited the policy significance of past CV studies and hence decreased the likelihood of future applications, is the general misunderstanding of the values estimated by the CVM. A numbes of CV analyses have presented their results as definitive statements of environmental values. The fact that the values so derived are truly "contingent", not only on the questionnaire design used and the survey practices adopted, but also on the conditions applying in the rest of the economy, has in many cases not been brought to the forefront as a caveat on the studies. It is quite probable that if this feature of CV analysis were better understood, a greater role in policy making could be established for the technique. One avenue of achieving this is to use the method to demonstrate the sensitivity of values to changing contingencies. Hence, rather than a single value being presented, a range of values, each associated with a particular set of circumstances could be developed. From that range, a policy maker could gain an appreciation of the factors affecting the value estimated and assess the magnitude of the value appropriate to the circumstances considered to be relevant to the choice at hand.

Given that policy makers will provide some continued impetus for CVM development and application in Australia, a number of improvements in design are readily identifiable. First, previous dichotomous choice CV studies have avoided the use of referenda style questions which essentially are framed in the context of a benefit-cost analysis. It has become clear that the alternative approach adopted – the concentration on just one side of the benefit-cost context should rather be harnessed as one within which respondents can logically consider their personal willingness to pay.

A second advance in CVM design would be the use of focus groups as a way of testing not only the communication aspects of the questionnaire but also some of the more difficult to detect biases. The specific communication aspects to be addressed relate to respondents' perceptions of the good being valued: does the questionnaire adequately convey to respondents an understanding of the good under consideration or are extraneous values being drawn in and relevant values excluded?

The issue of framing bias can also be addressed in focus groups. The commodity extent and the geographic extent of the good being valued are important factors involved in the determination of exactly what contingent circumstances are relevant to the decision being made. Focus groups can assist in defining at least the range of questions frames which are relevant through the in-depth probing of respondents' views as to likely substitute and complementary goods and the geographical area over which values are held.

12.6 Conclusions

Sinden (1991) concludes that "valuation in general, and contingent valuation in particular, is now being used instrumentally, for major landuse decisions". This is not a unanimous verdict. In fact, such has been the strength of criticism directed at what has been Australia's most ambitious, and arguably its most sophisticated, CVM application – the RAC's Coronation Hill study – that there has been considerable doubt thrown on the prospects for future applications.

The use of CVM is therefore at a crucial stage. A refusal of policy makers to consider future applications may well see the technique's use fade from prominence, whereas the acceptance of its use in a number of future studies could re-establish its rapid rise. Of course, the fate of the method in Australia will also be influenced by the overseas experience, especially as more evidence as to its success or failure is derived from countries other than the US. One feature of the Australian CVM debate has been the distinct lack of credence given to the many and varied US studies of the validity and accuracy of CVM estimates. It is apparent that many critics are convinced that there are sufficient cultural differences between the US and Australia to render the US validation studies useless for applications in the Australian context. If validity can be established across a wide variety of cultures, a strong argument in favour of CVM will be made. As part of this process, a series of Australian validation exercises should be an integral part of the techniques next phase of development. Whilst some of the early studies, such as Johnston (1982) and Bennett (1984), incorporated validation procedures, more recent work has almost taken validity for granted. This cannot be assumed, given the extent of recent criticism.

Future CVM application in Australia will need to be undertaken with great care and attention to the subtleties which are inherent in the method. Much of this case will need to be directed to ascertaining the appropriateness of the survey vehicle to the resource use decision being investigated. Establishing a range of values dependent on a range of contingent circumstances will allow policy makers to understand better the way in which CVM generated values can be used. The values obtained from any CV study are contingent upon the circumstances established in the hypothetical market set up by the questionnaire and the external circumstances. Dictating to policy makers the only set of contingencies which is relevant to the decision being made is highly likely to yield strong and usualy justified criticism. A cavalier approach will not only yield results which are useless to policy makers, but will also cause possibly irreparable damage to the methodology's future prospects.

References

Abelson, P. 1979: A study of property valuations in relation to market prices and the characteristics of properties. *Economic Record 55,* 328–338.

Bennett, J. 1984: Using direct questioning to value the existence benefits of preserved natural areas. *Australian Journal of Agricultural Economics 28* (2–3), 136–152.

Brunton, R. 1991: Will play money drive out the real money? *Environmental Background 2.* Institute of Public Affairs, Canberra.

Carter, M. Vanclay, F. & T. Hundloe 1987: *Economic and socio-economic impacts of the Crown of Thorns Starfish on the Great Barrier Reef. A report to the Great Barrier Reef Marine Park Authority.* Institute of Applied Environmental Research, Griffith University.

Carson, R. 1991: The RAC Kakadu Conservation Zone Contingent Valuation Study: Remarks on the Brunton, Stone and Tasman Institute Critiques, mimeo. University of California, San Diego.

Hundloe, T., McDonald, Blamey, Wilson & M. Carter 1990: *Socio-economic analysis of non-extractive natural resource uses in the Great Sandy Region. A report to the Queensland Department of Environment and Heritage.* Institute of Applied Environmental Research, Griffith University.

Imber, D., Stevenson & L. Wilks 1991: A Contingent Valuation Survey of the Kakadu Conservation Zone. *Resource Assessment Commission Research Paper Number 3.* Canberra.

Johnston, B. 1982: External benefits in rural research and the questions of who should pay. Presented to 26th Annual Conference of the Australian Agricultural Economics Society, 9–11 February 1982. University of Melbourne.

Moran, A. 1991: Valuing the Kakadu Conservation Zone. *Occasional Paper 138.* Tasman Institute, Melbourne.

Saddler, H., Bennett, J. Reynolds, I. & B. Smith 1980: *Public Choice in Tasmania,* CRES. Australian National University.

Sinden, J. 1991: An assessment of our environmental valuations. Invited paper, 20th Annual Conference of Economists. University of Tasmania.

Ulph, A. & I. Reynolds 1980: An economic evaluation of national parks, *CRES Report R/R4.* Australian National University.

Chapter 13

Israel–An early starter in environmental pricing

MORDECHAI SHECHTER

13.1 Introduction

This chapter reviews two studies on valuing environmental resources which were carried out in Israel, one during 1971–72 and the other during 1985–87. The first focused on the valuation of outdoor recreational services in Mt. Carmel National Park, and the second dealt with the valuation of air pollution-induced morbidity. Both studies were conducted by the author of this chapter, with the collaboration of colleagues from Israel and the United States. These are the only two studies in this particular economic "genre" of which I am aware. A good many studies were carried out in Israel in the field of water resources, but they have mainly focused on the value of water – a scarce resource in this semi-arid region – in agricultural uses.

13.2 Valuing natural resource services

13.2.1 BACKGROUND

In 1970, a public debate arose over a request by the Israel Cement Works to allow it to expand its limestone quarry (the source of the major raw material in cement production) past the border of the Carmel National Park and into the park proper. If granted, this expansion would have resulted in the destruction of one of the nicest recreational sections of the park. The Carmel National Park is situated in the northern part of the country, straddling the Carmel mountain range which runs along a south-north axis parallel to the Mediterranean coast. It covers an area of approximately 100 km². It is Israel's largest and oldest national park. A small part of the park has been set aside as a nature preserve for endemic flora. When the park was officially proclaimed in the early 1960's, a special exemption was granted to the factory allowing it to continue quarry operations at the park's border. If the expansion request were granted, the company would have obligated itself to re-landscape the area and construct a host of recreational facilities upon the termination of mining operations (after about 20–30 years). Indeed, it claimed that the area would then be much more attractive than in its natural state.

As expected, environmentalists and nature protection groups objected and protested vigorously. The company threatened that unless permission was granted, part of its labour force would have to be laid off and, in addition, the price of cement would rise appreciably as it would be necessary to haul inferior quality limestone from a more distant quarry. Consequently, the authorities concerned (the National Parks Authority, the Ministry of Tourism, the Interior Ministry, the Israel Lands Authority, and the cement company itself) jointly funded an interdisciplinary comparative evaluation study of various alternative quarrying sites (none of which involved natural areas) and the Carmel option (Enis & Shechter 1972; Enis & Shechter 1974). The evaluation study incorporated a cost-benefit analysis of the alternative quarrying sites. In the context of this analysis, the demand for and valuation of the recreational amenities (i.e., *use* values) of the park were estimated (Shechter, Enis & Baron 1974).

13.2.2 METHODOLOGY: CVM AND TCM

In connection with the recreation benefits valuation study, two sample surveys were carried out during 1971–72: a household survey and a site survey. The former consisted of a representative sample of about 2,000 households from Israel's urban areas (which then made up about 70% of the country's population). The site survey consisted of about 900 visiting units (families or groups travelling together), where one member of the group, randomly selected, was interviewed. The interviews were conducted at various recreation sites in the park. The site-survey questionnaire was shorter, but covered the same topics as the home questionnaire. In order to take into account the effect of seasonality, the survey was conducted on three different dates during the year. Since entrance to the park is free (there are no gates), the sample was supplemented with a count of all vehicles entering the park on the survey dates, as well as on three randomly selected additional days. That made it possible to estimate the sampling ratio, which turned out to be about 2 percent.

Contingent Valuation Method (CVM)

In both surveys, the questionnaire included Contingent Valuation (CVM) bidding game-type questions, designed to elicit maximum willingness to pay (WTP) values for a visit to the park in its present (undisturbed) state. In order to minimize strategic bias, the issue of quarrying was not mentioned in the questionnaire. The payment vehicle here was entrance fees. Respondents were asked about the highest entrance fee they would be willing to pay in order to visit the park (rather than not visit it).

Respondents were also asked to indicate their willingness to spend additional time travelling to the park (again in a bidding game framework). This was done after a base level had been established by asking them to indicate the amount of time it took them (or, in the home survey, thought it would take them) to reach the park. The payment vehicle here was travelling time. The scenario which served to elicit the responses in this case was that a road plan had been proposed which would result in limiting access to the park from existing roads, and therefore additional time would be needed in order to reach it. The time measure was converted to money terms by assigning a shadow price to travel time equal to the mean hourly wage rate. Variable transportation costs (chiefly the cost of gasoline) were added to the time cost.

In addition to valuing standard use benefits (i.e., resource services foregone by the quarry), the study also attempted to assess the impact of human congestion on the *quality* of these services. Respondents were again asked to state their WTP in terms of travel time, this time in order to avoid a crowded site.

Travel Cost Method (TCM)

The travel cost analysis was based on the site survey data. A Marshallian consumer surplus was calculated from the visit-rate equation by assigning a shadow price to travel time (a proxy for distance). As in the CVM analysis, this price was set equal to the mean hourly wage rate plus variable transportation costs.

Results

Mean WTP in the site survey was about 20% higher than the corresponding estimate in the home survey, probably due to sample selection bias: ceteris paribus, people who actually visit the park do it because they place a higher value on the visit. Multivariate logit regression analyses of WTP responses showed that in both surveys WTP in terms of additional travel time was better explained by socioeconomic variables than WTP in terms of entrance fees.

Table 13.1 summarizes the benefits obtained under the two CVM and TC-models. Due to the sample selection bias mentioned above, CVM measures were calculated only for the home survey. WTP in terms of travel time, as well as the TC measure, would be sensitive to the value assumed for the implicit price of travel time. If, for example, it was halved, as has sometimes been the practice, the results of both CVM and TCM would have been strikingly close!

Table 13.1 Valuation of use benefits (per visit, in 1972-US$)[1] using the Contingent Valuation Method (CVM) and the Travel Cost method (TCM)

Method	Use benefit per visit (1972-US$)
CVM – WTP in entrance fees – WTP in travel time	1.95 5.86
TCM	4.56

*Note:*1) To provide some perspective: the per capita national income was about US $1,700 in 1972.

When the lowest value from table 1 is used to arrive at national (population) estimates, the results indicated that if resource damages (reduced recreational amenities) were added as an *explicit* cost category to the total cost of quarrying in the park, then the cost difference in favor of the second best alternative was appreciably reduced; in fact, it practically disappeared. If it were possible (then) to quantify damages such as the loss of biological diversity and related ecological losses (which nowadays we would term "non-use", "existence" or "preservation" benefits), the preservation alternative would have turned out to be the socially efficient choice.

As an aside, in order to render the results more "concrete" for decision makers and the public at large, resource damage was expressed in terms of a (shadow) *price per acre* of the park (dividing total damages by the area which would have been affected by the decision). This was presented as the land price which should have been demanded by the owners (the public) as compensation for "selling" their rights to the *in situ* recreational amenities of the park (Shechter & Baron 1977).

Demand elasticities obtained from the travel-cost equations were also calculated and should be of some interest. Depending on income class, price elasticities ranged between 0.92 and 1.5, with higher income groups characterized by a higher elasticity (probably due to the fact that they usually enjoy a wider variety of recreational opportunities). Income elasticities ranged from 2.7–3.0 at the lower end of the income scale, to 0.3–0.5 at the higher end.

13.2.3 THE POLICY DIMENSION

The issue of quarry expansion was finally resolved by the Cabinet which – in rare cases – assumes the powers of a supreme Physical Planning Authority. It decided against allowing quarrying operations within the park boundaries. It is of course presumptuous to assume that this study was *the* major factor behind the final decision. There was a good deal of public pressure, a large demonstration in the park organized by the Nature Protection Society, media involvement (including editorials and articles which cited the findings of the study), and the usual political manipulations. One would have to engage in a separate study, with the collaboration of political scientists, to try to unravel the myriad forces which led to and shaped the final decision.

Post Script. Quarrying operations have since commenced at the second-best site recommended by the study. The price of cement did indeed rise, but as a consequence of the 1973–74 oil crisis (cement is an energy-intensive material). This price rise was much more significant than any price rise resulting from the shift to the new quarry which in itself had been calculated to be rather insignificant. And, even then, employment – which had been a major argument used by the company – was not affected at all.

13.3 Valuing an environmental amenity

13.3.1 BACKGROUND

In 1984, a group of Israeli researchers, collaborating with two US scientists[1] embarked upon a comprehensive, comparative study of environmental amenity valuation, specifically, air quality in relation to health damages. The aim was to carry out an investigation in which various valuation methodologies would be empirically tested and evaluated, and alternative welfare change measures estimated using the *same* primary, micro data base. The project was funded by the US-Israel Binational Science Foundation (a non-governmental public foundation).

Although this volume focuses on the contingent valuation method (CVM), the hedonic price method (HPM) and the travel cost method (TCM), two other methods used in the air quality study will be briefly mentioned here: the household production function (HPF) approach and a utility function model (UFM). The reason for this inclusion is that WTP measures obtained by *indirect* methods, i.e. methods based on observed economic behaviour in markets for related goods and services, provide an additional basis for evaluating CVM, and thus enable us to better assess the reliability of CVM. A more detailed account of the various indirect methods employed in the study can be found in Shechter (1991).

The study area selected for the empirical investigation was the Haifa metropolitan area. Haifa is an industrial city in northern Israel, with a population of about 350,000. Topography, meteorological conditions, and a concentration of heavy industry (power plant, oil refinery, petrochemical industry) have created conditions conducive to pollution in parts of the metropolitan region. In the past five years maximum mean 24-hour and maximum 1/2-hour concentrations of SO_2 ranged between 40 to 100, and 680 to 2,550 μ g/m^3, respectively. Air quality varies by season (higher in the spring and in the autumn). No pollution is imported from sources outside the region. Evidence has been accumulating that indicates a high prevalence of respiratory illnesses in the more polluted areas of the Haifa region (Epstein et al. 1991).

13.3.2 METHODS

The empirical investigation was based on a household survey of a stratified, cluster area probability sample of about 3,500 households. Data on socio-economic and demographic attributes as well as dwelling attributes (location, size, property tax assessment, and length of occupancy) were obtained. Respondents were asked to reply to open-ended questions dealing with the perception of air pollution in the neighbourhood and work place. Another set of questions dealt with (self-assessed) health status, present and past smoking habits, respiratory system symptoms and diseases (covering all household members), usage of medical services (primary clinic visits, medications), bed days during a two-week recall period, and hospitalization during the preceding year. The third part of the interview contained contingent valuation questions. The order of the CVM and health questions was randomized across respondents.

The Contingent Valuation Study

The CVM employed three elicitation procedures used in conjunction with different subsets of the sample: (a) open-ended, where respondents were asked to state maximum WTP for the postulated change in the amenity (to minimize the so-called starting point bias, they were instructed to select an appropriate percentage figure from a payment card); (b) a modified iterative bidding game, in which interviewees were asked whether they would have agreed to increase – and by how much – their initial WTP payment, had they been informed that the original, aggregated sum would not have been sufficient to accomplish the posited change in air quality; and (c) referendum-style binary choice, in which respondents were asked to state whether they would be willing to pay a stated percentage increase in their municipal tax assessments. The percentage categories were identical to those used in the payment card, and were randomly assigned to households. Although the binary choice procedure does not provide information regarding the sample distribution of WTP valuations, it nevertheless enables the estimation of its first moments, the mean and the median.

The elicitation procedure was conducted as follows: the interviewees were shown photographs of the city of Haifa on visibly polluted and on relatively clean days, and were told that cleaning the city's air would be an undertaking of city government. Furthermore, it was carefully explained to them that consumers invariably share in abatement costs, whether through taxes if government undertook the cleanup, or higher prices for goods and services if the polluting industries were required to do it. The municipal property tax, the sole local tax, served as the payment vehicle. In two separate scenarios respondents were asked to state their maximum WTP as a percentage of the annual tax (1) to prevent a 50% deterioration of current air quality levels if no action were taken (an equivalent surplus measure, denoted by WTP^e), and (2) for a 50% improvement of present levels (a compensating surplus measure, denoted by WTP^c). In each scenario, respondents who were not willing to pay any sum were queried for a reason, in order to distinguish between people who did not value environmental improvement (presumably because they did not think air quality was bad), and those who wished to register a protest for a variety of reasons.

Table 13.2 below gives the estimates of sample mean WTP^c and WTP^e, exclusive of zero protest bidders. In general, the results suggest that on average respondents were willing to pay more in order to prevent worsening of air quality (WTP^e) than to improve it (WTP^c). It has been shown (Loehman 1991) that in *this* type of comparison, there is theoretically no a priori reason to expect WTP^e > WTP^c, or the opposite; the direction of the sign depends on the shape of the indifference curves.

In relating the CVM results of this study to the conditions espoused by Cummings et al. (1986) and Mitchell and Carson (1989) for increasing the accuracy of CVM estimates, it should be noted that circumstances surrounding the survey have facilitated the task of obtaining reliable WTP responses. There has been public awareness of air pollution-induced morbidity. Moreover, because relatively small sums of money (per household) were involved strategic bias was probably absent. Respondents were familiar with the payment vehicle (city property tax), although naturally they had had no prior experience with valuing air quality in this particular manner. It is doubtful, however, whether another condition, namely the presence of little uncertainty, was satisfactorily met. Although the questionnaire attempted to reduce supply uncertainty (demand uncertainty is irrelevant in this case), it did not seek to ascertain it.

It is worth briefly mentioning two additional companion studies to the main CVM study. One attempted to assess the impact of psychological responses generated by perceived environmental pollution, specifically stress and anxiety, on WTP valuations (Shechter & Zeidner 1991; Zeidner & Shechter 1988). Questions which attempted to gauge these emotions were incorporated into the CV questionnaire, using standardized stress and anxiety tests. Another study was a preliminary attempt to investigate the influence of media exposure on CVM estimates (Shechter 1988). Articles in the national and local press dealing with air pollution, which had been published during the 12 month period corresponding to the duration of the survey, were coded according to a list of attributes (content, size, placement, etc.). The relevant items for each household, i.e. those which had appeared during a two-week or four-week period prior to the date of the interview were matched with the respective households. Multivariate regression analyses were carried out to assess the influence of this kind of media exposure on WTP responses (see also Bergstrom et al. 1989).

Indirect Valuation Methods
Economists are understandably inclined to derive valuations of goods and services, including environmental goods, in conditions where preferences are explicitly or implicitly revealed through consumer behaviour in real markets. Therefore, in addition to CVM, the project dealt with four indirect valuation methods: health production function, a utility function model, hedonic price model, and

cost of illness. The first three methods attempt to derive willingness to pay estimates for the environmental good by exploiting consumption relationships (or in the "production" of the consumption good by the household) between the environmental good and the market good(s). The fourth method, the cost of illness method, is based on a physiological relationship between the environmental good and health. This relationship is expressed by a dose-response function. (Clearly, TCM was not relevant in the present investigation.)

It should be emphasized that in dealing with pollution-induced health damages, *any* method, whether direct or indirect, which yields WTP measures – compensating or equivalent measures (i.e. all the above methods except cost of illness), is supposed to provide a complete assessment of pollution damages. In dealing with pollution-induced morbidity, a WTP measure consists of four components (Chestnut & Violette 1984): (1) savings in expenditure on health-care services; (2) reductions in restricted activity days or sick days; (3) lowering of avertive expenditures; and (4) lessening of pain, discomfort, and annoyance associated with either the physiological impact of pollution (ill health) and aesthetic impact of pollution (odours, smog and haze). The fourth category is sometimes referred to as "disutility" or "psychological costs".

In the *health production function* (HPF) method, the state of health rather than the environmental good itself enters the utility function as an argument (Bockstael & McConnell 1983; Berger et al. 1987; Cropper & Freeman 1991). Households are assumed to engage in the "production of health" by consuming preventive and curative health services. Environmental and market goods and services are inputs in the production of health. Better environmental quality may substitute or complement health care services. Thus, WTP for changes in the environmental good (clean air) may be derived indirectly through changes in the demand for substitute or complement goods specified in the production function relationship.

To the extent that housing prices capitalize pollution-induced health damages, then the *hedonic price model* (HPM) (Palmquist 1991) may also be used to unravel and estimate the benefits of environmental improvements. Interestingly, it has been shown by Feenberg and Mills (1980) that there is a formal equivalence between TCM and the hedonic price model. Moreover, one could view the travel cost method also as a form of the household production function model, where time, travel expenses, and equipment are combined to produce "recreational experience" (McConnell 1985; Smith 1991).

In this study, however, it was impractical to use the household survey to obtain hedonic prices, since that would have necessitated relying on households' self valuations, which may or may not correspond to market prices. Instead, the HPM valuations were based on a sample of 220 dwelling units in the same sample neighbourhoods, all owner-owned (the majority of apartments in Israel are owner-owned), which were on the market at the time of the study. Price information was obtained from the various real-estate agencies involved in handling these sales. However, there was a serious flaw in the data. Because of the paucity of data on transactions, not all of these observations were based on realized transaction prices; some were based on the agent's own valuations, which may or may not have been later realized. An additional flaw was a possible presence of serious distortions in reported prices due to tax avoidance considerations. In order to express the HPM results in terms comparable to those derived by the other methods, three steps were taken. First, the estimated implicit hedonic price for air pollution (table 2) was converted to its annualized equivalent, since the housing price differential due to pollution represents a capitalized value. Second, a total loss figure was calculated for the stock of housing in the Haifa area assumed to be affected by air pollution. Third, this total was divided by the total number of households in the entire Haifa area.

In the *utility function model* (UFM) approach, a flexible form of the (indirect) utility function is explicitly specified and estimated. In a certain sense, the UFM may also be considered a variant of the production function approach (Mäler 1989). This method had not previously been used to value environmental goods. Using the household survey data base, the UFM method attempts to unravel households' preferences for the environmental good from observed consumption and price relationships for related complement or substitute market goods (Shechter & Kim 1991). In this respect it is important to note that in the other indirect methods mentioned above (including TCM) it is not possible to extract the expenditure function from which the welfare change measures (compensating and equivalent variations) can be computed. Instead, they yield a consumers' surplus approximation to these measures.

Finally, the *Cost of Illness* (COI) method (Cooper & Rice 1976; Cropper & Freeman 1991) has often been used to assess the benefits from the provision of environmental goods. It is a variant of the human capital measure of welfare, and focuses on changes in expenditures on health care services as well as on the value of lost production, given a dose-response relationship between excess morbidity (or mortality) and pollution levels. As is well known, however, these expenditures do not necessarily measure all that households are willing to pay to avoid poor health (Harrington & Portney 1987; Chestnut & Violette 1984).

Comparative results from the different valuation methods
Since a notable feature of the study is the use of identical, primary, micro-data there is reason to believe that results yielded by the different methods are comparable. Table 13.2 summarizes the results of the different methods. One may indeed conclude that the similarity of values obtained under the different methods – direct or indirect – is rather encouraging. Note that HPF and UFM represent WTP of all respondents, while in the CVM valuations, only true bidders are included, i.e. positive plus "true" zero bidders. This is because the indirect methods are presumed to reveal the "true" valuations of everyone, including the protesters.

Ownership claim considerations (Knetsch et al. 1984; Kahneman et al. 1986) would have led one to expect that $WTP^e > WTP^c$, since for the WTP^e measure individuals were asked to value a good which they supposedly "owned" (current air quality level), while in the second case respondents were asked to "purchase" the improvement in air quality, thus implying that they did not already possess it. However, a non-parametric paired T-test (Hollander & Wolfe 1973) confirms the casual observation that while WTP^e is significantly greater than WTP^c in UFM, the two measures are not significantly different from each other in the case of CVM.

An important issue in using CVM for valuing environmental goods which involve human health considerations has been raised in this study. Economic theory suggests that the COI method should yield lower values than the CVM, or any other indirect method which yields a WTP measure. The results in Table 13.2 contradict this prediction but upon further reflection it should not come as a surprise. After all, COI measures better represent society's costs than individual valuations. The former includes components which would not be expected to enter into the individual consumer's valuation calculus, because households do not directly bear all the costs of pollution damages. The consumption of health care services is heavily subsidized by public medical insurance in Israel, as in all European countries. Salaried workers are usually entitled to paid sick-leave. Moreover, people clearly do not possess the kind of dose-response information available to the analyst which would have enabled them to fully assess the impact of pollution on their health (see also a recent paper by Cropper & Krupnick 1989).

This observation raises an interesting hypothesis regarding CVM namely, that – at least in cases involving environment and human

*Table 13.2 Comparisons among direct and indirect valuations of a
50% change in perceived air pollution levels in Haifa.
Stated as annual, mean willingness to pay (WTP) per
household (1986 US$).*

Method	Annual WTP per household (1986 US$)[1]	
	WTP^c	WTP^e
DIRECT VALUATION		
– CVM		
– Open ended	25.1	47.3
– Modified bidding games		
– 1st bid	17.6	42.8
– 2nd bid	45.2	59.3
– Binary choice	44.1	46.1
INDIRECT VALUATIONS		
– Utility function model (UFM)	6.5	48.9
– Health production (HPF)	60.5	
– Cost of Illness (COI)	123.3	
– Hedonic Price Model (HPM)	66.2	

Note: 1) Respondents were asked to state their maximum WTP as a percentage of the
annual tax (1) to prevent a 50% deterioration of current air quality levels if no action
were taken (an equivalent surplus measure, denoted by **WTP^e**), and (2) for a 50%
improvement of present levels (a compensating surplus measure, denoted by **WTP^c**).

health – CVM measures basically reflect WTP to reduce the disutility
associated with morbidity (i.e. the fourth benefit category mentioned
above). That is, CVM essentially measures the standard psychological costs associated with the environmental degradation. If
this is the case, then no double counting would be involved if CVM
valuations, or at least a major part of them, were *added* to COI valuations, in order to arrive at a total *social* cost of environmental pollution. In this sense, CVM and COI measures could be viewed as complementary, rather than alternative, measures.

13.3.3 THE POLICY DIMENSION

The cost-benefit ratio of pollution abatement in the Haifa bay area was much higher than one. When annual benefits from reducing pollution levels were capitalized, the resulting sum turned out to be much larger than the cost of abatement (such as scrubbers which, if installed, would have reduced emissions by much more than the 50 % postulated in the questionnaire).

Following a prolonged debate between the Ministry of Environmental Quality and the Ministry of Energy (which has effectively, if not officially, sided with the two major polluting industries in the area: the Israel Electric Power, a state enterprise, and the Oil Refineries), regarding the tightening of the ambient SO_2 standard, a compromise has recently been achieved. Steps to tighten (lower) air quality standards, and consequently reduce emissions, have finally been taken, again following a Cabinet-level intervention.

Although the drive to tighten the standard had begun some time before the authors embarked upon this study, it gained momentum when results of the epidemiological findings reached the media. The economic valuation findings have also received rather wide media coverage. As in the case of the Carmel Park study, it is difficult to surmise what weight, if any, was attached to these results in reaching the decision.

The role of the media touches on another issue which has probably been encountered in other valuation studies of this kind, namely the problem of how policy makers and the general public relate to environmental studies and their findings. It is not surprising that there was little interest on part of the general public in the methodological aspects of the study, for example, the comparison among alternative valuation methods. It was more concerned with the question of who stands to benefit from and who would bear the costs of pollution abatement. It was therefore an important task to explain what the numbers do say: that regardless of who eventually bears the cost of pollution abatement (consumers through higher prices, producers through reduced profits, or workers through lower wages or even some unemployment), or who stands to reap most of the benefits (obviously, the people who live in the polluted neighbourhoods), a significant reduction in pollution levels in the Haifa area would be a rational policy imperative. It has been the author's experience that these notions and concepts are not easily put through to the general public.

13.4 Some concluding observations

Given the situation in most European countries, Israel does not fare too badly if one compares the meager output of environmental valuation studies on, say, per capita basis. With this observation in mind, if one were permitted to draw some tentative conclusions from two studies, it seems that – from the point of view of successful impact upon policy – what counts most is the relevance of a valuation study to an issue which is high on the political agenda at the time of the study's appearance (as well, of course, as the quality of the product!). This is conducive to another essential element – gaining access to the media as an effective means of reaching the public and policy makers. At least in the Israeli case it has been our experience that it is not so much whether a study was commissioned by the concerned authorities (the Carmel Park study) or funded by an independent body (the air pollution study) which determined its impact upon policy decisions. Media (hopefully, undistorted) exposure seems to be a much more crucial element.

As valuation studies gain respectability in the profession and the public at large, we should expect a higher output rate in Israel as well as elsewhere. In this sense, the second study described here is probably more of a mainstream phenomenon. The earlier study (early by either US or European yardsticks) should be considered a kind of "outlier". Although it did have some impact upon policy decisions, it was produced in a professional climate which was not receptive to this kinds of studies. In retrospect, it can be supposed that this is probably why it remained without any sequel for almost 15 years.

Recently two additional studies have been carried out. One has dealt with the valuation of the provision of supplementary private health care services on the premises of public hospitals (Golan & Shechter 1991). For ideological reasons these services have not been available in the past, but there has been growing pressure on the government to sanction them. The other, still in a preliminary stage, is probably of more interest to the readers of this volume. It concerns the estimation of non-use values of a natural resource, and the Carmel National Park is again the subject of investigation. The study was prompted by a forest fire which had devastated in 1989 the very same area which would have been destroyed by the quarry. A drive was launched through the media to solicit contributions from the public for the rehabilitation of the park. Some of the people who contributed to the drive had never, or seldom visited (or planned to visit) the park. Were their contributions motivated by existence and preservation motives? This is what the study is out to discover.

References

Berger, M.C., Blomquist, G.C., Kenkel, D. & G.S. Tolley 1987: Valuing changes in health risks: a comparison of alternative measures. *Southern Economic Journal* 53, 967–984.

Bergstrom, J.C., Stoll J.R. & A. Randall 1989: Information effects in contingent markets. *American Journal of Agricultural Economics 71*, 685–691.

Bockstael, N.E. & K.E. McConnel 1983: Welfare measurement in the household Production Framework', *American Economic Review 73*, 806–814.

Chestnut, L.G. & D.M. Violette 1984: *Estimates of willingness to pay for pollution-induced changes in morbidity: a critique for benefit-cost analysis of pollution regulation.* United States Environmental Protection Agency, Washington, DC.

Cooper, B.S. & D.P. Rice 1976: The economic cost of illness revisited. *Social Security Bulletin 39*, 21–36.

Cropper, M.L. & A.J. Krupnick 1989: *The social costs of chronic heart and lung disease.* Proceedings of the AERE Workshop on Estimating and Valuing Morbidity in a Policy Context. Research Triangle Park, N.C.

Cropper, M.L. & A.M. Freeman 1991. Environmental health effects. In J.B. Braden & C.D. Kolstad (eds.); *Measuring the demand for environmental quality.* 165–212. North-Holland, Amsterdam.

Cummings, R.G., Brookshire, P.S. & W.D. Schulze 1986. *Valuing environmental goods – an assessment of the contingent valuation method.* Rowman and Allenheld, Totowa, N.J.

Enis, R. & M. Shechter 1972: *Quarries and landscape.* In Hebrew. Center for Urban & Regional Studies, Technion (Israel Institute of Technology), Haifa.

Enis, R. & M. Shechter 1974: Environmental analysis of quarrying: an Israeli experience. *Landscape Planning 1*, 289–302.

Epstein, L.; M. Shechter, A. Cohen & C. Biger 1991: Air pollution and morbidity in the Haifa Area. In Hebrew. *Ha'refuah (Medicine) 120*, 709–713.

Feenberg, D. & E.S. Mills 1980: *Measuring the benefits of water pollution abatement.* Academic Press, New York.

Golan, E.H. & M. Shechter 1991. Use of the contingent valuation method for calculating willingness to pay for health care services: valuation of supplemental health care in Israel. Discussion Paper, Natural Resources and Environmental Research Center, University of Haifa, Haifa.

Harrington, W. & P.R. Portney 1987: Valuing the benefits of health and safety regulation. *Journal of Urban Economics 22*, 101–112.

Hollander, M. & D. Wolfe 1973: *Nonparametric statistical methods.* Wiley & Sons, New York.

Kahneman, D., Knetsch, J.L. & R. Thaler 1986: Fairness as a constraint on profit seeking: entitlement in the market. *American Economic Review 76*, 728–741.

Knetsch, J.L. & J.A. Sinden 1984. Willingness to pay and compensation demanded: experimental evidence of an unexpected disparity in measures of value, *Quarterly Journal of Economics 94*, 507–521.

Loehman, E. 1991. Alternative measures of benefit for nonmarket goods which are substitutes or complements for market goods, Discussion Paper, Dept. of Agricultural Economics, Purdue University, Lafayette.

McConnell, K.E. 1985: The economics of outdoor recreation. In A.V. Kneese & J.L. Sweeney (eds.): *Handbook of natural resource and energy economics,* vol. 2, 677–724. North-Holland, Amsterdam.

Mäler, K.G. 1989: Valuation of costs and benefits from resource use. The World Bank. Mimeo.

Mitchell, R.C. & R.T. Carson 1989: *Using surveys to value public goods: the contingent valuation method.* Resources For the Future, Washington, DC.

Palmquist, R.B. 1991: Hedonic methods. In J.B. Braden & C.D. Kolstad (eds.): *Measuring the demand for environmental quality,* 77–120. North-Holland, Amsterdam.

Shechter, M. 1991: A comparative study of environmental amenity valuations. *Environmental and Resource Economics 1,* 129–155.

Shechter, M., Enis, R. & M. Baron 1974: Mt. *Carmel National Park: the demand for outdoor* recreation. In Hebrew. Center for Urban & Regional Studies, Technion (Israel Institute of Technology), Haifa.

Shechter, M. & M. Baron 1977: What is the value of land in the Carmel National Park? In Hebrew. *Ir Ve'Ezor (City and Region). No 4.*

Shechter, M. et al. 1988: *The benefits of morbidity reduction from air pollution. Final science report.* Natural Resources and Environmental Research Center, University of Haifa, Haifa.

Shechter, M. & M. Zeidner 1990: Anxiety: towards a decision theoretic perspective. *The British Journal of Mathematical and Statistical Psychology 43,* 15–28.

Shechter, M. & M. Kim 1991: Valuation of pollution abatement benefits: direct and indirect measurement. *Journal of Urban Economics 30,* 133–151.

Smith, V.K. 1991: Household production functions and environmental benefit estimation. In J.B. Braden & C.D. Kolstad (eds.): *Measuring the demand for environmental quality,* 41–76. North-Holland, Amsterdam.

Zeidner, M. & M. Shechter 1988: Psychological responses towards air pollution: some personality and demographic correlates. *Journal of Environmental Psychology 8,* 191–208.

Chapter 14
Benefit estimation and environmental decision-making

ONNO KUIK, STÅLE NAVRUD & DAVID W. PEARCE

14.1 Introduction

Environmental benefit and damage studies have been carried out in many countries since the late sixties or early seventies. A powerful stimulus for this kind of research came from the United States in 1981 when President Reagan's executive order #12291, issuing Regulatory Impact Analysis, made it mandatory for the Environmental Protection Agency (EPA) to perform social cost-benefit analysis for its major regulations. The order boosted research into environmental benefits in the United States, and this led in its turn to an increased attention for benefit studies in Europe.

Have public authorities in the United States and Europe actually used environmental benefit estimates in their policy decisions? For which types of decisions have they used them and which purposes did they serve? What are the main obstacles to their use? To answer questions like these, OECD in 1989 commissioned experts in six selected countries to evaluate the use of benefit estimates in decision making in their countries, to identify possible obstacles, and to suggest ways to overcome these obstacles (Barde & Pearce 1991). This chapter highlights some of the findings of these experts. It also focuses on the use of estimates derived with the help of the Contingent Valuation (CV) method, arguably the most controversial valuation technique.

This chapter is organized as follows: In the next section a distinction is made between the purposes of benefit estimates and the policy levels at which they may play a role. Illustrations are given from some of the OECD country case studies. The role of CV benefit estimates is indicated. The third section offers some generalizations on the issues which may influence the use of benefit estimates in decision-making. Finally, some remarks are made on the position of the Contingent Valuation method as a tool for environmental decision making.

14.2 Purpose of benefit estimates

Environmental benefit estimates may be used in several ways in public decision making. First, a distinction may be made between decisions in environmental policy and decisions in other policy areas. The objective of environmental policy is to create environmental improvements or to avoid environmental damage, or, in other words, to establish environmental benefits. Other policy areas have other objectives, but actions may impose positive or negative side-effects on the environment. These side-effects may influence the social desirability of these actions. Second, a distinction may be made between levels of policy. A rough distinction can be made between policies, regulations, and projects. Valuation is relevant at each level, but may be used more extensively at one level than another. Third, a distinction may be drawn between different purposes for which benefit estimates are used in the areas mentioned. The purpose of benefit estimation may be to:

- create public awareness for a particular problem by using money as a readily understandable indicator of environmental damage or potential environmental benefits;
- influence particular decisions either by using formal cost-benefit analysis or in a more informal way;
- identify decisons, that is, to establish a priority ranking between a number of potential actions;
- justify decisions, either *ex ante*, before a decision is made, or *ex post*, after a decision is made and support for it needs to be found; and,
- justify the existence or continuation of a particular programme and/or agency, by pointing at the positive side-effects of its activities on the environment.

A discussion on the use of benefit estimates in decision making may easily become confused in the absence of these distinctions. One reviewer may come to the conclusion that benefit estimates are not used in decision making because he or she looks at the use of formal cost-benefit analysis in environmental regulations, while another reviewer reaches the opposite conclusion on the grounds that benefit estimates have a significant influence on public awareness. This confusion is not uncommon. On the basis of the six country case studies mentioned above, it is possible to construct a matrix which indicates for which levels of policy and for which purposes benefit estimates are likely to be of use in environmental decision-making.

Table 14.1 Levels and purposes of benefit estimates

Purpose Level	Stimulate awareness	Influence decisions	Identify decisions	Justify
Policy	Yes	Possible	Unlikely	Unlikely
Regulation	Yes	Likely	Possible	Possible
Project	No	Yes	Likely	Likely

Table 14.1 suggests that at the general policy level benefit estimates may be used to stimulate public environmental awareness and that they may influence decisions on this level, but that it is unlikely that benefit estimates will be used to establish priority ranking between different policy areas or that they could justify environmental policy either *ex ante* or *ex post*. At the level of regulations, benefit estimates may influence decisions and trade-offs to a somewhat larger extent. The project level offers the best possibilities for benefit estimates to play an important role in the decision-making process.

Projects
The early development of benefit measurement methodologies involved the evaluation of individual projects. Therefore we would expect to find most environmental benefit estimates on the project level. This is certainly the case in the United States, but the situation in Europe differs across countries. Environmental Impact Assessment (EIA) which is required for large projects in the European Community does not require monetary valuation. Most (or all) EIAs in Europe describe environmental impacts verbally or quantify effects in physical units.

In a number of European countries Cost-benefit analysis (CBA) is used as a decision-tool in public work schemes, especially in road construction. Usually, environmental effects are not valued in monetary terms. An exception is Germany, where noise, exhaust-gas pollution, separating effects and the deterioration of living conditions and communication are valued within CBA. The valuation is mainly carried out on the basis of a cost-of-damage-abatement approach. For instance, the damage of increased noise is valued as the number of houses which will be exposed to a noise level above some threshold, multiplied by the market value of noise-absorbing windows (Schulz & Schulz 1991).

In the United Kingdom, public and quasi-public agencies are subject to strict budget constraints. The Treasury (and the Ministry which is responsible for the agency) applies economic criteria to expenditure plans. In general, agencies should provide their "parent" Ministry and the Treasury with an assessment of the net present value of proposed schemes or investments, based on discounted cash flows. "Intangible" costs and benefits may be given a money value, for instance by analyzing peoples' actual behaviour and declared or revealed preferences. These imputed money values can be used as if they were actual cash flows (UK Treasury 1984). In recent years this has led to a greater use of environmental benefit estimates by agencies in the areas of water and sewerage management, coastal defence and afforestation (see Markandya, Pearce & Turner 1991). It is interesting to note that the UK Treasury is inclined to accept monetary values that are estimated with the Contingent Valuation method, although with some apparent scepticism.

Regulations
The U.S. Environmental Protection Agency (EPA) carries out regulatory and other activities to implement the provisions of various statutes enacted by Congress. The criteria to be used by the EPA depend on the statute involved. In addition, the EPA must comply with a series of Executive Orders issued by the president that require certain analyses and establish regulatory decisions criteria. The most recent such Order was executive Order 12291, requiring "Regulatory Impact Analysis" for all major rules. A regulatory approach should be selected that "maximizes net benefits to society" to the extent permitted by law. In describing the use of benefit estimation in decision making in the USA, Froehlig et al. (1991) remark that "in theory (..) the U.S. government should be making extensive use of benefit estimates in deciding whether to regulate, and in designing regulations. In practice, however, the actual use of benefit estimates in regulatory decision-making varies widely".

In the first place, for a number of regulations, statutes do not allow for a consideration of cost and benefits as a decision criterion. This is for instance the case in the setting of standards for ambient air quality in the Clean Air Act, emission standards for hazardous air pollutants in the same Act, or the regulation of treatment, storage and disposal of wastes in the Resource Conservation and Recovery Act. In the Clean Water Act, effluent limitations are heavily influenced by the performance of available treatment technologies. Benefit (or risk) estimates may be used to establish more stringent standards, but they may never be used to require less stringent standards than those achieved by the "Best Practicable Technology".

Second, even if a comparison of costs and benefits is allowed to be used as a decision criterion, it may not always be possible to quantify and value the environmental effects. A review of fifteen RIAs performed by the EPA between 1981 and 1986 found that only six of the fifteen RIAs included a complete analysis of monetized benefits. However the same review argued that even if not all benefits could be monetized, the RIAs often led to more effective and efficient regulations (EPA 1987).

In Europe, comparisons of costs and benefits of environmental regulations have been made only in a small number of cases, and even less use was made of the results. A striking example of a case in which a CBA was carried out but not used, is the case of car emission regulation in Norway (Navrud 1991). In 1984 the Ministry of the Environment asked the State Pollution Control Agency (SPCA) to carry out a detailed impact analysis of stricter car emission regulations (USA standards). The SPCA carried out a CBA which showed that the stricter emission regulation would, with a reasonable degree of certainty, be profitable for society. In the study both total costs and benefits and their distribution between different interest groups were well documented. The quality of the study may be characterized as rather high. However, in the hearing that followed the completion of the CBA, SPCA did not fully back its own study against criticisms of interested parties (Ministry of Consumer Affairs, Motor Trade Organization, etc.). In 1986, the Norwegian Government decided in favour of the stricter regulation, but, in the argumentation with the Government ahead of this decision, the Ministry of the Environment did not mention the benefit estimate at all. In other European countries, researchers have had similar experiences.

The OECD case study of Norway also presents an example of a regulation in which benefit estimates did play a role. In Norway, the so-called Locally Adapted Regulatory Impact Analysis (LARIA) aims at giving a priority ranking of regulatory actions in areas with the greatest pollution problems. All possible regulatory actions aimed at reducing pollution in a given area are assigned a B/C ratio which is used to arrive at a priority ranking. Benefits of each regulatory action are calculated using a set of weights for different benefits (for instance, one person less living in an area where air pollution exceeds threshold values for SO_2, NO_x, CO, soot; one person less strongly affected by noise; one ton of reduced SO_2 deposition, etc.) multiplied by the reduction in the number of persons affected; the reduction in deposition, etc. The set of weights is constructed on the basis of expert opinion and (existing) monetary estimates. In this case, benefit estimates are used to rank regulatory actions, although in the presentation of the results, SPCA dit not explicitly mention this monetization of benefits, but, so to speak, "hid" it behind a set of normalized weights. An example of such weights is presented in table 14.2. Because of the inclusion of the benefit "1000 NOK saved costs" in table 14.2, one can easily assign a monetary value to all benefits. Although the LARIA approach has been criticized on the fact that the weights (benefit estimates) have been rather randomly chosen, it nevertheless seems a promising approach to incorporate benefit estimation in environmental decision making.

Table 14.2 Weights used to aggregate environmental and health benefits in a LARIA of reduced air pollution in the Sarpsborg/Fredrikstad area.

Benefits	Weight
1 person above the threshold for – SO_2 – NO_x – CO – Soot	2.0 4.0 6.0 4.4
1 person troubled by dust from industry	0.3
1 person troubled by smell from industry	0.4
1 person troubled by dust/smell from other sources	0.2
1 person "strongly affected" by noise	8.0
1 traffic accident with persons injured	1400.0
1,000 NOK saved costs	1.0
1 ton SO_2 emitted (with respect to acidification)	2.7
1 ton NO_x emitted (with respect to acidification)	1.4

Source: Navrud (1991) (modified from a Norwegian source, T.Syversen (1988) Weighting of different benefits (in Norwegian). State Pollution Control Authority).

Policy
Many environmental benefit or damage studies have been carried out in the Netherlands and Germany to stimulate awareness of environmental problems. The Netherlands have a long history in environ-

mental damage studies, the first studies beeing carried out in the early 1970s. Dutch benefit studies are not linked to a specified policy proposal, regulation or project, but relate to pollution categories (for example, air pollution, water pollution, acidification) and/or damage categories (for example, crops, materials, forests). Environmental decision makers do not use damage and/or benefit studies to trade-off costs and benefits of alternative government actions, but their use lies primarily in providing an additional justification of these actions to other government departments, and, to a lesser extent, to the general public. Efficiency criteria (maximization of net present value) play a minor role; the emphasis lies on the assessment of financial-economic benefits, i.e. forgone productivity losses, decreasing money outlays for protection, cleaning, repair, replacement, and so forth. Environmental decision makers in the Netherlands have a low appreciation for willingness-to-pay estimates. It is for instance remarkable to notice that the monetary value of acidification damage to Dutch forests that was published in a government document was based on the expected yield reduction of timber, while a CV study which assessed the willingness-to-pay of the Dutch population to maintain forests as a recreational facility was completely ignored in official publications. The annual benefits of the CV study were about 50 times higher than the benefits of the forgone yield reduction of timber (Kuik et al. 1991).

According to Schulz and Schulz (1991), environmental benefit/damage studies at the national level have played an important role in the political discussion in Germany. In the late 1970s, the Federal Environmental Agency commissioned ten "pilot studies for the assessment of the benefit to be derived from measures designed to improve the environment". The studies attracted much attention, resulting in parliamentary enquiries, scientific conferences and essays. Schulz and Schulz argue that environmental benefit studies have contributed to making the real dimensions of environmental pollution clear, and in putting the environmental debate on a rational basis. They have not helped much in making polluters aware of the costs of their own actions or in improving allocative efficiency.

One of the pilot studies – *Better air, how do we valuate it?* (Schulz 1986) – was carried out with the Contingent Valuation method. Given the good reception of this study, it may be concluded that CV is less controversial in Germany than in the Netherlands, at least at the level of the environmental ministries.

14.3 Aspects which influence the use of benefit estimates in decision making

A major aspect wich has influenced the use of benefit estimates thus far is the uncertainty of the correctness (or the low credibility) of the estimates. First of all this uncertainty stems from uncertainty about the most elementary physical dose-effect relationships. Second, because of the fact that preferences for environmental goods are not directly observable in the market place, there is always something hypothetical about the estimated money values. Third, a long period of time often elapses between sources and effects of environmental pollution. The problem of discounting costs and benefits which occur on different points in time to some present value has not yet been satisfactorily solved. This problem becomes even more complicated if impacts affect future generations. Fourth, the chain of effects of a pollution problem from source to final impacts may very well cross national borders. Although this may not affect benefit estimation in theory, it certainly complicates practical applications.

The doubts about the correctness of certain benefit estimates are not entirely unfounded, as may be illustrated with the following example. Both in Germany and the Netherlands national damage estimates of noise pollution have been calculated. Both estimates are based on house price differentials. However, expressed in dollars per capita, the German damage is a 100 times higher than the Dutch damage (respectively US$ 297 in Germany and US$ 3 in the Netherlands). The reason for this huge difference is not that the Netherlands is a much quieter country than Germany, but that Germany has chosen a threshold noise-level of 30 dB(A) and the Netherlands a threshold noise-level of 60 dB(A)(Oosterhuis 1990).

Other obstacles to the use of benefit estimates in decision making may be, *inter alia*:

- Administrative. It is not uncommon that statutory impediments preclude the use of benefit assessment in decision making. In section 2, a few examples of these impediments in the United States were cited. These examples may easily be augmented with examples from other countries. In Germany, for instance, charges on waste collection must be based on financial calculations, not on an assessment of welfare economic cost. Another administrative obstacle may be the lack of capability to perform benefit studies within the government or outside. Certainly this has been a major obstacle in many European countries, but one which can be rather easily overcome.

- Academic obstacles. Good benefit studies need a close collaboration between economists and scientists. Inter- or multidisciplinary research environments are still rather the exception than the rule.
- Political obstacles. Cost-benefit analysis forces politicians to reveal their preferences. Politicians may be opposed to this.

A general constraint on the usefulness of benefit estimates in the decision-making process is that their timing is often wrong. One of the major criticisms at the usefullness of benefit estimates in RIAs in the United States is that they are made up separately from the rule development. They are used as an *ex-post* justification of the rule. Major decisions about alternative options of the rule are therefore not influenced by the benefit estimates. To be of more use, benefit estimates should be made in a very early stage of the rule-making process. Of course, they can then be less elaborate, because not all the results of other scientific research which is stimulated by the rule development will be available. Clearly, a trade-off between usefulness and accurateness may exist in some situations. It also poses a dilemma. A major reason for not using benefit estimates is doubt of their "correctness". More scientific information is likely to increase the correctness of the estimates. However, because of the time constraint, their usefulness decreases if the estimation exercise is delayed to use more scientific information. It thus seems that either the estimate is not used because of doubts about its correctness, or the estimate is not used because it is made too late.

14.4 The position of the Contingent Valuation Method (CVM)

In environmental benefit studies, the Contingent Valuation Method (CVM) is used to estimate individuals' willingness to pay for an environmental improvement or individuals' willingness to accept an environmental degradation. For a general introduction and technical detail, see chapter 9, or, Mitchell and Carson (1989) and Cummings et al. (1986).

In this section, a few remarks on the position of CVM are made from three perspectives. First, the position of CVM in state-of-arts reviews of benefit estimation techniques is considered. Second, some observations of CVM experts themselves are put forward. Finally, the actual use that is made of CV estimates in environmental decision making is looked at, and a new potential use is sketched.

14.4.1 STATE-OF-THE-ART REVIEWS

State-of-the-art reviews of benefit estimation techniques usually consider CVM to be a method with great potential (e.g. Freeman 1979; Miltz; 1988, and Pearce & Markandya; 1989). Compared with other methods, CVM scores high on the criteria of "completeness" and "comprehensiveness". Completeness refers to the coverage of benefit studies in terms of categories of environmental changes/receptors affected. Comprehensiveness refers to the coverage of various elements of value that are potentially, relevant from a welfare perspective, i.e. use and non-use (existence) values. Because of the ability of CVM to cover more categories more comprehensively than other methods, CVM may, in principle, result in less biased estimates. However, the validity and stability of the method remain uncertain.

14.4.2 CV EXPERTS

CV experts are often concerned with the validity of the method. Of the three classes of validity suggested by Mitchell and Carson (1989, chapter 9), the criterion validity has the greatest potential for offering a definitive test of a measure's WTP. To assess this type of validity, we need a criterion which is unequivocally closer to the theoretical construct than the measure whose validity is being assessed. A criterion of central importance to CV studies is actual market prices. Even though market prices are rarely available for public goods, there have been some experiments comparing hypothetical CV results with outcomes of identical actual markets (see chapter 11 of this book). However, in general there are no suitable criteria for validating WTP amounts for environmental goods. Therefore, there have been more tests of convergent validity, i.e. looking at whether the measure is correlated with other measures of the same theoretical construct for environmental goods which also can be valued by other methods, such as the Hedonic Price Method or the Travel Cost Method. Comparisons of the results of CV estimates and other estimation techniques on particular environmental goods have often shown close resemblances (cf. Cummings et al. 1986).

CV theorists have formulated recommendations which researchers should take into account in order to obtain valid results. Hoevenagel (1991) formulates the following recommendations with respect to the good to be valued, although he makes it clear that it is not yet possible to give an indication of what the divergence would be when these recommendations are not met (see also chapter 9 of this book for a more comprehensive list of recommendations):

- Environmental goods should be used with which respondents are familiar (Cummings et al. 1986.);
- Environmental goods should be used for which the research population feels a kind of commitment to pay. Hence, environmental goods for which a small number of "polluters" can be easily pointed out, are not recommended.
- Environmental goods which are subject to highly politically charged policy questions are not recommended (Freeman 1986).
- Environmental goods should be used in which the research population is, as much as possible, equivalent to the population that benefits from the good.
- Environmental goods should be used in which the amounts obtained are related to *user-values*, with a minimum ideological content (Kahneman 1986).

One can immediately sense that these recommendations lead to a neglect of just those categories and value elements which have made the above-mentioned benefit estimation reviewers so enthusiastic about CVM. Therefore, a dilemma exists between, on the one hand, the validity issue (and hence the credibility of the method), and, on the other hand, the issue of completeness and comprehensiveness which makes CV, in principle, such a powerful measurement instrument.

14.4.3 ACTUAL USE OF CV ESTIMATES

The actual use that is made of benefits which are estimated using CVM varies between countries. The method has been more or less accepted in the United States and is beginning to gain acceptance in the United Kingdom. Perhaps with the exception of the Scandinavian countries, its acceptance on the continent seems to be much lower. The reasons for this variation in acceptance are not quite clear. If it is a matter of ignorance on the part of the recipients, more information on the methodology and practical applications of the method on environmental problems may change its acceptance. It is also possible that the low acceptance of CVM is in some way related to a low priority for economic efficiency in the decision-making processes in some countries, especially if efficiency is defined in welfare economic terms. For example, the decision-making processes in the Netherlands seem almost exclusively concerned with distributional effects of environmental measures.

However, despite this possible lack of interest in questions of efficiency, policy makers in the environmental field desperately need to
assess the effects of their programmes in some comprehensive way,
and need to be guided in making trade-offs between different environmental goals. This need is presently often formulated as a need
for aggregate environmental indicators. In constructing aggregate
indicators, different environmental effects have to be compared with
each other in some way. CV estimates might be used to provide (a
number of) weights, as in the Norwegian LARIA example cited
above. Opschoor and Reijnders (1991) have suggested that CV might
be able to assist indicator development in the Netherlands. Hope and
Parker (1990) have developed a conceptual framework for a UK Environment Index, in which public opinion polls would be a crucial element in weighting various environmental issues. Very important in
their argument is that if it is not the public that sets priorities, experts
will. They do not believe that experts have a claim to superior knowledge at the aggregate level; the major threats to the environment are
socially determined. This argument holds, of course, for the entire
benefit discussion. Benefit estimates may be less than ideal, but what
is the alternative?

14.5 Conclusions

The following conclusions related to the use of benefit estimates in
environmental decision making can be drawn from this discussion:

1. Benefit estimates play a role in environmental decision making,
   not only in the United States but also in Europe.
2. The purpose of benefit estimates varies: they may be used to stimulate awareness of environmental problems, to influence or
   identify decisions, or to justify decisions.
3. The various purposes show some correlation with the policy level
   at which the estimates are used. The more ambitious purposes
   (i.e. CBA) usually coincide with lower policy levels (i.e. public
   projects).
4. The extent and purpose of use of benefit estimates varies across
   countries. The extent to which benefit estimates are used in
   Europe to influence environmental policy decisions is negligible.
   However, they are used at the project level in some sectors in a
   number of European countries.
5. Uncertainty about the correctness of the estimates is a major
   obstacle in the use of the estimates in decision making. Valuation

is only one element of uncertainty; the most elementary physical dose-effect relationships are often missing. However, in some cases the uncertainty may also be attributable to the inability of government officials to understand fully the methods used.

6. Other obstacles may be administrative, academic, political, or bad timing. Timing is not easy. If a benefit study is made too early in some policy process, the study may lack credibility because many essential physical data were not yet available. If the study is made too late, it may be credible, but it is too late to influence the policy process.

Concerning the use of Contingent Valuation (CV) estimates, in particular, we have reached the following conclusions:

7. The acceptance of CV estimates across countries varies considerably. The acceptance in the Netherlands seems to be very low. The reasons for this variation are not quite clear. Research might show interesting results.

8. State-of-the-art reviews on benefit estimation techniques usually consider CVM to be a method with great potential because of its ability to cover many environmental goods (completeness) and to cover many elements of value (comprehensiveness).

9. However, the validity issue (does CV measure what it intends to measure?) compels CV experts to restrict the number of goods that may be valued and to restrict the valuation to the estimation of use-values.

10. The challenge for CV researchers is to find ways to use CVM beyond the project level, i.e. to estimate benefits of national policy decisions. Interesting in this respect is the development of an aggregate environmental indicator, in which priorities and trade-offs between environmental problems have to be assessed.

References

Barde, J.-P., & D.W. Pearce (eds.) 1991: *Valuing the Environment: Six Case Studies.* Earthscan Publication Ltd, London, 271 p.

Cummings, R.G., Brookshire, D.S. & W.D. Schulze (eds.) 1986: *Valuing environmental goods.* Rowman and Allanheld, Totowa, N.J., 270 p.

EPA 1987: EPA's use of benefit-cost analysis: 1981–1986. U.S. Environmental Protection Agency, Washington D.C., 46 p.

Freeman, A.M. 1979: *The benefits of environmental improvement: theory and practice.* The John Hopkins University Press, Baltimore, 272 p.

Freeman, A.M. 1986: On assessing the state of the art of the contingent valuation method of valuing environmental goods. In: R.G. Cummings et al. (eds.): op. cit., 148-161.

Froehlig, M., Hufford, D.J.C. & N.H. Hammett 1991: The United States. In: J.-P. Barde & D.W. Pearce (eds.): op.cit., 236-265.

Hoevenagel, R 1991: An Assessment of the Contingent Valuation Method. Paper prepared for the European Science Foundation workshop, February 14-17, 1991, Charmey, Switzerland, 37 p.

Hope, C. & J. Parker 1990: Environmental information for all. The need for a monthly index. *Management Studies, Research paper number 5/90,* Cambridge University. Cambridge, 18 p.

Kahneman, D. 1986: Comments. In: R.G. Cummings et al. (eds.): op. cit., 185-194.

Kuik, O.J., Jansen, H.M.A. & J.B. Opschoor 1991: The Netherlands. In: J.-P. Barde J.-P., and D.W. Pearce (eds.): op.cit., 106-140.

Miltz, D. 1988: The use of benefit estimation in environmental decision making. *OECD, report ENV/ECO/88.8.* Paris, 57 p.

Mitchell, R.C. & R.T. Carson 1989: *Using surveys to value public goods: the Contingent Valuation Method.* Resources for the Future, Washington D.C., 463 p.

Markandya, A., Pearce, D. K. Turner 1991: The United Kingdom. In: J.-P. Barde & D.W. Pearce (eds.): op.cit., 203-235.

Navrud, S. 1991: Norway. In: J.-P. Barde, & D.W. Pearce (eds.): op.cit., 141-202.

Oosterhuis, F.H. 1990: Batenstudies in Europa (Benefit studies in Europe). In Dutch. In: O.J. van Gerwen (ed.): *De Financiering van het Milieubeleid* (Financing environmental policy). *Publication RMNO no. 52,* Rijswijk, 187-191.

Opschoor, J.B. & L.Reijnders 1991: Towards indicators of sustainable development. In: O. Kuik & H. Verbruggen (eds.): *In search of indicators of sustainable development.* Kluwer Academic Services. Dordrecht, 7-27.

Schulz, W. 1986: Better air, how do we valuate it?. Paper prepared for OECD, W.8614H, Paris, 58 p.

Schulz, W. & E. Schulz 1991: Germany. In: J.-P. Barde & D.W. Pearce (eds.). op.cit., 9-63.

UK Treasury 1984: *Investment appraisal in the public sector: a technical guide for government departments.* HM Treasury, London, 48 p.

List of Contributors

Ian Bateman	School of Environmental Sciences, University of East Anglia, U.K.
Jeff Bennett	Department of Economics and Management, University of New South Wales, Australian Defence Force Academy, Australia
Francois Bonnieux	Economie et Sociologie Rurales, Institut National de la Recherche Agronomique, Rennes, France
Birgitte Desaigues	Université de Bordeaux, Pessac, France
Ruud Hoevenagel	Institute for Environmental Studies, Free University, Amsterdam, The Netherlands
Per-Olov Johansson	Stockholm School of Economics, Stockholm, Sweden
Bengt Kriström	Stockholm School of Economics, Stockholm, Sweden
Onno Kuik	Institute for Environmental Studies, Free University, Amsterdam, The Netherlands
Kristin Magnussen	Norwegian Agricultural Economics Research Institute, Oslo, Norway.
Erkki Mäntymaa	Research Institute of Northern Finland, University of Oulu, Kajaani, Finland
Ståle Navrud	Norwegian Centre for International Agricultural Development (NORAGRIC), Agricultural University of Norway, Ås, Norway.
Ville Ovaskainen	Department of Forest Economics, The Finnish Forest Research Institute, Helsinki, Finland.
David W. Pearce	London Environmental Economics Centre, (LEEC)/University College London, London, U.K.
Werner W. Pommerehne	Deparment of Economics, University of Saarland, Saarbrücken, Germany, and University of Zürich, Zürich, Switzerland
Anselm U. Römer	University of Saarland, Saarbrücken, Germany
Mordechai Shechter	Natural Resources and Environmental Center, University of Haifa, Haifa, Israel.
Tuija Sievänen	Department of Forest Economics, The Finnish Forest Research Institute, Helsinki, Finland.
Jon Strand	Department of Economics, University of Oslo, Oslo, Norway
R. Kerry Turner	Center for Social and Economic Research on the Global Environment (CSERGE) University of East Anglia, U.K.
Dominique Vermersch	Economie et Sociologie Rurales, Institut National de la Recherche Agronomique , Rennes, France.